THE FILMS

OF

LON CHANEY

THE FILMS
OF
LON CHANEY

Michael F. Blake

VESTAL PRESS, INC.
LANHAM, MD., & LONDON
1998

VESTAL PRESS, Inc.

Published in the United States of America
by Vestal Press, Inc.
4720 Boston Way
Lanham, Maryland 20706

British Library Cataloguing in Publication Information Available

Library of Congress Cataloging-in-Publication Data

Blake, Michael F. (Michael Francis), 1957–
    The films of Lon Chaney / by Michael F. Blake.
       p.   cm.
    Includes bibliographical references.
    ISBN 1-879511-26-6 (cloth : alk. paper)
    1. Chaney, Lon, 1883–1930.   I. Title.
PN2287.C48B57   1998
791.43′028′092—DC21   97-34935
                                                          CIP

ISBN 1-879511-26-6 (cloth : alk. paper)

♾ ™ The paper used in this publication meets the minimum requirements of
American National Standard for Information Sciences—Permanence of
Paper for Printed Library Materials, ANSI Z39.48–1984.
Manufactured in the United States of America.

CONTENTS

Acknowledgments

Writing a book relating to the cinema, even though only one name may appear as the author, is never a one-person operation. Many people have extended a helping hand, suggestions, and words of encouragement as this volume came to life.

Therefore, I wish to extend my appreciation and thanks to Robert G. Anderson, Brian Anthony, Liliane Broadbent, Harold Casselton, Connie Chaney, George Chaney, Lon R. Chaney, the Cinema and Television Library at the University of Southern California, Mary and Bert Clark, Ned Comstock, James Cozart, Oliver Dernberger, Vladimir Dmitriev of the Gosfilmofond Archive (Russia), William N. Dunphy, Larry Edmunds Bookshop, Sam Gill, Arja Grandia of the Netherlands Film Museum, Robert Grasso, the late John Hampton, the Margaret Herrick Library of the Academy of Motion Picture Arts and Sciences, Robert Israel, Dana Kalionzes, the Library of Congress, the Louis B. Mayer Library of the American Film Institute, Vladimir Opela at the Narodni Filmovy Archive (Czechoslovakia), Tina Rainey, Christopher Shannon at the George Eastman House, Beth Werling, Bret Wood, and Patrick Wood.

Thank yous are also in order to my supportive friends who have shared my triumphs and tribulations: Sandi Berg, James Curtis, Beverly Diehl, Mike Hawks, Michael Holland, Loren Harbert, Kevin Joy, Mark Kineavy, Philip Leibfried, Cheryl Pappas, James Peers III, James Pepper, David C. Smith, Elaine Stuart, Steve Tanner, Takashi Teshigawara, Mitch Trimboli, the late Lamar D. Tabb, and Tom Weaver. A special tip of the cap goes to my friend George Wagner, who has always been willing to run a movie projector or offer his opinion.

It is with a great sadness that I must thank, posthumously, Lawrence Austin of the Silent Movie Theatre. The support he gave to my previous books, and to me, was most generous. Silent movies, and their admirers, lost one of their true champions to a senseless act of greed.

Last, but certainly not least, a big thank you to my wife, Linda. She has demonstrated the patience of a saint while reading through several revisions, offering her opinion on photographs and sitting through countless screenings of Chaney films. It was my good fortune to stumble across her.

Preface

He stared at me from the pages. The face, covered in varying amounts of greasepaint, putty, and crepe hair, seemed to be always looking at me. It was as if the figure in the photograph were saying, "Come with me. I'll show you something you haven't seen." And he was right.

Many of Lon Chaney's admirers were first introduced to this wizard of character roles by a picture upon a printed page. Before we saw the movies, we had memorized the photographs. Most of us had not yet seen his image flashed on a movie screen, and it was the photographs that graced various books and magazines that piqued our interest and ignited our passion. For it was through these pictures that we became familiar with the man behind the faces. Even the lack of hard facts did little to sway his fans' adulation of him; in most cases it served only to fuel the fire, leaving us eager to know more about him.

Through the many photos that dotted the various cinema books and monster magazines, we became fascinated by what this man could do to his face with greasepaint. No doubt the many over-embellished and misleading stories that developed around his accomplishing these feats helped to knight Lon Chaney with an almost mystical godlike stature that, along with these photographs, whetted our appetites to see his films.

Because I was fortunate enough to have seen some of his movies, I was approached with a sense of awe by those Chaney admirers who had yet to see these treasures. If you had seen any of Chaney's rare M-G-M films in the early 1970s, you had bestowed upon you the reverence reserved for a distinguished war veteran. You had been there. You had seen him in action. He performed for you, while others had only a still picture or two to entice them. If you had seen a film, you had a duty to share Chaney's exploits with those less fortunate. Today, thanks to the video revolution and cable television, many of Chaney's admirers can see his performances. But when the film has ended and the screen fades to darkness, it is the still photograph that remains with us. Whether the picture is in our mind, or in a book, or is a glossy eight-by-ten that we hold greedily in our hands, the image speaks directly to us. Each picture says something different to the person gazing upon it. To some, those lucky enough to have seen his performances, it may bring back memories of a film or a portrayal that was astounding. Others who have yet to see these films look at these pictures much like the first fans who stood in the lobbies of movie theatres in the 1920s and stared at the same illustrations, wondering what the film would hold in store for them. And for a certain few, these pictures are inspirations, the spur needed for them to try to replicate the look of Chaney's make-up with the help of their own make-up cases.

To a film buff or a cinema historian, the unposed, behind-the-scenes photographs are equally important. They capture a moment on the set of a film, showing that our heroes and heroines are really much like the rest of us. They may be in a deep discussion with the director, taking home movies on the set, getting their make-up touched up, or laughing at some event to which we will never be privy. But these illustrations allow us to see the "real" side of our favorite stars and, in many cases, they speak volumes more than scene stills do. They allow us, if only for a moment, to join that magical world of making motion pictures. We are no longer "outside looking in"; we are part of the action. They allow us to become closer to our subject, maybe even getting a feel for what he or she was like while making a movie.

Then there are those films that none of us will ever see, the films that are lost forever. Because of these "missing links" in the chain of cinema history, the photographs from those pictures become even more important. They, along with any surviving memorabilia (posters, lobby cards, etc.), are the last tangible illustrations of what once was. Like the old, fading images in grandfather's photo album, these pictures document a moment in time, even if it was merely an illusion or fantasy. They allow us to look back and wonder, using our imagination to envision what the rest of the film might have been like.

The purpose of these various photographs was publicity. They, along with the posters and lobby cards, were displayed in front of the theatre, to entice moviegoers to patronize a certain studio's film. By the early 1920s, these forms of promotion had become not only an art but also a full-time business. Fan magazines published a two-page layout with pictures of an upcoming film, hoping to spark that ever-necessary word of mouth. Some magazines would publish photos from films that were still in production, usually featuring a behind-the-scenes picture or a star shaking hands with a visiting dignitary. A theatre lobby of the

1920s would be a dream come true for a collector of film memorabilia today. In large theatres, posters of various sizes would be displayed along with colorful lobby cards and perhaps a cut-out display. Amongst these treasures would be the eight-by-ten glossy pictures, about a dozen adorning a glass case. Patrons would eagerly crowd around these displays before the picture, trying to guess what the movie was about. After the movie, they would again gather to remind their friends of a certain scene or, in Chaney's case, stare at his remarkable make-up.

Then there were the fans who wrote to their favorite stars, hoping to get an autographed picture. When one arrived in the mail, little did the recipient realize that it wasn't really the star's handwriting on it, but probably that of a secretary in the studio's publicity department. These portrait photographs were sent by the thousands to eager fans and fan magazines. As the business continued to grow, many studios employed only the best photographers to capture that "certain look" they wanted for their stars. The portrait photograph, especially those taken by Hollywood's greatest (George Hurrell, Ruth Harriet Louise, and Clarence Bull), are much-sought-after items by memorabilia collectors. They had a style all their own, and it was many of these photographs of Chaney that have intrigued his most recent group of fans. These portraits stare back at us and make us wonder how he accomplished his make-ups and what type of characters he played.

Over a span of seventeen years, Lon Chaney emerged from the obscure ranks of a movie extra to become Hollywood's first character star. No other actor could have taken such a variety of characters and literally transfixed the entire world of moviegoers. While many of his portrayals were not, at first glance, the type to which one would expect an audience to warmly respond, Chaney was able to cross the barrier of a role's less-than-admirable traits and win viewers' sympathy.

In film after film, Lon Chaney displayed his dexterousness by portraying a Russian peasant, a tough Marine sergeant, a century-old mandarin and his grandson, a tragic clown, a shrewd police detective, a crippled magician, a legless criminal, three different Chinese roles, a deformed bell ringer, a mysterious phantom, a Swedish farmer who becomes senile, a blind pirate, a deranged surgeon and his botched experiment (a half-ape/half-man), a scheming country lawyer, a veteran train engineer, and even a ventriloquist who masquerades as an old woman. Each time audiences would fill the theatres to be thrilled by his uncanny talent, causing one critic to ask, "What *can't* this man do?"

Striving to find a place in the early days of motion pictures, Lon Chaney was quick to grasp the fact that being a character actor could provide a long and steady career compared to those of actors playing leading man or juvenile roles. With that observation in mind, Chaney executed a variety of performances, including an occasional foray as a leading man or juvenile. His ability to play assorted roles eventually led to his becoming one of the most prolific and admired character actors in Hollywood in the early 1920s. With the release of *The Hunchback of Notre Dame*, Lon Chaney ascended from character actor to Hollywood's only character *star*. Until his untimely death in 1930, he reigned as one of Hollywood's biggest stars. Proof of his popularity can be measured not in his amount of fan mail but in the fact that all of the eighteen films he made at Metro-Goldwyn-Mayer studios (in a six-year period) turned a profit. Additional proof of his popularity is that, in 1928 and 1929, as silent movies were being superseded by sound films and audiences lining up to buy tickets, Lon Chaney, who continued to appear in silent movies, nevertheless was voted by theatre exhibitors as the most popular actor in motion pictures.

When you read the synopses and look at the photographs from his films, many of which are considered lost, you will see that there was more to Lon Chaney than merely his being considered a "horror actor" (only a small handful of his films are of that genre) or simply an actor who could do anything with make-up. In his relatively short career, Lon Chaney appeared in 157 films. Unfortunately, only 44 survive today in either complete or partial form.

Many of those that have survived are not in the best condition, falling victim to decomposing nitrate film stock. In some cases, entire reels are missing or, at best, only fragments remain of the original print. As the years pass, the chances of finding a "lost" Lon Chaney film grow remote. It always remains the optimistic hope of film historians and Chaney fans that more of his work will be found, allowing us to observe another facet of his unique talent. But time continues to be a film's greatest foe. Nitrate film stock does not age well, and many movies from both the silent and sound eras are gone forever. Efforts are being made by preservationists to transfer films produced on this delicate stock to a stable film base, but the cost of this process is monumental. Compounding this problem are the agonizing decisions that must be made: should the money be expended to restore a little-known motion picture or a lost Lon Chaney or Greta Garbo film?

But just when we think the chances of finding a missing Chaney film have all but gone the way of the dodo bird, a happy accident will occur. I have detailed other such finds in my previous two books on Chaney, but some of the most exciting happened while I was putting the finishing touches on this volume. For years, we all thought that *Thunder*, Lon Chaney's last silent and fifth-highest grossing M-G-M film, was lost forever. Then came the telephone call from Lawrence Austin of the Silent Movie Theatre. He was looking through several reels containing miscellaneous film clips that the former owner and founder of the theatre, John Hampton, had preserved, and lo and behold—a small fragment of the film (running sixty to ninety seconds) was on the reel! And as fortune would have it, the entire sequence featured Chaney. Shortly after this discovery, I received word that a portion of nitrate footage from *Thunder* (approximately 530 feet) was found at the Library of Congress. As we speak, the legal and financial hurdles for restoring this footage are almost completed, and restoration will be under way.

Just as soon as I got over the excitement of learning about *Thunder*, several European film archives responded to my letters of inquiry. Believe it or not, four more films (*The Wicked Darling* [1919], *When Bearcat Went Dry* [1919], *Paid In Advance* [1919], and *Riddle Gawne* [1918]) previously thought to be missing turned up, including the first film Chaney made with director Tod Browning. A few months later, the American Film Institute announced that a film collector had donated two rare silent films, *Richard III* (1912) and another print of *When Bearcat Went Dry*. Unfortunately, the latter print is, according to published reports, not in the best condition, but it is hoped that it will be restored soon.

These recent finds have ignited my hopes that more discoveries will continue. Maybe one of the many rumors about *London After Midnight*'s existence will finally come to fruition. With the recent find of *Thunder*, I remain hopeful that prints of many other titles have somehow been carefully preserved and are lying quietly in someone's basement or garage, awaiting discovery. Until then, the remaining 44 films and this book will help to fill the void. And let's not forget those pictures. Many of them were taken over seventy years ago, but they still intrigue us. They are worth a thousand words—and a thousand faces.

Michael F. Blake

A Note about the Reviews

The reviews herein are taken from the various industry trade journals and fan magazines of the day. *Motion Picture News, Exhibitors Trade Review, Harrison's Reports, Moving Picture World, Variety, Wid's Film Daily* (which was later shortened to *Film Daily*), and *Film Spectator* were published exclusively for industry executives, film exhibitors, and theatre owners. Keeping this fact in mind will help the reader when such terms as "a $2 picture" (the highest price charged for a ticket) or "best for large-sized houses" (big movie palaces) are used.

These trade magazines also included articles and photographs of various publicity gimmicks used by theatre owners to attract their patrons. Detailed articles related to problems encountered by theatre owners and projectionists, and offered solutions. But perhaps the most important aspect of these journals was the records they gave of the percentage of an audience each major star attracted. This type of report, along with the financial tally of a film's performance at the box office, dictated the popularity of a star, *not* the fan mail.

The fan magazines, on the other hand, spoke directly to the patrons of the silver screen. They told their loyal readers whether some star's picture was worth their spending 25¢ to $2. *Photoplay* was one such publication. Each month the magazine chose certain pictures and performers' portrayals as their choices of the month. Annually the magazine would select, as did many trade journals, their top ten films and performances of the specific year.

Of Chaney's numerous appearances in movies from 1913 to 1918, I have restricted the reviews to one per film, the exceptions being the six he directed in 1915 and the career-boosting films *Hell Morgan's Girl* and *Riddle Gawne*. Lest anyone accuse me of whitewashing Lon Chaney's films or performances, I have included reviews that were less than laudatory. For some of the early Universal films (1913–1918), the reader may find no review after a synopsis. This is not an omission; unfortunately, no review could be found in any of the journals available.

Behind-the-scenes information about the films, wherever applicable, may be found in the *Notes* section.

CHAPTER ONE

1913

Poor Jake's Demise

IMP/Universal, 1 reel. *Released:* August 16, 1913. *Production Code No.:* 0006. *Director:* Allan Curtis. *Scenario:* Not credited.

CAST
Lon Chaney.

SYNOPSIS
Jake comes home and surprises his wife and Willy Mollycoddle in a compromising position. He tosses Willy out of the house and scolds his wife, threatening to kill himself. His wife, fearing he will carry through his promise, calls the police, begging them to intercede. While the police are searching for him, Jake stops at a bar to drown his sorrows before carrying out his threat and sees Willy. With the aid of a seltzer bottle, Jake takes his revenge on his wife's Romeo.

CRITICS' CORNER
This is simply horse play without any special appeal, though it is harmless and lacks vulgarity. *Moving Picture World*

NOTES
This is the first known screen credit Lon Chaney received. Some film historians contend that Chaney appeared in unbilled roles in *Honor of the Family* (1912) and *Suspense* (1913) prior to *Poor Jake's Demise*. This author has been able to examine photographs or footage from both of these films and is confident that Chaney does not appear in either title.

The Sea Urchin

Powers/Universal, 1 reel. *Released:* August 22, 1913. *Production Code No.:* 0101. *Director:* Edwin August. *Scenario:* Jeanie MacPherson.

CAST
Lon Chaney (*Barnacle Bill*); Robert Z. Leonard and Jeanie MacPherson (*The Lovers*).

SYNOPSIS
Barnacle Bill is a hunchback fisherman in love with the young girl. When she falls in love with Bob, he becomes enraged and plots revenge against the young man. All this changes when the young girl is almost drowned and Bill, risking his own life, saves her. When she offers to marry him out of gratitude, Bill realizes that her happiness is foremost and reunites the young lovers.

CRITICS' CORNER
A memorable offering, with some vivid scenes along a picturesque coast. *Moving Picture World*

NOTES
This is the first known film in which Chaney played a character role. Robert Z. Leonard and Chaney had worked together in musical comedies with the Ferris Hartman Troupe three years earlier. Leonard would later direct Chaney in *Danger—Go Slow* (1918), starring Leonard's then-wife, Mae Murray.

The Blood Red Tape of Charity
Powers/Universal, 1 reel. *Released:* September 26, 1913. *Production Code No.:* 0119. *Director:* Edwin August. *Scenario:* Not credited.

CAST
Edwin August, Lon Chaney.

SYNOPSIS
William Weldon, a telephone line man, has a hard time making ends meet for his large family. It becomes increasingly difficult when he is laid off because of an injury. The family applies for charity, but the red tape involved delays the family's receiving any support. Mark, a gentleman thief who lives in the same building as the Weldons, meets the Weldon's invalid daughter, who explains their plight. Mark endeavors to aid the family by forcing a doctor to treat the daughter. He also plots and carries out a robbery of society people at a ball. Mark pawns the stolen jewelry and gives the money to the Weldons. With Mark's help, the family recovers, but the thief realizes he must turn himself in

to the police. He goes to jail with a clear conscious because of the charity he had bestowed.

CRITICS' CORNER
Edwin August has written a brilliant two-part drama along this theme and acted and produced it in a manner that will fasten the public's attention. *Moving Picture World*

NOTES
Chaney did not receive screen credit, but appears in a trade paper ad playing a Jewish pawnbroker.

Shon the Piper

101-Bison/Universal, 3 reels. *Released:* September 30, 1913. *Production Code No.:* 0168. *Producer:* Otis Turner. *Scenario:* Not credited. *Photographer:* William Foster.

CAST
Robert Z. Leonard (*Shon*), Marguerite Fisher, Lon Chaney.

SYNOPSIS
In the late 18th century in Scotland, Shon, a rich duke, seeks adventure in the Highlands to escape the girl who wants to marry him for his wealth. In the Highlands, disguised as a piper, Shon meets Madge. The two fall in love but her father objects to Shon favoring instead the rich Laird. When the girl relates her father's wishes, Shon tells her not to despair. At the wedding of Madge and the Laird, Shon, playing his pipes, rescues Madge, spiriting her away to his castle. To help in their escape, Shon summons his clan to cover their tracks, and they do battle with the pursuing clan. When Madge's father learns of Shon's real title, he consents to his daughter's wishes, and all ends well.

CRITICS' CORNER
This three-reel photoplay produced by Otis Turner can best be described as a poetic melodrama, rich in local color. . . . not even a Scotchman can say that the exterior scenes were not laid in the Highlands. *Universal Weekly*

NOTES
While he did not receive screen credit, Chaney played a member of one of the Scottish clans.

The Trap

Powers/Universal, 1 reel. *Released:* October 3, 1913. *Production Code No.:* 0157. *Director:* Edwin August. *Scenario:* Not credited.

CAST
Lon Chaney, Cleo Madison.

SYNOPSIS
Lon is engaged to Jane, a social butterfly whose financial desires are impossible for him to fulfill. Seeking help from his brother Chance, he is flatly turned down. Lon attempts to steal from his brother but is caught and turned away. Days later, Lon tries to explain the situation to Jane but is rebuffed. Chance finds Jane in tears and puts his arms around her to comfort her. Chance's wife, Cleo, sees her husband embracing another woman but cannot identify her. She later dabs some paint on the sleeve of her husband's overcoat in an attempt to entrap him. Chance and Lon meet again and an argument erupts, with Chance leaving his overcoat on the beach. Lon puts on the coat and happens upon Jane, who then accepts his explanation and forgives him. They embrace, with the paint still on the sleeve of the coat. Returning to the house, Lon and Chance reconcile, but when Cleo finds paint on Jane's dress, she accuses her husband of infidelity. Lon is able to explain the situation and all is resolved.

CRITICS' CORNER
The story is not overly strong, though some of the scenes are attractive.
Moving Picture World

NOTES
According to the Universal Picture Code Book the film's release date is October 26, 1913.[1]

The Restless Spirit

Victor/Universal, 3 reels. *Released:* October 27, 1913. *Production Code No.:* 0199. *Director:* Allan Dwan. *Scenario:* Not credited. *Photographer:* Walter Prichard.

CAST
Warren Kerrigan (*The Husband*), Pauline Bush (*The Wife*), Jessalyn Van Trump (*The Woman*), William Worthington (*The Stranger*), Lon Chaney.

SYNOPSIS
Living in a village, the husband idles and dreams away his time while his wife and child come to want. He believes himself capable of greater

things than the village offers. He finally leaves the village, resolving to find power and glory in the world beyond. His wife and child move in with her father, who hopes she will leave her husband and marry the rich stranger. In the desert, the husband collapses from exhaustion. He is found by a woman who nurses him back to health while he relates his ambitions and hopes. Listening to him, she realizes what his problem is and shows him the vanity of illusions such as he has, of trying to conquer the world when his own village remains unconquered. He returns to his family and comes to be respected and loved in his own village.

CRITICS' CORNER
The picture is different from anything yet attempted; it is unique in the extreme, a beautiful piece of artistic work that will stand among the best pictures ever put out. *Universal Weekly*

NOTES
While Chaney did not obtain billing in the cast list, he is clearly identifiable in a photograph (sporting a fake beard) on cover of the October 25 issue of *Universal Weekly*.

An Elephant on His Hands

Nestor/Universal, 1 reel. *Released:* November 21, 1913. *Production Code No.:* 0175. *Director:* Al Christie. *Scenario:* Not credited.

CAST
Lon Chaney (*Eddie*).

SYNOPSIS
Eddie hates animals and his wife loves them. Eddie's uncle sends him an elephant to care for from his bankrupt circus. Although Eddie protests vigorously, his strong-headed wife forces him to go to the train station to pick up the animal. After paying a stableman an enormous fee to care for it, Eddie goes to the train station, but it's just one problem after another when the stableman refuses to board the beast. Eddie decides to leave the elephant in his back yard, but havoc erupts. In the end, Eddie and his wife hitch up the elephant to a furniture van and all three walk off into the sunset.

CRITICS' CORNER
In this comedy, it is probable that most of the fun will come from the antics of the animals, two of which are featured—a monkey and an

elephant. The oscillatory feats of the former are bound to convulse any house. *Moving Picture World*

Almost an Actress

Joker/Universal, 1 reel. *Released:* November 15, 1913. *Production Code No.:* 0141. *Director:* Allan Curtis. *Scenario:* Not credited.

CAST
Louise Fazenda (*Suzie*), Max Asher (*The Director*), Edward Holland (*The Heavy*), Lee Morris (*Lee*), Lon Chaney (*The Cameraman*), Silvon de Jardins (aka Bobby Vernon; *Benny*).

SYNOPSIS
Suzie is a stage-struck young girl who refuses her boyfriend's proposal of marriage, planning instead to become a famous actress. A film company just happens to be in town, having its own calamity: the leading lady's false teeth have broken and the director needs a new lead. Suzie, on an errand for her mother, is pressed into service by the quick-thinking director. Benny, Suzie's brother, is sent to find her, and when he sees her in the clutches of a villain, he attempts to save her by spreading the word of his sister's peril. When the neighbors arrive, Suzie is about to be burned to death. The fire department, along with her boyfriend, arrive, creating a small deluge while attempting to put out the fire. The movie company demands that the fire department and neighbors leave. The next scene requires Suzie to be tied up on the beach as the tide rises. Meanwhile, the neighbors summon the sheriff, who arrests the film company but forgets about Suzie, leaving her to drown in the rising tide. Her boyfriend rescues her, and the director offers her a job as a regular, which Suzie vigorously declines.

CRITICS' CORNER
A very laughable production of the low comedy type, full of chuckles and free from offense. . . . The scenes are all of burlesque nature and furnish plenty of genuine amusement. *Motion Picture World*

NOTES
Silvon de Jardins, who later became a popular silent-film comedian under the name Bobby Vernon, was a member of the 1913 Kolb and Dill company in which Chaney also appeared. This was the same company that was playing in Los Angeles when Chaney's first wife, Cleva, attempted suicide in the wings of the theatre.

Back to Life

Victor/Universal, 2 reels. *Released:* November 24, 1913. *Production Code No.:* 0223. *Director:* Allan Dwan. *Scenario:* M. de la Parella.

CAST

Pauline Bush (*The Wife*), J. Warren Kerrigan (*Destiny's Victim*), William Worthington (*The Gambler*), Jessalyn Van Trump (*The Charmer*), Lon Chaney (*The Rival*).

SYNOPSIS

A gambler brings his sick wife to the mountains but soon tires of caring for her and finds comfort in one of the women in the nearby saloon. The wife finds out about her husband's cheating and leaves him, heading into the forest, where she hopes to die. She comes upon a wounded man, Jim, and helps him. Jim takes her to an old couple's cabin, where she rapidly regains her own health. The wife decides to return to her husband. On the way back to her cabin, she discovers him dying from a gunshot wound he has suffered in a saloon brawl. After her husband's death, the wife is reunited with Jim, and they make plans to face the future together.

CRITICS' CORNER

Like all of director Allan Dwan's features, it has tons of action throughout. *Universal Weekly*

Red Margaret, Moonshiner

Gold Seal/Universal, 2 reels. *Released:* December 9, 1913. *Production Code No.:* 0299. *Director:* Allan Dwan. *Scenario:* Jeanie MacPherson.

CAST

Pauline Bush (*Red Margaret*), Murdock MacQuarrie (*Government Agent*), James Neill (*The Sheriff*), Lon Chaney (*Lon*).

SYNOPSIS

Red Margaret is the leader of a band of moonshiners who defy the law. Authorities know that if she were caught, the rest of her band would surely surrender. The government sends in an agent to work undercover, and Margaret falls in love with him. Margaret's suitor figures out the agent's true identity and captures him, and Margaret notifies the deputies that the agent is in danger. A big shoot-out erupts, during which her father is killed and the agent is wounded. Margaret leads the agent back to the sheriff's office, where she surrenders after having saved the agent's life.

CRITICS' CORNER
Pauline Bush gives a good portrayal. . . . It is a disagreeable part and a hard one, but she makes much of it. There are good mountain backgrounds. *Moving Picture World*

NOTES
Chaney played an old moonshiner in this film, sporting a wild beard and long hair. It shows that early on in his film career, Lon was using make-up for various roles.

Bloodhounds of the North

Gold Seal/Universal, 2 reels. *Released:* December 23, 1913. *Production Code No.:* 0314. *Director:* Allan Dwan. *Scenario:* Not credited.

CAST
Pauline Bush (*His Daughter*), William Lloyd (*The Embezzler*), James Neill (*The Refugee*), Murdock MacQuarrie, Lon Chaney (*Mounties*).

SYNOPSIS
An out-of-the-way spot in the mountains is a refuge for many wanted by the law. An embezzler and his daughter find their way into this encampment and the embezzler eventually becomes the guiding spirit of the colony. But two mounties are on the embezzler's trail. He positions some of the colony's men to ambush the mounties. In the shoot-out, one of the mounties is wounded. The embezzler's daughter cares for him. The other mountie follows the girl to her father and tries to force himself upon her, but the wounded mountie interferes. The bad mountie learns who the girl's father really is and arrests him. The girl pleads with the wounded mountie, saying she will do anything if he will save her father. When he attempts to shoot his partner, the refugee mistakes his intention and they kill the bad mountie. In the gunfire, the embezzler dies. The wounded mountie is himself near death when another mountie arrives to help. The girl realizes the mountie is a man to love and respect.

CRITICS' CORNER
This two-reel drama gives a good account of the Canadian Mounted Police. . . . Some splendid woods and mountain settings occur. *Moving Picture World*

Notes

This production was filmed on location in Mt. Lowe, California.

On location, Dwan's company was confined by heavy rains at the Ye Alpine Tavern on Mt. Lowe. While the rain idled the company, they rehearsed scenes for the up-coming *Richelieu*. After five days, the company completed filming this production and another film, *The Honor of the Mounted* (1914), in two days.[2]

Location filming was not without its mishaps. Chaney and actor Arthur Rosson became lost in a deep canyon and it wasn't until late in the evening that the two men were found by rescue teams.[3]

CHAPTER TWO

1914

The Lie

Gold Seal/Universal, 2 reels. *Released:* January 6, 1914. *Director:* Allan Dwan. *Scenario:* Jeanie MacPherson.

CAST

Murdock MacQuarrie (*Auld MacGregor*), Pauline Bush (*His Daughter*), William Lloyd (*Mac's Brother*), Lon Chaney (*Young MacGregor*), Richard and Arthur Rosson (*More Fortunate Youths*), Fred McKay (*Their Father*), James Neill (*The Gambler*).

SYNOPSIS

The two children of Auld MacGregor wish their father would treat them better and spend more money on them. A gambler, hoping to get his hands on MacGregor's fortune, works up a friendship with his son. The boy lies to his father about his sudden winnings. His lie is exposed by Arthur, who has fallen foul of the gambler. Young MacGregor gets into a saloon fight with the gambler, and his sister and Arthur fire their guns at the gambler at the same moment. However, Arthur's shot goes unnoticed and young MacGregor's sister is accused of the gambler's death. The boy pleads with his father to lie and secure an alibi to save his sister, which Auld MacGregor does.

CRITICS' CORNER

This is a very good two reel production. . . . The story is interestingly presented and holds interest from the beginning. It is perhaps a little drawn-out in places, but on the whole the film is a commendable one. *Motion Picture World*

The Honor of the Mounted

Gold Seal/Universal, 2 reels. *Released:* February 17, 1914. *Production Code No.:* 0317. *Director:* Allan Dwan. *Scenario:* Arthur Rosson.

CAST
Pauline Bush (*Marie Laquox*), Murdock MacQuarrie (*A Mountie*), Lon
Chaney (*Jacques Laquox*), James Neill (*Post Commander*).

SYNOPSIS
Mac, Jacques, and his sister, Marie, grow up together in the mountains.
Mac and Marie are in love but he wishes to better himself, so he moves
to the city to seek an education. Tiring of city life, however, Mac returns
and joins the mounties, although everyone looks down on him, including Marie. Forrest is a mountie sent to Mac's hometown to investigate
smuggling. While there, he meets Marie and tries to force himself upon
her. He is killed by Jacques and Mac is sent to investigate the murder.
An enemy of Jacques tells Mac that it was Jacques who killed the
mountie, and Mac is forced to arrest his best friend. But when the
townspeople attack Mac, Jacques fights beside his old friend. Mac refuses to take Jacques in and they quarrel, which leads to their falling to
their deaths on the treacherous "Devil's Slide."

CRITICS' CORNER
Lon Chaney and Mr. MacQuarrie . . . hold the center stage, acting out
the great drama that strives to loosen their friendship. *Universal Weekly*

NOTES
This production was filmed back to back with *Bloodhounds of the North*
(1913) on location at Mt. Lowe, California.[4]

Remember Mary Magdalen

Victor/Universal, 2 reels. *Released:* February 23, 1914. *Production Code
No.:* 0409. *Director:* Allan Dwan. *Scenario:* Not credited.

CAST
Pauline Bush (*The Woman*), Murdock MacQuarrie (*The Minister*), Lon
Chaney (*The Half-Wit*).

SYNOPSIS
Returning to her hometown years after making a foolish mistake in her
youth, a worn-out woman finds her parents have died. Villagers shun
her, and news of her return quickly spreads. The new minister is asked
to have her ordered out of town, but she refuses to leave and stays at
her parents' home. The minister is taken by her repentance and courage. When the townspeople try to drive her out of town, the woman
goes out to meet the crowd but is met with jeers and stones. The minis-

ter, as well as a half-witted man, defend the woman, but the man is hit with one of the stones and dies. This tragic accident causes the crowd to disperse, and later the minister and the woman find happiness with each other.

CRITICS' CORNER
A good drama which presents several morals. *Motion Picture News*

Discord and Harmony

Gold Seal/Universal, 3 reels. *Released:* March 17, 1914. *Production Code No.:* 0354. *Director:* Allan Dwan. *Scenario:* Arthur Rosson.

CAST

Pauline Bush (*The Girl*), Murdock MacQuarrie (*The Composer*), Allan Forrest (*The Artist*), James Neill (*The Symphony Conductor*), Lon Chaney (*The Sculptor*).

SYNOPSIS

Old Felix, a struggling composer, finally sells one of his symphonies. A young girl who lives in the same building as Felix and has just lost her mother seeks the help of the old man, who is so touched by her he adopts the girl as his ward. A local sculptor falls in love with her. To complicate matters, an artist also desires the girl, but she shuns the artist's advances. Felix has raised enough money for the sculptor to go to Europe to study, but before leaving, he marries the young girl with only Felix's knowledge. The artist overhears the young couple making plans for their future, not knowing about their marriage, and spreads a rumor about the girl's dishonor. Felix's friends confront him about the rumors and, becoming upset, the old man drives them from his apartment. The strain of both losing his friends and struggling to complete his latest symphony are too much, and the old man dies. The girl tells his old friends about Felix's death and they gather to play his unfinished work, hoping to be forgiven. When the now-famous sculptor returns from Europe, Felix's old friends discover the marriage between the couple.

CRITICS' CORNER

A very melancholy production somewhat similar in certain respects to a number of its predecessors yet vastly different than others. Excellent make-up and good direction are responsible for its telling points. . . . A splendid finale is registered. *Motion Picture News*

The Menace to Carlotta

Rex/Universal, 2 reels. *Released:* March 22, 1914. *Production Code No.:* 0442. *Director:* Allan Dwan. *Scenario:* Lon Chaney.

CAST

Pauline Bush (*Carlotta*), William C. Dowlan (*Tony*), Murdock MacQuarrie (*His Father*), Lon Chaney (*Giovanni Bartholi*), John Burton (*The Vulture*).

SYNOPSIS

Tony is a bootblack who is finally able to bring his father and sister, Carlotta, to the United States from Italy. He introduces his friend, Giovanni Bartholi, to his family. One night Giovanni loses his money to the Vulture while gambling, and Tony and his family take him in, treating him like one of their own. The Vulture suggests to Giovanni that he bring Carlotta to a certain dive where he can make some money for himself and retrieve his lost fortune. Giovanni refuses, but the Vulture persists, and eventually Giovanni agrees to the plan. He brings the unsuspecting Carlotta to the appointed dive, but she is rescued by Tony.

CRITICS' CORNER

The fight between Giovanni and the old father is very realistic, almost too much so. *Motion Picture News*

NOTES

This is Chaney's first known credit for a scenario. The film's working title was *Carlotta the Bean Stringer*.

The Embezzler

Gold Seal/Universal, 2 reels. *Released:* March 31, 1914. *Production Code No.:* 0421. *Director:* Allan Dwan. *Scenario:* Not credited.

CAST

Pauline Bush (*His Daughter*), Murdock MacQuarrie (*John Spencer*), William C. Dowlan (*Arthur Bronson*), Lon Chaney (*J. Roger Dixon*), William Lloyd (*William Perkins*), Richard Rosson (*The Penman*).

SYNOPSIS

John Spencer is idolized by his daughter, who is unaware of his criminal past. Roger Dixon knows of Spencer's past and begins to blackmail him. As time passes, the blackmailer's demands become bolder. He threatens to reveal Spencer's past if he cannot have his daughter's hand in marriage. She is involved with a young attorney, Arthur, and Spencer agrees to discredit the young man in his daughter's eyes. Meanwhile, Dixon plots with two other criminals to frame Arthur by stealing the options. Spencer's daughter overhears the plan and notifies her father, who then confesses his past crimes and Dixon's grip on his life. To save her father, she agrees to marry Dixon. When Dixon pays off the two criminals, an argument erupts and he is killed. With Dixon's death, the skeleton in the Spencer family closet also expires, and happiness follows.

CRITICS' CORNER
The story is well constructed, but not very fresh in the subject matter. *Moving Picture World*

NOTES
The Universal Picture Code Book lists the film's release date as March 24, 1914.[5]

The Lamb, The Woman, The Wolf
101-Bison/Universal, 3 reels. *Released:* April 4, 1914. *Production Code No.:* 0431. *Director and Scenario:* Allan Dwan.

CAST
Pauline Bush (*The Woman*), Murdock MacQuarrie (*The Lamb*), Lon Chaney (*The Wolf*).

SYNOPSIS
The Lamb is a kind man who loves the Woman but does not expect her to share his burden of caring for his invalid mother. The Wolf, a virile mountaineer, has returned after a five-year absence and seeks to renew his love affair with the Woman. They marry and move to the mountains, where he works for the stage line and mining company. The Woman soon realizes that she has made a mistake in marrying the Wolf, who is very brutal to her. After the Lamb's mother dies, he ventures into the mountains to nurse his sorrow. He falls in with a band of outlaws and becomes a member of their group. By now the Wolf has tired of the Woman and makes plans to steal the mining company money and abandon her. The Lamb has also made plans to steal the payroll. The Lamb arrives at the office first but is not recognized by the Woman, who has been left alone to guard the money. The Lamb lays his gun on the table in order to calm her fears. Meanwhile, the Wolf, whose face is masked, sneaks in and startles the Woman, who grabs the gun and kills the in-

truder. She then recognizes the Lamb and realizes that happiness lies ahead for them.

CRITICS' CORNER
The production as a whole is one of about average merit. *Moving Picture World*

The End of the Feud

Rex/Universal, 2 reels. *Released:* April 12, 1914. *Production Code No.:* 0461. *Director:* Allan Dwan. *Scenario:* Not credited.

CAST
Murdock MacQuarrie (*Hen Dawson*), Pauline Bush (*June*), Lon Chaney (*Wood Dawson*), William Lloyd (*Jed Putnam*), William C. Dowlan (*Joel*).

SYNOPSIS
For fifty years the Dawsons and Putnams have been feuding, but a new minister convinces the two families that it is ungodly to fight. Peace and harmony abound until Wood Dawson finds out that his sweetheart, June, is in love with Joel Putnam. Wood confronts Joel about the romance and a fight erupts, ending with Wood's death. Hen Dawson, determined to kill Joel in revenge, finds him with his daughter. Hen is about to murder Joel when the minister, intervening, settles the feud by marrying Joel and June.

CRITICS' CORNER
Drama of the south, beautiful scenery throughout. . . . A good love story with unusual editing. *Motion Picture News*

The Tragedy of Whispering Creek

101-Bison/Universal, 2 reels. *Released:* May 2, 1914. *Production Code No.:* 0524. *Director and Scenario:* Allan Dwan.

CAST
Murdock MacQuarrie (*The Stranger*), Pauline Bush (*The Orphan*), William C. Dowlan (*Bashful Bill*), Lon Chaney (*The Greaser*), George Cooper (*The Kid*), Mary Ruby (*His Sweetheart*), John Burton, Doc Crane and William Lloyd (*Prospectors*).

SYNOPSIS
In a small mining community lives an orphan girl engaged to a miner known as Bashful Bill. A degenerate Mexican known as the "Greaser"

proves to be a menace to the community. Bill finds the Greaser threatening a young couple and gives him a well-deserved beating. A young stranger who has wounded himself while cleaning his weapon comes into camp, and the orphan girl takes him to her cabin to dress his wounds. There she is attacked by the Greaser but is saved by the stranger. Unaware of her engagement to Bill, the stranger has fallen in love with her, but when he learns the truth, he decides to go, leaving her behind. As he turns to look back down the mountain, the stranger spots the Greaser about to shoot the girl and Bill from a cliff. The stranger attacks the Greaser and both men are killed in the fight.

CRITICS' CORNER
And then there is Mr. Chaney in the role of the Greaser. Mr. Chaney has used his own ideas in working out the character, a pervert, in this play and what he has given us is startling to an unusual degree. True, he paints a horrible picture for us—one that is apt to cause a feeling of revulsion. But, that is as it should be. In fact Mr. Chaney has created a new character—one that will live long—that will be copied as a newer standard for others. *Universal Weekly.*

The Unlawful Trade

Rex/Universal, 2 reels. *Released:* May 14, 1914. *Production Code No.:* 0532. *Director and Scenario:* Allan Dwan.

CAST
Pauline Bush (*Amy Tate*), William Lloyd (*Old Tate*), George Cooper (*Young Tate*), William C. Dowlan (*Neut*), Murdock MacQuarrie (*The Revenue Man*), Lon Chaney (*The Half-Breed*).

SYNOPSIS
Although he is a moonshiner, George Tate is a good man. He possesses the qualities that many a hero is made of. A half-breed has murdered his father and continually harasses George's sister, Amy, then leads revenue men to the moonshiner's hideout. A shootout begins. In the heat of battle, George, Amy, and Neut Haigh, who loves Amy, retreat to the Tate cabin. As the battle continues, George opens a trap door and orders his sister and her lover to escape while he holds off the revenue men, a gesture that costs him his own life.

CRITICS' CORNER
Undoubtedly one of the best pictures Universal has made. . . . The story of the moonshiners and their war on the revenue men, yet is different from the thousand or so others of this class. *Motion Picture News*

The Forbidden Room

101-Bison/Universal, 3 reels. *Released:* June 20, 1914. *Production Code No.:* 0469. *Director:* Allan Dwan. *Scenario:* Not credited.

CAST

Murdock MacQuarrie (*Dr. Gibson*), Pauline Bush (*His Sister/His Niece*), William C. Dowlan (*Prosecuting Attorney*), Lon Chaney (*John Morris*), John Burton (*Dr. Jarvis*).

SYNOPSIS

Dr. James Gibson promises his dying mother that he will seek out Pauline, his sister, but finding her brings no joy; she has gone insane. He brings Pauline and her daughter home to live with him but keeps Pauline in a locked room. Her daughter seems oblivious to the conditions. Dr. Gibson and his wealthy neighbor, John Morris, share an interest in hypnotism, and one night the doctor places his niece under hypnosis to prove a point with Morris. He instructs his niece to kill Morris, who is her enemy. Instead of a knife, she is given a piece of paper and goes through the motions of stabbing him. Later, Pauline catches a glimpse of Morris and realizes that it was he who caused her ruin. She escapes from her room, taking her daughter's shawl, and goes next door to kill Morris. The next day, Gibson is summoned to the Morris house, where his niece's shawl is discovered. The niece is arrested and convicted of the murder. Later, Pauline is discovered dead in her room, clutching Morris' watch. This piece of evidence leads to the daughter's acquittal.

CRITICS' CORNER

The feature of this picture is a mystery which throughout sustains the interest of the audience. *Motion Picture News*

The Old Cobbler

101-Bison/Universal, 2 reels. *Released:* June 27, 1914. *Production Code No.:* 0589. *Director:* Murdock MacQuarrie. *Scenario:* Not credited.

CAST

Murdock MacQuarrie (*The Cobbler*), Richard Rosson (*His Son*), Agnes Vernon (*Jess*), Lon Chaney (*Wild Bill*).

SYNOPSIS

Old Nathan, a cobbler, finds his son going through his purse one day and so turns him out of the house, hoping his son will change. Nathan's wife is all he has left, but he finds her dead. After her funeral, Nathan heads west and settles in a mining town. Wild Bill visits Nathan and rudely asks him to repair a boot. Nathan stands up to the man and a friendship grows between them. Jess, a dancehall girl and sweetheart of Bill, needs a slipper repaired. Nathan performs the task and places a touching note in the slipper. The note strikes a chord in Jess and she gives up the dance hall. The old cobbler shows Bill a picture of his son and relates his son's history. When Bill catches the highwayman from a stage robbery, he recognizes the criminal as Nathan's son. Bill claims that the robbers dropped the money and got away, clearing the son's name, and Nathan and his son are reunited.

CRITICS' CORNER

The supporting cast, with Lon Chaney and Mr. Rosson at the head, gives a telling account of itself. The settings, for the most part, are western, picturesque and beautifully photographed. *Moving Picture World*

A Ranch Romance

Nestor/Universal, 2 reels. *Released:* July 8, 1914. *Director:* Not credited. *Scenario:* Not credited.

CAST

Murdock MacQuarrie (*Jack Deering*), Agnes Vernon (*Kate Preston*), Lon Chaney (*Raphael Praz*), Seymour Hastings (*John Preston*), E. Keller (*Don Jose Praz*).

SYNOPSIS

Ranch owner John Preston owes a large sum of money to Don Jose Praz. The don's son, Raphael, steals some of Preston's cattle and urges his father to press the issue of the debt so that he may marry Preston's daughter, Kate. The girl is in love with ranch foreman Jack Deering. Unable to force Preston's consent to marry his daughter, Raphael kidnaps Kate. When Kate's horse returns to the ranch, Jack and the cowboys follow her trail. Jack confronts Raphael at the cabin and in the fight, Raphael is killed.

CRITICS' CORNER

The plot is conventional but is enacted in a manner that makes it most interesting. There is an excellent fight scene between the two men. *Motion Picture News*

Hopes of a Blind Alley

101-Bison/Universal, 3 reels. *Released:* July 4, 1914. *Production Code No.:* 0560. *Director:* Allan Dwan. *Scenario:* Not credited.

CAST
Pauline Bush (*Pauline*), Murdock MacQuarrie (*Jean Basse*), William C. Dowlan (*The Unsuccessful Artist*), Lon Chaney (*Vendor*), George Cooper (*The Little Janitor*).

SYNOPSIS
Old Jean Basse manages a meager living by selling miniature statuary, barely supporting himself and his granddaughter, Pauline, who is in love with an unsuccessful artist. Old Jean's one desire is to own a fine silk hat. His dream comes true when he inherits a small fortune from a relative. Unfortunately, the entire estate has been attached by creditors, with the exception of a few worthless items, including an old painting. Pauline's boyfriend recognizes the painting as an original Van Dyke, worth a great deal of money. Old Jean takes the painting to a vendor, who attempts to buy it for two dollars, but the old man refuses. The vendor tries to steal the painting, but his plans are defeated. Meanwhile, Pauline's sweetheart begins to sell his own paintings and they plan to marry. Old Jean, dying, gives Pauline the valuable painting as a wedding gift. At his death bed, the young couple present him with a silk hat, which he insists on wearing as he dies.

CRITICS' CORNER
This story seems to ring true to human feelings. . . . The plot is powerful. The action does not drag. *Motion Picture News*

Her Grave Mistake

Nestor/Universal, 2 reels. *Released:* July 15, 1914. *Production Code No.:* 0614. *Director:* Not credited. *Scenario:* Not credited.

CAST
Murdock MacQuarrie (*Roger Grant*), Agnes Vernon (*Isabel Norris*), Seymour Hastings (*Her Father*), Lon Chaney (*Nunez*).

SYNOPSIS
Roger Grant is the foreman of the "Circle S" ranch and is engaged to Isabel Norris, daughter of the ranch owner. Prior to a dance, Grant receives a note from the national guard warning him about an impending attack on the reservoir by the Mexicans. He is requested to arm

his cowboys and guard the reservoir until the guard arrives. Nunez, a Mexican spy, learns of the letter and plans to steal it from the ranch house. Grant and Isabel return from the dance; she tells him to wait for her signal, then come to the ranch house. Isabel makes the signal, but Nunez comes out of hiding and chokes the girl into unconsciousness, steals the letter, and escapes just as Grant arrives. He is blamed for assaulting Isabel but escapes. Isabel finds a piece of clothing belonging to Nunez and, with the theft of the letter, comes to the conclusion that it was Nunez who attacked her. She follows the cowboys to stop them from going after Grant. Meanwhile, the Mexicans have attacked the reservoir and Grant holds them off single-handedly until Isabel and the cowboys arrive. Nunez is captured and Grant is vindicated.

CRITICS' CORNER
The story is not at all original but Mr. MacQuarrie has a way of putting anything over he tries. *Motion Picture News*

By the Sun's Rays

Nestor/Universal, 2 reels. *Released:* July 22, 1914. *Production Code No.:* 0619. *Director:* Not credited. *Scenario:* Not credited.

CAST
Murdock MacQuarrie (*John Murdock*), Lon Chaney (*Frank Lawler*), Seymour Hastings (*John Davis*), Agnes Vernon (*Dora Davis*), Dick Rosson (*Bandit*).

SYNOPSIS
Detective John Murdock is sent to investigate the numerous gold shipment robberies from a Colorado mine. Frank Lawler, a clerk in the mine office, is in love with the superintendent's daughter, Dora. She, however, does not share the same feelings for Lawler. Dora is taken with the handsome new detective, whose identity remains unknown to Lawler. When another gold shipment is sent out, Murdock and Dora, who are hiding in the hills, observe Lawler using a mirror to signal the bandits. Murdock instructs Dora to keep Lawler busy at the office while he and the posse catch the bandits. At the office, Dora is attacked by Lawler but saved by the intervention of Murdock, who finds the mirror in Lawler's desk. Lawler attempts to escape but is killed by the posse.

CRITICS' CORNER
An old plot but the novel manner in which it is worked makes it interesting. . . . The picture will appeal more to the lovers of westerns than others. *Motion Picture News*

NOTES
This is the earliest existing film featuring Lon Chaney in a major role.
For years, 8mm prints of this film were sold to collectors by Break-
speare Films of England. Several 16mm prints exist in private film collections. Kino International released *By the Sun's Rays* on videotape in
1995.

The Oubliette

101-Bison/Universal, 3 reels. *Released:* August 15, 1914. *Production Code
No.:* 0647. *Director:* Charles Giblyn. *Scenario:* L. G. Stafford, from a story
by George Bronson Howard. *Photographer:* Lee Bartholomew.

CAST
Murdock MacQuarrie (*Francois Villon*), Pauline Bush (*Philippa de An-
nonay*), Lon Chaney (*Chevalier Bertrand de la Payne*), Harry F. Crane
(*King Louis XI*), Chet Withey (*Colin*).

SYNOPSIS
Francois Villon, a vagabond and poet, is on his way to Paris with his
friend Colin. They intercede in the eviction of an elderly couple from
their home and empty their purses to help pay the couple's debts.
When hunger finally overcomes them, they steal the purses of two
monks, for which they are eventually caught and imprisoned. Villon
manages to escape but his friend Colin meets his fate at the gallows.
While Villon pays his respects to his dead friend on the gibbet, the
Chevalier de Soissons mocks the corpse. Villon, enraged, attacks the
knight, killing him, then dons the Chevalier's armor. He encounters
Philippa de Annonay and the Chevalier Bertrand de la Payne at an inn.
She is being held against her will and yells for help. Villon and de la
Payne engage in a sword fight, resulting in de la Payne's death. Villon
returns Philippa to her castle and continues on to Paris. King Louis XI
tests Villon's loyalty by having him arrested. Disguised as a convict, the
king offers to help the poet escape if he will aid him in overthrowing
Louis. Villon snubs the offer, proving his loyalty, and the king reveals
his identity. Villon is knighted for his loyalty to the throne.

CRITICS' CORNER
The camera becomes a veritable magic mirror to us in this delightful
picture of the days of Francois Villon. . . . Indeed it is remarkable how
convincing and like real human life these scenes from the long dead
past are. Here we have men in armor behaving like real flesh and blood

people. And we quite forget that we are not contemporaries with them. *Moving Picture World*

NOTES

This was the first of four 3-reelers about the *Adventures of Francois Villon*. Chaney also appeared in the second episode, *The Higher Law* (1914).

In 1983, a print of this film was found under a farm porch in Georgia in good condition.[6] It was restored by the American Film Institute. Prints of *The Oubliette* can be found at the Library of Congress and in several private film collections. Kino International included clips from this film in their videotape documentary, *Lon Chaney: Behind the Mask* (1995).

A Miner's Romance

Nestor/Universal, 2 reels. *Released:* August 26, 1914. *Production Code No.:* 0628. *Director:* Not credited. *Scenario:* Not credited.

CAST

Murdock MacQuarrie (*Bob Jenkins*), Agnes Vernon (*Lucy Williams*), Lon Chaney (*John Burns*), Seymour Hastings (*Dave Williams*).

SYNOPSIS

Chased by a bear, John Burns falls off a cliff. Bob Jenkins, a miner, discovers the unconscious Burns and takes him to his cabin. The injured man recovers, and he and Bob become friends. Dave Williams and his daughter, Lucy, arrive in town, and Lucy and Bob fall in love. Burns also falls for Lucy, but his advances are repelled. Burns is so consumed with jealously that, to kill Bob, he rigs up a gun with a string running from the trigger to the latch of Bob's cabin door. Fate steps in when two mice gnaw through the string. Bob finds the gun and realizes the treachery that had been planned for him. When he fires the gun, Burns believes Bob has fallen victim to his plan. He hurries to Lucy and drags her away, determined to have her, but Bob and the townsmen kill Burns, saving Lucy.

CRITICS' CORNER

The story contains some old features, but holds the attention. *Moving Picture World*

Her Bounty

Rex/Universal, 1 reel. *Released:* September 13, 1914. *Production Code No.:* 0716. *Director:* Joseph de Grasse. *Scenario:* Ida May Park.

CAST
Pauline Bush (*Ruth Braddon*), Joe King (*David Hale*), Lon Chaney (*Fred Howard*), Beatrice Van (*Bessie Clay*).

SYNOPSIS
Ruth Braddon's interest in conditions for workers is fueled by a letter she receives advising her on matters in her own father's factory. Her father has Fred Howard, his junior partner and Ruth's finance, show her around. While on the tour of the factory, Ruth comes across a young worker who has fainted. When another employee, David Hale, asks Howard for better conditions, he is ordered back to work. Ruth is impressed by the young man and says she will speak to her father. David explains to his sweetheart, Bessie, that he is expecting a raise and so will soon be able to marry. Ruth visits David in the tenements and he shows her the poverty that is so apparent there. She asks him to help her and eventually breaks her engagement to Howard because she has fallen in love with David. Ruth goes to her father's office to ask for money for her project and there discovers a letter from David addressed to her father, asking for a raise and explaining his desire to marry Bessie. Realizing her mistake, Ruth tells David that she cannot marry someone beneath her, freeing him to return to Bessie.

CRITICS' CORNER
A fine drama and very appropriate Sunday release. . . . Pauline Bush and Lon Chaney are the principals. *Motion Picture News*

NOTES
This is the first film Chaney appeared in for the husband-and-wife filmmaking team, Joseph de Grasse and Ida May Park.

The Higher Law

101-Bison/Universal, 2 reels. *Released:* September 19, 1914. *Production Code No.:* 0676. *Director:* Charles Giblyn. *Scenario:* Not credited. Based on a story by George Bronson Howard.

CAST
Murdock MacQuarrie (*Francois Villon*), Pauline Bush (*Lady Eleyne*), Harry F. Crane (*King Louis XI*), Lon Chaney (*Sir Stephen*).

SYNOPSIS
King Louis XI of France offers a peace gesture to Edward IV of England. His companion, Sir Stephen, advises Edward IV to reject the

offer. Edward seeks the counsel of Francois Villon, who suggests that in order for peace to be achieved, Sir Stephen must be removed. Villon is sent to England to deal with Sir Stephen. Villon enlists the aid of Sir Haco Hubba. Sir Haco's daughter is enlisted to seduce Sir Stephen and lure him to their castle. Sir Stephen succumbs to her seduction and, at the castle, is quickly dispatched by Villon and Sir Haco's men. Villon then returns to France to report on the success of his expedition.

CRITICS' CORNER
An excellently produced and absorbing tale as set before the observer in these two reels. . . . The picture does not rely solely on its meticulous costumes and atmosphere for success. There is sufficient scheming, brawls, duel scenes and the like to appease the appetites of keen lovers of sensationalisms. *Motion Picture News*

Richelieu

101-Bison/Universal, 4 reels. *Released:* September 26, 1914. *Production Code No.:* 0345. *Director:* Allan Dwan. *Technical Director:* Frank D. Ormstron. *Scenario:* Not credited. Based on the play of the same title by Edward George Bulwer-Lytton.

CAST
Murdock MacQuarrie (*Cardinal Richelieu*), Pauline Bush (*Julie de Mortemar*), William C. Dowlan (*Adrien de Mauprat*), Robert Chandler (*Sieur de Beringhen*), Edna Maison (*Marion de Lormer*), James Neill (*The King*), Lon Chaney (*Baradas*), Richard Rosson (*Francois*), Edna Chapman (*The Queen*), William Lloyd (*Joseph*), Frank Rice (*Huget*).

SYNOPSIS
In seventeenth-century France, Cardinal Richelieu sends Adrien de Mauprat, his ward's lover, to fight the Spanish. Adrien's victory infuriates Baradas, a favorite of King Louis XVI. Baradas is also in love with Richelieu's ward, Julie. Planning to kill the cardinal and snatch the throne, he convinces Adrien that the cardinal is against him. Richelieu, however, has learned of the plot, and after speaking with Adrien, they agree to let Baradas think his plan has worked. Adrien is jailed and Baradas tries to seize Julie. Richelieu saves both Julie and Adrien by going to the king and threatening to resign. King Louis relents, releases Adrien, and has Baradas jailed. Julie and Adrien are reunited and Richelieu regains his position.

It is hardly necessary to say that he (Allan Dwan) has succeeded in really reproducing this section from this momentous and troublous time in France. *Motion Picture News*

The Pipes of Pan

Rex/Universal, 2 reels. *Released:* October 4, 1914. *Production Code No.:* 0739. *Director:* Joseph de Grasse. *Scenario:* Not credited.

CAST
Pauline Bush (*Marian*), Joe King (*Stephen Arnold*), Carmen Phillips (*Caprice*), Lon Chaney (*Arthur Farrell*).

SYNOPSIS
Painter Stephen Arnold dreams of a pastoral love scene between a faun and a wood-nymph that is interrupted by the daughter of Pan. Stephen is determined to capture the image on canvas and searches for a suitable model. He meets Caprice, a dancer, who reminds him of the spirit of the daughter of Pan. She agrees to pose for him and he soon becomes enamored of her. Stephen becomes so caught up in his work that he neglects his wife, Marian. He even refuses her entrance to his studio. Marian seeks comfort from her husband's best friend, Arthur Farrell, who willingly obliges; but Marian changes her mind. Finishing the painting, Stephen cannot let Caprice go and, in a passionate love scene, he wins her. Marian goes to his studio to tell her husband she is leaving him and finds the painting for which Caprice has posed. In a rage, she slashes the painting to ribbons, and Caprice's mysterious hold over Stephan is broken. The repentant artist returns to his forgiving wife.

CRITICS' CORNER
The husband's conscientious scruples were rather too sudden to be very convincing. This holds the interest throughout, but it undoubtedly steps over the line of delicacy to an extent. *Moving Picture World*

NOTES
The sequence in the film telling the history of Pan were hand colored.

Virtue Its Own Reward

Rex/Universal, 2 reels. *Released:* October 11, 1914. *Production Code No.:* 0747. *Director:* Joseph de Grasse. *Scenario:* L. G. Stafford, from a story by John Barton Oxford.

CAST

Pauline Bush (*Annie Partlan*), Gertrude Bambrick (*Alice*), Tom Forman (*Seadley Swaine*), Lon Chaney (*Duncan Bronson*).

SYNOPSIS

Annie, the sole support of her family, works long hours at the local canning factory to help pay for the education of her sister, Alice. Unknown to Annie, Alice is engaged to Seadley Swaine, the son of a wealthy businessman. After graduation, Alice goes to work at the canning factory without her sister's knowledge to save for a wedding dress. At the factory, Alice catches the eye of the department manager, Duncan Bronson, who has an unsavory reputation. Bronson wins Alice's attention even after Annie warns her about him. Taking matters into her own hands, Annie shows up at work one day in a fancy new dress purchased with the money she has diligently saved. Bronson quickly turns his attention to Annie, finding her more attractive than her flighty sister. Alice goes on to marry Swaine and, the danger past, Annie returns to her plain clothes. At the factory, everyone gossips about Annie, but she is happy knowing that she has saved her sister from a life of misery.

CRITICS' CORNER

There is some very good acting in this number on the part of all principals and it gets up to a strong interest. . . . Some real life in this number. *Moving Picture World*

NOTES

Tom Forman, who played Seadley Swaine, later directed Chaney in *Shadows* (1922).

Her Life's Story

Rex/Universal, 2 reels. *Released:* October 15, 1914. *Production Code No.:* 0727. *Director:* Joseph de Grasse. *Scenario:* James Dayton, from the poem "The Cross" by Miriam Bade Rasmus.

CAST

Pauline Bush (*Carlotta*), Laura Oakley (*Sister Agnes*), Ray Gallagher (*Don Manuel*), Lon Chaney (*Don Valasquez*), Beatrice Van (*The Wife*), Felix Walsh (*The Child*).

SYNOPSIS

Carlotta, the daughter of lowly parents, is adopted by the nobleman Don Valasquez. She and the don's son become childhood friends and, growing up, they fall in love. The son, Don Manuel, goes off to join the king's court. Six years pass, and he returns with a wife and child. Carlotta becomes bitter and obsessed with hatred for the wife and child. One day she sees the child reaching for a rose by the window sill. When the child loses his balance, Carlotta does nothing to help, and the boy falls and is killed. Overcome with remorse, Carlotta joins a convent. Thirteen years later, she confesses to Sister Agnes that the spirit of the dead child appears to her on the anniversary of his death, each time with a cross of blood displayed on his forehead. The day she confesses this to Sister Agnes is the anniversary of the child's death. This time, when the apparition holds out his hands to her, Carlotta recognizes him as the Christ child and realizes that, because of her confession, she has been forgiven.

Small Town Girl

101-Bison/Universal, 3 reels. *Released:* November 7, 1914. *Production Code No.:* 0575. *Director:* Allan Dwan. *Scenario:* Not credited.

CAST
Murdock MacQuarrie (*The Snob's Father*), Pauline Bush (*The Girl*), William Lloyd (*Her Father*), Lon Chaney (*Procurer*), Richard Rosson (*The Girl's Boyfriend*), Rupert Julian (*The Snob*).

SYNOPSIS
Ruth, a small-town girl who is dissatisfied with her life, yields to the persuasions of a snob, who takes her to the city. He supports her despite his parents' denouncement of the girl but in time abandons her and goes west, where he is made into a real man. The snob returns to Ruth, who now has a child, but she scorns him. Ruth finds happiness with the faithful lover of former days.

CRITICS' CORNER
This drama featuring Pauline Bush and Rupert Julian contains just a plain story and nothing of the impossible. But in its plainness it is extraordinary. . . . The whole drama will appeal more to the serious and better educated of the average audience. *Motion Picture News*

NOTES
The Universal Picture Code Book lists the film's release date as January 17, 1915.[7] Rupert Julian, who played the Snob, later directed Chaney in *The Kaiser, The Beast of Berlin* (1918) and *Phantom of the Opera* (1925).

Lights and Shadows

Rex/Universal, 2 reels. *Released:* November 29, 1914. *Production Code No.:* 0760. *Director:* Joseph de Grasse. *Scenario:* Not credited.

CAST

Pauline Bush (*Mother/Daughter*), Lon Chaney (*Bentley*).

SYNOPSIS

Eve has learned that her mother was married to Bentley, the son of a wealthy man who disinherited him for wedding a stage performer. On the night of her birth, her father deserted them. After her mother's death, Eve is raised by the family nurse. When she grows up, she discovers letters that suggest where she might find her father. But, on her way to find him, Eve is robbed of her ticket and money and is left penniless. She joins a traveling stage troupe and falls for the leading man, James Gordon, but he is married. Eve finally locates her father, who has made a fortune for himself. While her father makes plans for her to marry, James Gordon lands an important theatrical job in New York. Eve learns that Gordon's wife has died and travels to New York to be reunited with him, leaving her father and his plans behind.

CRITICS' CORNER

This story is slightly too complicated to make a good picture and too much time is covered. The ending is abrupt and one is left to speculate upon the final outcome. *Motion Picture News*

The Lion, The Lamb, The Man

Rex/Universal, 2 reels. *Released:* December 6, 1914. *Production Code No.:* 0815. *Director:* Joseph de Grasse. *Scenario:* Not credited.

CAST

Pauline Bush (*Agnes Duane*), Lon Chaney (*Fred*), Millard K. Wilson (*Bert*), William C. Dowlan (*The Reverend*).

SYNOPSIS

Agnes returns home from college to learn that her parents have chosen an effeminate minister to be her husband. Because she laughs at their choice, her parents send her to live with her uncle in Kentucky. She meets two brothers who fall in love with her. The younger brother, Fred Brown, is cunning and tries to force himself upon Agnes but is stopped by his older brother, Bert. She flees from the brothers and meets a reverend, who turns out to be a real man. Agnes has found the one man she can truly love.

CRITICS' CORNER
Produced in a telling manner by Joseph De Grasse. Pauline Bush, Lon Chaney and M. K. Wilson are well cast. . . . The two reels are always entertaining. *Motion Picture News*

NOTES
Millard K. Wilson became a close friend of Chaney's and later worked on a number of his M-G-M pictures as an assistant director.

A Night of Thrills

Rex/Universal, 2 reels. *Released:* December 13, 1914. *Director:* Joseph de Grasse. *Scenario:* Not credited.

CAST
Lon Chaney.

SYNOPSIS
Hazel and Jack are deeded a mansion belonging to her late Uncle Howard. Days before the couple's impending marriage, Hazel hears some unkind rumors about Jack. After confronting him about the gossip, she runs away without giving him a chance to explain. Staying in the mansion alone, Hazel finds two crooks robbing the house. When the crooks go into the wine cellar, Hazel seizes the opportunity to escape, only to run into Jack in the hallway. Mistaking him for another crook, she screams and faints. The crooks hear her cries, think the house in haunted, and make a hasty retreat, leaving their loot behind. When Hazel is revived, she and Jack resume their argument. But then the spirit of Uncle Howard appears to restore peace, and the two leave the mansion to get married.

Her Escape

Rex/Universal, 2 reels. *Released:* December 13, 1914. *Production Code No.:* 0770. *Director:* Joseph de Grasse. *Scenario:* Lon Chaney.

CAST
Pauline Bush (*Pauline*), William C. Dowlan (*Her Lover*), Lon Chaney (*Pete*), Richard Rosson (*Dope Fiend*).

SYNOPSIS

Fed up with her family of career criminals, Pauline runs away, only to be followed by her brother, Pete. The fight that ensues catches the attention of Paul, a miner, who comes to Pauline's aid, freeing her from her brother. They eventually fall in love and marry. Pete, who is blind from another fight, learns of his sister's marriage to the rich miner. He enlists the help of a dope addict to lead him to Pauline. Confronting his sister, Pete threatens her life unless she gives him money. Pauline manages to get away from her brother, who attempts to follow but stumbles down a flight of stairs, killing himself.

CRITICS' CORNER

Not many dramas are as intense and full of action as this. . . . Produced by Joseph De Grasse this film bears the marks of fine direction. *Motion Picture News*

NOTES

The Universal Picture Code Book lists the film's release date as December 27, 1914.[8] Judging by photographs in industry trade journals, Chaney played the blind man by simply rolling his eyes up for the duration of the scene, similar to the method he used as Blind Pew in *Treasure Island* (1920).

CHAPTER THREE

1915

The Sin of Olga Brandt

Rex/Universal, 2 reels. *Released:* January 3, 1915. *Production Code No.:* 0842. *Director:* Joseph de Grasse. *Scenario:* Not credited.

CAST

Pauline Bush (*Olga Brandt*), William C. Dowlan (*Rev. John Armstrong*), Lon Chaney (*Stephen Leslie*).

SYNOPSIS

To raise money for her handicapped sister, Olga sells herself to lawyer Stephen Leslie. Years later, Olga marries Reverend John Armstrong. Happiness abounds until the screening of a movie entitled *Shall We Forgive Her?* causes a commotion in their small town. The movie brings back the memories of Olga's indiscretion with Stephen Leslie. When the townspeople and the deacon lead an effort to have the film censored, the film's owners hire Stephen Leslie to represent them. Recognizing Olga, the lawyer threatens to expose Olga's past unless she returns to him. Olga writes a confession to her husband who, with Leslie, has gone to the theatre to see the film and decide if it should be censored. Unaware of his wife's situation, the reverend praises the moral of the picture, which encourages forgiveness. Leslie is overcome by the film and tracks down Olga at the train station, begging her to return to her husband. He promises to forget the past and never bother her again. The reverend reads Olga's letter and, remembering the moral of the picture, forgives her.

CRITICS' CORNER

A delicate story handled in a manner which will not offend by Joseph De Grasse's company headed by Pauline Bush, Lon Chaney and William Dowlan. *Motion Picture News*

NOTES
The Universal Picture Code Book lists the film's release date as January 5, 1915.[9]

Star of the Sea

Rex/Universal, 2 reels. *Released:* January 10, 1915. *Production Code No.:* 0796. *Director:* Joseph de Grasse. *Scenario:* Phil Walsh.

CAST
Pauline Bush (*Mary*), Laura Oakley (*Janice*), William C. Dowlan (*Mario Brisoni*), Lon Chaney (*Tomasco*).

SYNOPSIS
Sculptor Mario Brisoni has secured a commission to sculpt a statue of the Madonna and Child for a church in Naples. He leaves behind his jealous girlfriend, Janice, who eventually follows him to Naples. She is furious to learn that he has fallen in love with a young widow, Mary, who with her baby is posing for Mario. Janice enlists the aid of the disgruntled hunchback fisherman Tomasco, who had dreams of marrying Mary himself. The two plot on destroying the statue the evening before its dedication. When he sees the statue, however, Tomasco is overcome by its beauty and cannot destroy it. Janice nevertheless tries to do so, but when the statue opens its eyes with a painful look, she too cannot bring herself to destroy it. Mario is hailed as a great sculptor, and he and Mary are married.

CRITICS' CORNER
Played by Pauline Bush, William Dowlan and Lon Chaney this drama presents a fine story and excellently produced by Joseph De Grasse. Some very pretty scenes have been caught. The action is slow yet always absorbing. *Motion Picture News*

The Measure of a Man

Rex/Universal, 2 reels. *Released:* January 28, 1915. *Production Code No.:* 0781. *Director:* Joseph de Grasse. *Scenario:* Not credited.

CAST
Pauline Bush (*Helen MacDermott*), William C. Dowlan (*Bob Brandt*), Lon Chaney (*Mountie Lt. Jim Stuart*).

SYNOPSIS
Helen MacDermott has been brought up by her protective father. Bob Brandt, a handsome gambler, becomes acquainted with Helen. The girl

falls for his charms and elopes with him despite her father's opposition. Six months later, Helen learns that her husband is nothing more than a cheat, but she cannot return to her father. Later, when Bob accidentally shoots himself, he is befriended by Lt. Jim Stewart of the mounties, who takes the wounded man and his wife back to his cabin, where they stay until Bob is well. The two men become friends, and Jim secures a place on the force for Bob. Jim slowly realizes that he is falling in love with his best friend's wife and resigns from the force. Meanwhile, Helen has been keeping a secret diary, which Bob finds and reads. Accepting the that fact that Helen is in love with Jim, Bob tracks Jim down and brings him back to unite the two lovers.

CRITICS' CORNER
The action of this drama is rather slow but a good story runs through it and it will be enjoyed by those who care for a little action. *Motion Picture News*

Threads of Fate

Rex/Universal, 2 reels. *Released:* February 21, 1915. *Production Code No.:* 0870. *Director:* Joseph de Grasse. *Scenario:* Not credited.

CAST
Pauline Bush (*The Wife*), William C. Dowlan (*Her Lover*), Lon Chaney (*The Count*).

SYNOPSIS
Prior to marrying the count, his wife had a brief but happy love affair with a violinist. Going against her own desires, the wife marries the count, but it is a loveless marriage. Never far from her memory is her love for the violinist, whom she happens to meet at a place she and the count frequent. Meeting secretly, the two former lovers realize that they cannot live without each other and plan to run away. The count, jealous at being overthrown for a musician, follows them, causing the two to drive their car off a cliff, and they are killed.

CRITICS' CORNER
A psychological drama of the unconventional nature made by Joseph De Grasse. . . . The subtitles are extractions from the works of Pope, Horace, Whittier, Steadman, Taylor, Tennyson, Dryden and Milton. *Motion Picture News*

NOTES
The opening and closing scenes featuring the three Fates weaving the threads of mankind were hand colored.

When the Gods Played a Badger Game

Rex/Universal, 2 reels. *Released:* February 28, 1915. *Production Code No.:* 0961. *Director:* Joseph de Grasse. *Scenario:* Not credited.

CAST

Pauline Bush (*The Chorus Girl*), Lon Chaney (*The Property Man*).

SYNOPSIS

A chorus girl has all but made up her mind to accept the offer of marriage of a wealthy man when the man's wife comes to her and begs her not to marry her husband and ruin their marriage. The girl sympathizes with the wife and pretends that she is married, as well. The wealthy man is so disgusted by the chorus girl, he returns to his wife, believing she is the only pure woman in the world.

CRITICS' CORNER

A very strong offering made by Joseph De Grasse in a company headed by Pauline Bush and Lon Chaney, who plays the property man instead of his accustomed role of heavy. . . . This is very well acted and constructed and will draw considerably on the sympathies of all. *Motion Picture News*

NOTES

The film's working title was *The Girl Who Couldn't Go Wrong*.

Such is Life

Rex/Universal, 2 reels. *Released:* March 4, 1915. *Production Code No.:* 0926. *Director:* Joseph de Grasse. *Scenario:* Not credited.

CAST

Pauline Bush (*Polly*), William C. Dowlan (*Will Deming*), Lon Chaney (*Tod Wilkes*), Olive Golden (*Olive Trent*).

SYNOPSIS

Polly, the maid at Mrs. Jennings' boarding house, forms a romantic attachment to the actor Will Deming. Will is the only one at the boarding house to give her a kind glance, let alone the time of day. Olive Trent, an aspiring actress, takes a room at the boarding house in hopes of breaking into show business. One day Will meets Olive at a theatrical agency and he is taken by her beauty. He sympathizes with her distress but she rebuffs him, mistaking Will's motive. Tod Wilkes, a burlesque performer who is also a resident at the house, offers Olive a job in his company. The job is far from Olive's aspirations and she refuses his offer. But when her money runs out, she reconsiders Wilkes' offer. He invites her to his room to run through the part, and when the rehearsal is over, he makes passionate but unwanted advances to her. Olive breaks free of Wilkes and runs to her room. Will and Polly see her, and Will remembers her from the agency. He offers Olive a job in his company, which she accepts, and they leave the boarding house with neither a good-bye nor a backward glance to Polly.

CRITICS' CORNER

This comedy-drama features Pauline Bush. . . . The picture contains a number of pathetic themes and others which are equally humorous. A nice combination. *Motion Picture News*

Where the Forest Ends

Rex/Universal, 2 reels. *Released:* March 7, 1915. *Production Code No.:* 0910. *Director:* Joseph de Grasse. *Scenario:* Not credited.

CAST

Pauline Bush (*Rose*), William C. Dowlan (*Jack Norton*), Lon Chaney (*Paul Rouchelle*), Joseph de Grasse (*Silent Jordan*).

SYNOPSIS

Rose meets painter Paul Rouchelle in the forest. Paul is charming and induces Rose to follow him back to the city with promises of a life of excitement. But Rose quickly tires of city life and returns to her home in the mountains and to her sweetheart, Jack, who is a ranger. Jack learns of Rose's indiscretion when Paul comes to the mountains to persuade Rose to return to the city with him. Enraged, Jack attempts to kill Paul, but Paul gets away. Silent Jordan, an old ranger, takes Jack to the grave of the woman he once rejected, an act he has regretted ever since. Jack realizes he has judged Rose too harshly and so forgives her, and they are married.

CRITICS' CORNER

This story is old but it is so artistically told that it appears new. . . . Lon Chaney is excellent as the heavy. *Motion Picture News*

NOTES

The Universal Picture Code Book lists the film's release date as February 6, 1915.[10]

Outside the Gates

Rex/Universal, 2 reels. *Released:* March 14, 1915. *Production Code No.:* 0925. *Director:* Joseph de Grasse. *Scenario:* Not credited.

CAST
Pauline Bush (*Sister Ursula*), William C. Dowlan (*Manuel*), Lon Chaney (*Perez*).

SYNOPSIS
Sister Ursula is a novice in a convent in southern Spain. Opening the door of the convent one day to allow Perez the peddler to come in, she catches a glimpse of Manuel, a young cavalier, who is riding past. As she struggles with her feelings, Ursula is further tempted when Perez asks her if he might display the rich cloth he will use for the altar. She confesses her sins to the abbess, who in turn gives Ursula a penance of kneeling before the altar in an all-night vigil. Weariness overcomes her and she falls asleep. In her dream, Perez offers her fine clothes, jewelry, and Manuel for a lover. Ursula follows Perez and encounters a series of horrid events. Bandits accost her, a troupe of dancing girls jeer at her, and finally even Manuel turns from her. She awakens and, realizing that it was all a nightmare, is now thoroughly content with her place in the convent.

CRITICS' CORNER
One of Joseph De Grasse's productions in which the writer evidently put in a lot of thought but some of the actions of the characters will be more apt to strike the spectator as humorous than serious. However the story is very well constructed. . . . Lon Chaney gets some fine character work as the peddler. *Motion Picture News*

All for Peggy

Rex/Universal, 1 reel. *Released:* March 18, 1915. *Production Code No.:* 0972. *Director:* Joseph de Grasse. *Scenario:* Ida May Park.

CAST
Pauline Bush (*Peggy*), William C. Dowlan (*Will Brandon*), Lon Chaney (*The Stable Groom*).

SYNOPSIS
Will Brandon is engaged to Peggy, the daughter of the stable groom for his father's horse, Ladybird. James Brandon, Will's father, does not approve of his son's pending marriage because of Peggy's low station.

But Will is determined and so agrees to a wager with his father. If Lady-bird wins the race the following day, Will must forego the marriage. He plans to turn the tables on his father, however, by asking Peggy's brother, the jockey who will ride the horse in the race, to feign illness. Within an hour of the race, Peggy cannot rouse her brother, so she dons his jockey suit and takes his place. After Ladybird wins the race, Will and James Brandon approach the jockey. When they discover that Peggy is the jockey, James Brandon is so tickled by his son's failed plan and the girl's courage that he consents to their marriage.

CRITICS' CORNER
This is an enjoyable comedy-drama produced by Joseph De Grasse. Pauline Bush is Peggy and she shows herself an expert horsewoman in the race. William C. Dowlan is her lover, while Lon Chaney has a small part as the girl's father. *Motion Picture News*

The Desert Breed

Rex/Universal, 2 reels. *Released:* March 28, 1915. *Production Code No.:* 0899. *Director:* Joseph de Grasse. *Scenario:* Tom Forman.

CAST
Pauline Bush (*Jessie*), Lon Chaney (*Fred*), William C. Dowlan (*Jack, Fred's Partner*).

SYNOPSIS
Fred and Jack make a hasty retreat from the town of Rawhide, just a step ahead of the sheriff's posse. At the edge of the desert, they come upon the cabin of Jessie, who lives alone. Afraid of the two men, she locks her door, and when Jessie points her gun in their direction, they quickly decide to leave. But the two men come back when they hear her cries for help. Fred and Jack overpower three members of the sheriff's posse who are attempting to attack Jessie. Fred and Jack confess to Jessie that they are fugitives and ask her to guide them across the de-sert. Grateful for their help, she agrees to escort them. They leave just before the arrival of the sheriff, who decides not to follow the trio, knowing they will not make it across the barren desert. In the desert, Fred, who was wounded in the fight at the cabin, hallucinates that Jack is the enemy. To add to their problems, the only waterhole has dried up. But Jessie finds water and the three survive their trip across the desert. Waving good-bye to the two men, Jessie heads home.

CRITICS' CORNER
An original drama of decidedly pleasing nature relying on the more clearly drawn characters for interest rather than the plot, which if analyzed would prove almost nil. . . . Mr. Chaney gets in an excellent piece of character work in his part. *Motion Picture News*

Maid of the Mist

Rex/Universal, 1 reel. *Released:* April 1, 1915. *Production Code No.:* 1033. *Director:* Joseph de Grasse. *Scenario:* James Drayton.

CAST

Pauline Bush (*The Girl*), Ray Gallagher (*The Boy*), Lon Chaney (*The Postmaster*).

SYNOPSIS

Ray, a young novelist, goes to the mountains in search of local color for his book. His millionaire father has written in his will that Ray cannot marry until the age of twenty-five. Pauline works as a maid in the local hotel in the mountains. She and Ray fall in love and, despite his father's warnings, he marries the girl, hoping to keep it a secret, then is called back to the city on urgent business. The local postmaster is in love with Pauline and is so jealous over her marriage that he makes sure she never receives any letters and that none of her letters gets mailed. Pauline's father moves to a distant mining region, taking her with him, and when Ray returns, he cannot find his bride. He publishes his novel, *Maid of the Mist*, with a photo of Pauline on the flyleaf. Meanwhile, she has given birth to a child, and her father swears vengeance upon the man responsible. He finds a copy of Ray's book and tracks down the young man, but when he finds Ray, Ray shows him the marriage certificate, and he and his new family are happily reunited.

CRITICS' CORNER

A strong one-reel subject, with Lon Chaney, Pauline Bush and Ray Gallagher in the cast. . . . This a pleasing subject throughout. *Moving Picture World*

The Girl of the Night

Rex/Universal, 2 reels. *Released:* April 8, 1915. *Director:* Joseph de Grasse. *Scenario:* Ida May Park.

CAST
Pauline Bush, Hilda Slomen, Lon Chaney.

SYNOPSIS
Nance is rescued from an abusive childhood by Jerry, a kind-hearted thief. Years later, Jerry is arrested for burglary, and his gang worries that a powerful attorney, Arthur Langham, will produce evidence to convict them all. Jerry asks Nance to steal the documents from Arthur's house. She agrees but is caught by the lawyer. She tells him Jerry's kindness, and he agrees to help Jerry if they promise to lead better lives. As the trial nears, Nance overhears the gang's plan to kill Arthur. She goes to his house to leave him a warning and walks in on the attorney's wife and his best friend, who are having an affair. When Arthur comes home unexpectedly, Nance takes some of the wife's jewels and steps forward, pretending to be a thief. Arthur is about to turn Nance over to authorities when his guilt-ridden wife intervenes. She gives Nance some money to help her to go straight, and she and Jerry plan a new life for themselves.

CRITICS' CORNER
The story of these two reels is presented in a wonderfully gripping manner. All the scenes are effectively worked out and the spectator finds himself wrapped up in the story from the start . . . Lon Chaney has a small part as a crook, who reforms and finally wins her [the girl]. *Motion Picture News*

The Stool Pigeon

Victor/Universal, 2 reels. *Released:* April 9, 1915. *Production Code No.:* 1054. *Director:* Lon Chaney. *Scenario:* L. G. Stafford.

CAST
J. Warren Kerrigan (*Walter Jason*), Vera Sisson (*Mildred*), George Periolat (*Oswald Trumble*).

SYNOPSIS
Walter Jason, a country boy, arrives in the big city hoping to find a big job, but fails to do so. He is befriended by Oswald Trumble, a master crook, who plans to use Walter in one of his crimes. Walter and Oswald attend the fashionable masked ball given by the wealthy Moore family, where Oswald plans to steal the family's jewelry. Walter meets the Moore's daughter, Mildred, and they strike up a conversation. As they walk outside, Oswald calls Walter back inside the mansion. Moments

later, Mildred is kidnapped, and a look-alike young woman from Oswald's gang takes her place. When Walter returns, he notices that the young lady does not now have a certain beauty mark on her arm. He excuses himself and alerts the police at the house, who question the girl. She confesses. Oswald is arrested and Mildred is freed. Mildred forgives Walter and they become engaged.

CRITICS' CORNER
This is Lon Chaney's first picture made with the Kerrigan-Victor Company and his success with it marks him as a capable director. The story is replete with situations of tense character and is so constructed that the climax can hardly be foretold until it arrives. A great point in its credit. That it will be heartedly appreciated by the most critical audience is certain. *Motion Picture News*

A crook story by L. G. Stafford of unusual interest in two reels. . . . The story is cleverly worked out and holds interest firmly. *Moving Picture World*

NOTES
The Universal Picture Code Book lists the film's release date as April 19, 1915.[11]

The Stool Pigeon marked Lon Chaney's directorial debut. It was the first of six films (*The Stool Pigeon, For Cash, The Oyster Dredger, The Violin Maker, The Trust,* and *The Chimney's Secret* all released in 1915) that he would direct for the Victor Company at Universal. I. G. Edmonds, author of *The Big U,* claims that Chaney was to direct another film for the Victor Company entitled, *The Service of the Sword.* However, neither *Motion Picture News* or *Moving Picture World* mentions anything of Chaney either directing or appearing in the production. Also, according to the Universal picture code list, the film was apparently shot, but never released.

The Grind

Rex/Universal, 3 reels. *Released:* April 11, 1915. *Production Code No.:* 1007. *Director:* Joseph de Grasse. *Scenario:* Ida May Park.

CAST
Pauline Bush (*Jean Chesney*), Queenie Rosson, Helen Rosson (*Her Sisters*), Lon Chaney (*Henry Leslie*).

SYNOPSIS
After her mother's death Jean Chesney raises her two sisters, Rita and Lily. Rita, a secretary, confides to her younger sister, Lily, that her boss,

Henry Leslie, is interested in her. Both girls are thrilled at the attention, not realizing the danger because Leslie is married. Leslie's son, Bob, is attracted to Jean but she ignores his attention. Leslie offers to take Rita to his country home for dinner and she accepts. Meanwhile, Leslie's wife has a heart attack and his son is desperate to find him. Jean finds out from Lily that Rita has gone to Leslie's country home and so she is off to save her. After dinner, Leslie makes advances upon Rita, only to be stopped by Jean with the news of his wife, who has died. Later, a inebriated Bob is robbed and dumped on the street. Jean, not knowing his identity, finds him and helps him to recover. When she realizes who he is, Jean is angered, but eventually they become friends and she forgives him for his actions.

CRITICS' CORNER
Such an offering is sure of keeping the interest up all the time and the subject is handled in such a delicate manner that the picture is suitable for exhibition in any theatre including those of neighborhood and family patronage. *Motion Picture News*

For Cash

Victor/Universal, 2 reels. *Released:* May 3, 1915. *Production Code No.:* 1079. *Director:* Lon Chaney. *Scenario:* W. M. Caldwell.

CAST
J. Warren Kerrigan (*The Artist*), Vera Sisson (*The Girl*).

SYNOPSIS
The old father of a mountain girl dies after the excitement of attempting to shoot his daughter's suitor. The orphaned girl is then adopted by a rich cousin, so she moves to the city, where she is introduced to the life of society. An artist who loves the girl cannot find her after painting her portrait. He falls on hard times and, in order to survive, he is forced to sell the girl's portrait to another artist, who is also a blackmailer. Thinking better of his deed, he returns to find the blackmailer assaulting the girl. His timely rescue lays the foundation for a happy marriage.

CRITICS' CORNER
Lon Chaney directed this while Warren Kerrigan and Vera Sisson are the principals. The two reels have been photographed well and some pretty scenes have been obtained. The story becomes more vague as

the action progresses and the main idea is hard to grasp. *Motion Picture News*

This is very conventional and not particular attractive in settings. The principals are interesting but their work furnishes the chief strength of the production. *Moving Picture World*

An Idyll of the Hills

Rex/Universal, 2 reels. *Released:* May 3, 1915. *Production Code No.:* 0816. *Director:* Joseph de Grasse. *Scenario:* Not credited.

CAST

Pauline Bush (*Kate Graham*), Millard K. Wilson (*Dick Massey*), Lon Chaney (*Lafe Jameson*).

SYNOPSIS

Dick Massey wants to better himself but keeps it a secret from the mountain community of Kentucky where he lives. Kate, whom Dick loves, mocks his interest in educating himself. Dick is so hurt by Kate's ridicule that he hides his book under a log. Kate meets Collins, a well-bred man from the city, visiting the mountains. They become very friendly, and Lafe Jameson becomes jealous of the "furriner's" attention to one for whom he has his own desires. Collins realizes his friendship with the girl could be dangerous and writes a letter to Lafe letting him know he cares nothing for an ignorant girl. Lafe thinks the man is from the revenue department, and Dick is chosen to kill him. After speaking with Collins, however, Dick cannot carry out the deadly deed. But Collins accidently shoots himself and Dick is falsely accused of the action, until Collins reveals that it was an accident. Kate is so impressed with Dick's sincerity that she falls in love with him.

CRITICS' CORNER

The story of this is very good but there is hardly enough action to sustain the interest over two thousand feet. A few of the episodes of the story are none too clearly put. The photography and the scenes are very good. *Motion Picture News*

NOTES

The Universal Picture Code Book lists the film's release date as March 13, 1915.[12]

The Stronger Mind

United/Universal, 2 reels. *Released:* May 15, 1915. *Director:* Joseph de Grasse. *Scenario:* Not credited.

CAST

Murdock MacQuarrie (*A Crook*), Pauline Bush (*The Girl*), Lon Chaney
(*The Crook's Pal*).

SYNOPSIS

A crook and his pal are interrupted while robbing a bank. Fearing capture, the crook flees to a Western mining town, where he meets a girl
who ministers to the needs of others. The crook assumes the disguise
of a minister and, through the influence of the girl, he renounces his
past. He writes to his pal and tells him of his rejuvenation. His pal
shows up, doubting his partner's new faith, and persuades his former
partner to rob the local bank, where the girl's father works as a guard.
The crook's pal is killed and the crook realizes that "the straight and
narrow" is the only way to walk.

CRITICS' CORNER

A two reel production which in its finished condition. . . . promises to
be unusually interesting. *Moving Picture World*

The Oyster Dredger

Victor/Universal, 2 reels. *Released:* June 7, 1915. *Production Code No.:*
1104. *Director and Scenario:* Lon Chaney.

CAST

J. Warren Kerrigan (*Jack*), Vera Sisson (*Vera*).

SYNOPSIS

While on vacation at the seaside, Vera, an heiress, meets Jack, an oyster
dredger. She takes a fancy to his way of life and arranges with her lawyer to trade places with the fisherman. Jack agrees to change places,
too, and tries to accustom himself to his new lifestyle. Vera's lawyer, who
has absolute control of her finances, tries to force the girl to marry
him. Vera refuses to accept his offer. While the lawyer broods over his
misfortune in a bar, Jack enters, tired of the life that is so different from
what he knows. He overhears the lawyer speaking badly about Vera and
is about to attack him when the lawyer steps backward and falls into the
sea. Jack and Vera reunite and profess their love for each other.

CRITICS' CORNER

This two-part drama featuring Warren Kerrigan and Vera Sisson is a
good, interesting picture, well acted and ably directed. *New York Dramatic Mirror*

Rather impossible, yet the presence of Jack Kerrigan and Vera Sisson in the principle role serves to lift it from the ordinary. There are many bits of comedy throughout the two reels which make the film doubly enjoyable. The scenes and photography are good. *Motion Picture News*

NOTES
The Universal Picture Code Book lists the film's release date as June 14, 1915.[13]

Steady Company

Rex/Universal, 1 reel. *Released:* June 29, 1915. *Production Code No.:* 1216. *Director:* Joseph de Grasse. *Scenario:* Ida May Park, from a story by Julius G. Furthman.

CAST
Pauline Bush (*Nan*), Lon Chaney (*Jimmy*).

SYNOPSIS
Nan and Jimmy take the same trolley car home every evening. Jimmy always offers the girl his seat, and Nan always refuses. One rainy night, however, she accepts, and at their stop, they walk home together, sharing Jimmy's umbrella. Nan promises to go to the park with him that weekend. During their walk in the park, they come across a drunken man being accosted by a group of boys. To Nan's horror, the drunken man is her father. Jimmy chases the boys off and offers to see her father home. Nan is sure her romance with Jimmy is over and goes home crying. When Jimmy arrives with her father, he tells Nan that they still have half a bag of peanuts to finish in the park. Nan realizes that Jimmy doesn't care about her background and truly loves her.

CRITICS' CORNER
This is one of the best one reel comedy-dramas that we have seen for a long time. It was produced by Lon Chaney, who plays one of the principal parts opposite Pauline Bush . . . the wealth of pleasingly realistic, incidental touches unite to make the reel one of the most gratifying program releases. *Motion Picture News*

NOTES
The Universal Picture Code Book lists the film's release date as July 6, 1915.[14] There is a question as to whether Chaney or Joseph de Grasse directed this picture. Most filmographies credit de Grasse as director, but the *Motion Picture News* review lists Chaney as "producing" the pic-

ture. The term "Produced by" was commonly used in the early days of motion pictures as a euphemism for director. No other existing trade journals list Chaney as the director.

The Violin Maker

Victor/Universal, 1 reel. *Released:* July 9, 1915. *Production Code No.:* 1186. *Director:* Lon Chaney. *Scenario:* Milton M. Moore.

CAST
Lon Chaney (*Pedro*), Gretchen Lederer (*Marguerita*).

SYNOPSIS
Marguerita, the sweetheart of Pedro, a violin maker, is overheard playing the violin by Maurice, the director of a theatre. He is so taken by the girl's talent that he offers her a chance to perform on stage. Her first appearance is a great success, and Pedro uses all his talents to craft the finest violin for her. When he goes to the theatre to present it to her, she and Maurice are walking out, holding hands. Pedro disguises himself as a blind beggar and follows them. When he plays the violin on the street corner, Marguerita and Maurice are attracted to his music. They ask whether they can buy the violin but Pedro refuses, saying it was made for his sweetheart. He then reveals himself to the couple and breaks the violin over his knee. Later, Pedro enters into a cafe where Marguerita is playing a violin. She sees him, and while still playing, goes to his table and asks his forgiveness. Pedro realizes that the violin she is playing is the same one he made for her but had broken. The two lovers make up and are once again happy.

CRITICS' CORNER
A stronger character portrayal is here rendered by Lon Chaney in the role of an Italian violin maker. The story is original in many ways and pleases all the time by its strong heart interest action. *Motion Picture News*

The Trust

Victor/Universal, 1 reel. *Released:* July 16, 1915. *Production Code No.:* 1168. *Director:* Lon Chaney. *Scenario:* Katherine M. Kingsherry.

CAST
Vera Sisson (*Florence Allison*), William Quinn (*Mr. Allison*), Lon Chaney (*Jim Mason*)

SYNOPSIS

Jim Mason's home life is ruined because of his wife's extravagances, and he is driven to become a thief. While robbing Florence Allison's home, he is confronted by the woman. She relates how her marriage is about to break up because of her husband's disinterest. Mason is so moved that he helps her in a plot to restore her husband's love. Florence tells Mason that he may keep the pearls he has taken, but he promises to return them if their plan fails. When the husband arrives home, he finds his wife bound and gagged. The shock of his wife's life in jeopardy rekindles his love for her. Meanwhile, Mason is injured in a fight with another thief, who knows he has the pearls. Hurt, Mason drags himself to the Allison home to return the pearls, thinking the plan has failed. He finds the Allisons happy, and they reward him with the pearls.

CRITICS' CORNER

This story is rather ineffective as it develops with undo rapidity. Lon Chaney, Vera Sisson and William Quinn carry the principal roles. *Motion Picture News*

There is some vagueness in the construction, but as a whole the story proves quite entertaining and has some novelty to it. *Moving Picture World*

Bound on the Wheel

Rex/Universal, 3 reels. *Released:* July 19, 1915. *Production Code No.:* 1231. *Director:* Joseph de Grasse. *Scenario:* Ida May Park, from a story by Julius G. Furthman.

CAST

Elsie Jane Wilson (*Cora*), Lon Chaney (*Tom*), Lydia Yeamans Titus (*Mrs. Coulahan*), Arthur Shirley (*Hans*).

SYNOPSIS

Cora Gertz and Tom Coulahan live with their respective parents in a tenement. Although Cora's parents are poor, they are happy. In contrast, Tom's parents continually fight, and his father is an alcoholic. Tom proposes to Cora, saying they will live with his parents. Cora, despite the warnings of her parents that Tom could turn out to be a drunk like his father, marries him. They move in with his parents and Cora's family returns to Germany. Tom's father dies, and his mother and Cora take in washing to help make ends meet. True to her parents' warnings,

Tom spends most of his time in saloons. His mother is taken ill and given medicine. One drop is prescribed; any more would be fatal. Hans, a family friend of Cora's parents, comes from Germany to visit. Hans has a sizable bankroll, with which he hopes to invest in a business. When Tom sees the money, he plans to rob their visitor. Realizing her husband's plan and feeling the situation hopeless, Cora, with suicidal intentions, fills a glass of water and puts in three drops of the medication prescribed for Tom's mother. But she changes her mind and finds Hans to warn him of her husband's plot. When she returns, she finds her husband dead, having drunk the glass of water containing the medicine. Later, Cora and Hans marry.

CRITICS' CORNER

A strong drama that goes right to the point. . . . This is produced very well with much attention being paid to the tenement district. Lon Chaney as the husband does some excellent character work. *Motion Picture News*

NOTES

The Universal Picture Code Book lists the film's release date as July 25, 1915.[15]

Mountain Justice

Rex/Universal, 2 reels. *Released:* August 6, 1915. *Production Code No.:* 1247. *Director:* Joseph de Grasse. *Scenario:* Ida May Park, from a story by Julius G. Furthman.

CAST

Elsie Jane Wilson (*Nora*), Arthur Shirley (*Angus McDonald*), Lon Chaney (*Jeffrey Kirke*), Grace Thompson (*Mary*).

SYNOPSIS

Angus McDonald and Jeffrey Kirke are partners in a moonshine still. Kirke is married to Mary, whom he treats with disrespect. Angus finds himself in love with Mary and ignores the affections of Nora. During a raid, Jeffrey kills a revenue man. Angus turns his partner over to the law with hopes of having Mary for himself. Angus' act of treason infuriates the other mountain people, who plan to hang him. Nora pleads for his life and, with her father's help, they save Angus. It is then that Angus realizes Nora's love for him.

CRITICS' CORNER
There's gorgeous mountain scenery in this, while the originality of the
story and the good acting unite to make the picture very desirable.
Motion Picture News

NOTES
The Universal Picture Code Book lists the film's release date as August
15, 1915.[16]

Quits

Rex/Universal, 1 reel. *Released:* August 10, 1915. *Production Code No.:*
1246. *Director:* Joseph de Grasse. *Scenario:* Ida May Park, from the story
"Sheriff of Long Butte" by Julius G. Furthman.

CAST
Arthur Shirley (*John Sloan, the Sheriff*), Lon Chaney (*Frenchy*).

SYNOPSIS
John Sloan, the sheriff of Long Butte, was once in love with a girl who
fell in love with a Frenchman. He still keeps a picture of the girl in his
cabin. One day Sloan accidentally falls into quicksand and is rescued by
a man named 'Frenchy.' Frenchy confesses that he is a fugitive from
the law and pleads with Sloan for protection. Sloan decides to repay his
debt by giving the man shelter in his cabin for the night and promises
to help him get out of the territory the next day. That night, Frenchy
sees the picture of Sloan's former lover and is haunted by the photograph. It is the face of his wife, whom he has murdered. The next morning, the sheriff's deputies come to the cabin. They recognize the
murderer and arrest him. In jail, Frenchy pleads with Sloan to help
him escape. After the escape, Sloan has a change of heart, and he and
his deputies chase the criminal and assume they have killed him as he
paddles away in a canoe. As the story ends, however, Frenchy, full of
mocking laughter, peers out from behind some boulders.

CRITICS' CORNER
This picture adapted from a magazine story is positively one of the
strongest single reel dramas that we have ever seen. . . . Lon Chaney as
Frenchy gives one of those remarkable character portrayals which he is
best. . . . This is a *real* drama and deserves to be highly featured. *Motion
Picture News*

NOTES

The Universal Picture Code Book lists the film's release date as August 14, 1915.[17] The film's working title was *The Sheriff of Long Butte*. The production was filmed on location at Big Bear Lake, California.

The Chimney's Secret

Victor/Universal, 1 reel. *Released:* August 18, 1915. *Production Code No.:* 1195. *Director and Scenario:* Lon Chaney, based on a story by Milton M. Moore.

CAST

Lon Chaney (*Charles*), Gretchen Lederer (*Mary*).

SYNOPSIS

By the flickering light of a candle, an old peddler hides his bundle of cash in the chimney of his hovel. In a house nearby live Mary and her invalid sister. She befriends the old peddler one day when children throw stones at him. Mary's hopes of saving enough money to move her sister to a better climate grow as she saves her money. She opens a savings account at the bank and becomes acquainted with the cashier, Charles, who secretly is greedy and covets the bank's money. Later, Mary learns that the bank has failed and Charles has absconded with the money. The peddler sees Mary pounding on the bank doors in desperation. Out of fear, he takes his money from the chimney and prepares to leave when Mary comes to his door. Showing signs of insanity, the old peddler tosses the money on the table and tells her he has robbed the bank. He rips off his beard and hair and reveals himself as Charles. Telling her to return the money, Charles has another fit of insanity and tries to stop her, only to have a seizure and die.

CRITICS' CORNER

This is novel and well played by Lon Chaney as the cashier and Gretchen Lederer as the girl. *Motion Picture News*

This story of the young bank cashier who masquerades as a miserly peddler is not entirely new, but will offer a surprise to many observers. It is quite dramatic in its way and well constructed. Lon Chaney and Gretchen Lederer play the leads. *Moving Picture World*

NOTES

The Universal Picture Code Book lists the film's release date as August 23, 1915.[18]

The Pine's Revenge

Rex/Universal, 2 reels. *Released:* September 19, 1915. *Production Code No.:* 1312. *Director:* Joseph de Grasse. *Scenario:* Ida May Park, from her story "The King's Keeper."

CAST

Cleo Madison (*Grace Milton*), Lon Chaney (*Black Scotty*), Millard K. Wilson (*Dick Rance*), Arthur Shirley (*John Harding*).

SYNOPSIS

Ranger Dick Rance saves Grace Milton from an overturned canoe. This is the same girl he was to marry years earlier, before John Harding broke up the romance. Grace doesn't realize who the ranger is and upon her recovery goes to his cabin to thank him. John Harding finds out about this and wants to kill the ranger, his old enemy. He meets with the criminal Black Scotty, who also wants revenge against the ranger, and they plan to trap him in a forest fire. Receiving a note to meet Grace at Pine Cove, Rance finds himself in the trap. He escapes and is able to call for help to fight the forest fire, in which Black Scotty dies. Harding is caught and confesses his crime, and Grace and Rance resume their romance.

CRITICS' CORNER

This is an average story. . . . Its northern scenes and photography are most satisfying. *Motion Picture News*

NOTES

The film's working title was *The King's Keeper*. The *Motion Picture News* review credits Nell Shipman as scenarist.

The Fascination of the Fleur de Lis

Rex/Universal, 3 reels. *Released:* September 26, 1915. *Picture Code No.:* 1265. *Director:* Joseph de Grasse. *Scenario:* Bess Meredyth.

CAST

Cleo Madison (*Lisette*), Arthur Shirley (*Antoine Gerome*), Millard K. Wilson (*The King*), Lon Chaney (*Duke of Safoulrug*).

SYNOPSIS

Lisette's peasant mother loved the fleur-de-lis flower so much that when her daughter was born, she had a natural birthmark in the shape of the flower. When Lisette matured, her love for the flower became as obsessive as her mother's before her. She forsakes her true love, Antoine, for the worldly pleasures as the wife of the Duke of Safoulrug. Their marriage is an unhappy one, ending with the duke's suicide after finding his wife in the arms of the king. Lisette becomes the king's mistress. The king falls gravely ill and in need of a life-or-death operation. It is performed by Antoine, who ignores Lisette. She realizes that the curse of the fleur-de-lis has caused her such unhappiness and burns her birthmark off with a hot poker. She leaves the king and returns home to find her father has died. At her parents' graveside, she is reunited with Antoine.

CRITICS' CORNER
An effective drama written by Bess Meredyth. Photographic work and scenes, all of which transpire in a mythical European country are exceedingly good. Joe De Grasse produced it so the beautiful locations are easily accounted for. *Motion Picture News*

Alas and Alack

Rex/Universal, 1 reel. *Released:* October 10, 1915. *Picture Code No.:* 1346. *Director:* Joseph de Grasse. *Scenario:* Ida May Park.

CAST
Arthur Shirley (*Charles Holcombe*), Cleo Madison (*Jess*), Lon Chaney (*Her Husband*).

SYNOPSIS
Jess, the wife of a fisherman, daydreams of what she would do with a million dollars after seeing a fine yacht in the harbor. The yacht's owner, Charles Holcombe, is married to a self-centered woman who cares more for her lap dog than she does him. To escape the nagging of his wife, Holcombe rows ashore. There he finds Jess and her daughter. He overhears Jess explaining to her daughter what makes the noise in a seashell. She says that a beautiful girl was imprisoned by a bad fairy because she dared to love her handsome prince, and the noise is the cry of the imprisoned girl. Holcombe is amazed by the pretty woman who toils so hard. He introduces himself and, to find an excuse for standing around, he picks a bouquet of flowers. With no other reason to stay, Holcombe reluctantly returns to his yacht and his nagging wife, dreaming of being married to the young girl. The yacht sails away and Jess waits for her husband to return with more fishing nets to repair.

CRITICS' CORNER
Written by Ida May Park and taking a decidedly pessimistic attitude towards life . . . This is interesting with Cleo Madison, Lon Chaney and Arthur Shirley in the principal roles. *Motion Picture News*

NOTES

A print of *Alas and Alack* is housed at The National Film and Television Archive in London.

A Mother's Atonement

Rex/Universal, 3 reels. *Released:* October 17, 1915. *Production Code No.:* 1319. *Director:* Joseph de Grasse. *Scenario:* Ida May Park.

CAST

Cleo Madison (*Alice, wife/Jen, daughter*), Lon Chaney (*Ben Morrison*), Arthur Shirley (*James Hilton*), Wyndham Standing (*Wilbur Kent*), Millard K. Wilson (*John Newton*).

SYNOPSIS

Old Ben Morrison and his daughter, Jen, live on an island not far from the mainland. Jasper Crane asks her father for Jen's hand in marriage. Ben says that Jen is much like her mother, who abandoned him and his daughter for another man. Learning of the impending marriage plans, Jen escapes to the mainland, where she seeks protection from Mrs. Hilton and her daughter, Dorothy. The son, James, has fallen in love with Jen. Wilbur Kent also covets the girl but is thwarted by James. When Mrs. Hilton learns of her son's interest in the girl, she insists that Jen leave. She does, with financial help from Kent. Jen's mother, Alice, had run off years earlier with the wealthy John Newton but the affair did not last. Unable to secure work in the city, Jen contacts Kent for help. He is engaged to marry Dorothy Hilton and throws a lavish bachelor party. Newton shows up at the party, not knowing that Kent has invited Alice, and their old emotions rekindle. Kent invites Jen to the party. Alice recognizes her daughter but does not reveal her identity. James Hilton is also at the party, and he takes Jen away from the crowd so that they may lead a happy life together. Newton asks Alice to allow him to atone for his past and begs her to lead a life worthy of her daughter.

CRITICS' CORNER

This is not a picture for the unsophisticated as it makes no pretense of hiding its true colors. The first scenes photographed in the environs of the lake are ideal, being well chosen and excellently filmed. *Motion Picture News*

NOTES

In this film, Chaney is seen as an old man of the mountains and in flashbacks as the character at a younger age.

Only reels one and two of *A Mother's Atonement* survive, and are housed at the Library of Congress.

Lon of Lone Mountain

Rex/Universal, 1 reel. *Released:* October 19, 1915. *Production Code No.:* 1366. *Director:* Joseph de Grasse. *Scenario:* Ida May Park.

CAST

Marica Moore, Arthur Shirley, Lon Chaney, George Burrell.

SYNOPSIS

Melissa lives in the mountains with her stern stepfather, Dan Hadley. Her suitor, Lon, is appalled by the cruelty of her stepfather. The new male schoolteacher, who is quite popular with the women of the community, acts as Melissa's protector on more than one occasion and finally persuades the girl to attend school. Lon views this gesture with jealousy, and he persuades the other men to help him drive the teacher from their mountain community. However, when Lon learns the schoolmaster's true worth, he shields him from the attack, and by doing so is injured himself. Melissa comes to know Lon's true love for her and is grateful to him for saving the life of her friend.

CRITICS' CORNER

Lon Chaney endows this backwoods love story with a strong character study. Joe De Grasse produces so its artistic qualities can best be imagined. It surely is a worthy one reeler in every one of its major respects.
Motion Picture News

The Millionaire Paupers

Rex/Universal, 3 reels. *Released:* October 26, 1915. *Director:* Joseph de Grasse. *Scenario:* Ida May Park.

CAST

Grace Thompson (*Enid*), Gretchen Lederer (*Mabel*), Lon Chaney (*Martin*), Arthur Shirley (*Allan*), Millard K. Wilson (*George*), Marsha Moore.

SYNOPSIS

Mrs. Burne-Smith and Mrs. Winthrop have planned that their two children should marry despite the fact that the two have never met. Both Enid and Allan have different ideas. Enid leaves home, moving into a tenement house that Allan owns. Allan, who suspects his building manager, Martin, of being unscrupulous, disguises himself and takes an apartment to keep an eye on him. Enid befriends a young couple, George and Mabel. She notices that Mabel is too familiar with the landlord and learns that Mabel has coaxed him into putting off the rent so that she can buy her wedding clothes. Enid and Allan meet and strike up a romance, not knowing of their parents' plan. Mabel confesses to Enid her problems with Martin, and Enid pawns her last piece of jewelry to release Mabel from the landlord's clutches, taking responsibility for buying the clothes in order to save Mabel and George's relationship. Allan also snubs Enid, and she returns home to carry out her mother's wishes. Allan fires Martin and places George in charge of the building. Allan's search for Enid to make amends is to no avail. He accompanies his mother to meet his planned match and is happily introduced to Enid.

CRITICS' CORNER
For the most part this is a delightful picture. The story by Ida May Park has received excellent interpretation and realistic atmosphere. Each member of the cast . . . deserves praise. *Motion Picture News*

NOTES
The film's working title was *Fate's a Fiddler*. Small portions of this film exist in some private film collections.

Under a Shadow
Rex/Universal, 2 reels. *Released:* December 5, 1915. *Production Code No.:* 1384. *Director:* Joseph de Grasse. *Scenario:* F. McGrew Willis, from his story "A Secret Service Affair."

CAST
Gretchen Lederer, Lon Chaney, Arthur Shirley, Millard K. Wilson.

SYNOPSIS
Thera Dufre, a former secret service agent, is now hiding from government agents. She receives a message to deliver a sealed packet to De Serris of the service. In the same city lives Mrs. Irving, who bears a strong resemblance to Thera. De Serris has a photo of Thera, and by chance, when Mrs. Irving passes him at the appointed meeting spot, he accosts her, demanding the package of which she has no knowledge. He tries to force himself into her auto, but she escapes. Witnessing this event, Thera flees. That evening, Mrs. Irving retrieves her daughter's doll from the patio and is again accosted by De Serris. Her husband

hears the commotion and arms himself. His wife tries to stop him from firing his revolver, but it discharges and the bullet strikes their daughter. Rushing the child to the hospital, the Irvings' car hits Thera, who is on her way to the train station, but she is not seriously hurt. Mr. Irving notices the resemblance between the two women and orders his butler to take Thera to their home. At the Irving home, De Serris confronts Mrs. Irving again and they struggle. Thera kills the man, and Mrs. Irving faints. Thera plants the gun next to the unconscious woman and is about to leave when the phone rings. She answers the phone and receives word from Mr. Irving that their daughter is fine and he begs forgiveness. Thera realizes she cannot frame Mrs. Irving and accepts the penalty for her deeds.

CRITICS' CORNER
A fair melodrama that contains as its strong point much exciting action. . . . The double exposure scenes are not very well handled. *Motion Picture News*

Stronger Than Death

Rex/Universal, 2 reels. *Released:* December 17, 1915. *Production Code No.:* 1419. *Director:* Joseph de Grasse. *Scenario:* Bess Meredyth.

CAST
Louise Carbasse, Lon Chaney, Arthur Shirley, Millard K. Wilson.

SYNOPSIS
June Lathrop is under the guardianship of Rupert Spaulding, a rejected suitor of her deceased mother. June learns of the love her guardian bears for her and how he loved her mother. He has faithfully followed her mother's request that he take care of her upon her mother's death. He now asks June to allow him to care for her all through life by marrying him. She reluctantly consents, giving up her love for John Henshaw, a surgeon. Shortly before his death, Spaulding has June sign a promise that she will never marry again. After Spaulding's death, Henshaw calls on June, but she is reminded of her written promise. The stress of this impossible promise causes her to suffer from sleepwalking, and one night she falls from a balcony, suffering a brain concussion. Henshaw conducts the delicate surgery, during which June's spirit meets her dead husband, who now sees her unhappiness and offers to free her from her promise. He takes the promise from the other legal papers and it becomes ashes before her eyes. After the surgery,

June orders her lawyers to bring her the legal documents and they find that the written promise enacted by her late husband has turned to ashes. She is now free to marry the man she loves.

CRITICS' CORNER
This drama is based on a strong theme, but as produced with a great number of fantastical, visionary scenes is rather confusing at times. . . . Withal it will please, though the visionary scenes might possibly be made clearer. *Motion Picture News*

NOTES
The Universal Picture Code Book lists the film's release date as December 26, 1915.[19]

Father and the Boys

Broadway/Universal, 5 reels. *Released:* December 20, 1915. *Picture Code No.:* 1444. *Director:* Joseph de Grasse. *Scenario:* Ida May Park, from the play of the same title by George Ade. *Photographer:* Edward Ullman.

CAST
Digby Bell (*Lemuel Morewood*), Louise Carbasse (*Bessie Brayton*), Harry Ham (*William Rufus Morewood*), Colin Chase (*Thomas Jefferson More-wood*), Yona Landowska (*Emily Donelson*), Mae Gaston (*Frances Berkeley*), Lon Chaney (*Tuck Bartholomew*), Hayward Mack (*Major Bellamy Didsworth*), H. Davenport (*Tobias Ford*).

SYNOPSIS
Lemuel Morewood wishes his two sons, Billy and Tom, would learn the family business, marry, and settle down. However, Billy is infatuated with a woman of the "smart set," and Tom is more interested in boxing. Lemuel hires Bessie Brayton to entertain at a party he is giving and, at her urging, he wins a large amount of cash by gambling with Major Didsworth. He leaves with Bessie to spend the money. Concerned that he has fallen prey to a golddigger, his sons follow them. A wild chase ensues, with the sons learning that their father only went with Bessie to help her raise money for a supposedly worthless mine and that he has no intention of marrying Bessie, who is engaged to Tuck Bartholomew. The boys agree to learn the family business and settle down.

CRITICS' CORNER
An excellent five reel comedy. . . . Digby Bell, the veteran character actor is seen in the leading part. He is supported by a good cast. . . . A very pleasing comedy number. *Motion Picture News*

The Restless Spirit (1913). A previously unknown title in Lon's filmography. He is standing to the left, wearing a large goatee. (*Courtesy of the Academy of Motion Picture Arts and Sciences*)

Almost an Actress (1913). One of a few comedies Lon Chaney made during his years at Universal. Lon as the cameraman (far left), Max Asher, Silvion de Jardins, Lee Morris, and Louise Fazenda. (*Courtesy of Sam Gill*)

The Pipes of Pan (1914). Lon and Joe King.

The Stronger Mind (1915).
Murdock MacQuarrie
and Lon.

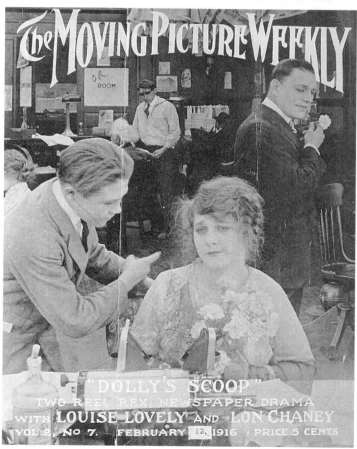

Dolly's Scoop (1916). Cover from the Universal Studios trade weekly.

The Grip of Jealousy (1916). In this film, Lon's character (standing at right) ages from a young man to one in his late fifties. Louise Lovely (center) stands next to a Caucasian actor playing a black, sporting a blackface makeup and a primitive bald cap/wig.

Tangled Hearts (1916). Hayward Mack, Louise Lovely, Lon, and Agnes Vernon.

The Gilded Spider (1916). Gilmore Hammond, Lon, Louise Lovely, and Hayward Mack.

Bobbie of the Ballet (1916). Lon hands over Louise Lovely to Jay Belasco (standing, back to camera).

The Grasp of Greed (1916). C. N. Hammond, an unidentified player, Lon, and Jay Belasco.

Mark of Cain (1916). Lon, Frank Whitson, and an unidentified player.

Place Beyond the Winds (1916). Ad from *Moving Picture Weekly*, Universal's trade journal.

The Piper's Price (1917). William Stowell, Maud George, and Lon. Note that Lon grayed his temples to signify advanced age.

Hell Morgan's Girl (1917). Alfred Allen, Dorothy Phillips, Lon, and William Stowell.

The Girl In the Checkered Coat (1917). Dorothy Phillips and Lon. While the set appears to be an interior, it was actually shot on one of Universal's outdoor stages. Note the brightness of the set and the overhead shadows—features that would appear only from shooting outdoors.

The Flashlight (1917). Dorothy Phillips, William Stowell, and Lon. This film marked the first time Chaney played a dual role (two brothers) in a motion picture.

A Doll's House (1917). Lon, Dorothy Phillips, and an unidentified player.

Triumph (1917). Lon, Dorothy Phillips, and William Stowell.

Pay Me (1917). Lon (center, holding gun), Dorothy Phillips, and William Stowell.

The Grand Passion (1918). Lon (center) points to newspaper.

A Broadway Scandal (1918). Lon and Carmel Myers (right).

Riddle Gawne (1918). E. B. Tilton, Lon, and Katherine MacDonald.

The Wicked Darling (1919). Kalla Pasha, Lon, and Priscilla Dean. This was Chaney's first movie with director Tod Browning.

The False Faces (1919). Lon, Mary Anderson (center), and Henry B. Walthall.

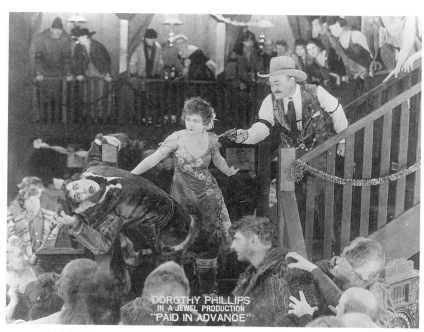

Paid In Advance (1919). Lon, Dorothy Phillips, and Joseph Girard.

The Miracle Man (1919). Thomas Meighan, Lon, J. M. Dumont, and Betty Compson.

The Miracle Man (1919). Left to right: Lon, Frankie Lee, Joseph Dowling, Elinor Fair, Betty Compson, W. Lawson Butt, Thomas Meighan, and J. M. Dumont.

Victory (1919). Bull Montana, Lon, and Wallace Beery.

Treasure Island (1920). Shirley Mason (center) finds herself surrounded by pirates, including Lon (right, with moustache).

Nomads of the North (1920). Lon and Betty Blythe.

The Penalty (1920). James Mason, Lon, and Wilson Hummel.

The Penalty (1920). Lon and Charles Clary.

CHAPTER FOUR

1916

Dolly's Scoop

Rex/Universal, 2 reels. *Released:* February 20, 1916. *Picture Code No.:* 1557. *Director:* Joseph de Grasse. *Scenario:* Ida May Park, from a story by Hugh Weir.

CAST

Louise Lovely (*Dolly Clare*), Lon Chaney (*Don Fisher*), Marjorie Ellison (*Mrs. Fairfax*), Mae Gaston (*Helen*), Laura Praether (*Maid*), Hayward Mack (*James Fairfax*), Millard K. Wilson (*Philip*), Edward Nes (*Jap Boy*).

SYNOPSIS

James Fairfax, owner of the *Morning Argus*, will stop at nothing to get a story for his paper. Anything that is news is property to him, no matter whom it hurts. He is jealously in love with his wife, Alice. Philip Ainsworth still carries his love for Alice, even though she is married. At the urging of one of Philip's sisters, Alice goes to see him to ask him to stop drinking. During the visit, Philip tries to grab Alice, falling to the floor and making a great deal of noise in the apartment house. Fearing she'll be caught, she grabs a bundle of old love letters and leaves. Dolly Clare, a reporter for the newspaper, sees a heavily veiled woman leaving Philip's apartment. Going into Philip's room, she finds a photo of Alice and takes it, not knowing who she is. She calls her boss at home to report the story and relays it to Alice, who tells Dolly the truth and begs her to destroy the photo. Dolly tries to suppress the story, but Fairfax orders the photo to be run on the front page. Another reporter, Dan, has a photo of a woman who has committed suicide but cannot be identified. Dolly exchanges the picture of Alice for the unknown woman, thus saving Alice.

CRITICS' CORNER

To the general public newspaper stories always have a certain fascination and so *Dolly's Scoop*, a melodramatic number of that sort, will

doubtless appeal despite the fact that judged from a reportorial standpoint it is unreal. *Motion Picture News*

NOTES
A print of *Dolly's Scoop* is housed at The National Film and Television
Archive in London.

The Grip of Jealousy

Bluebird/Universal, 5 reels. *Released:* February 28, 1916. *Picture Code
No.:* 1499. *Director:* Joseph de Grasse. *Scenario:* Ida May Park, from her
story "Love Thine Enemy."

CAST
Louise Lovely (*Virginia Grant*), Lon Chaney (*Silas Lacey*), Grace Thomp-
son (*Beth Grant*), Jay Belasco (*Harry Grant*), Hayward Mack (*Philip
Grant*), Colin Chase (*Hugh Morey*), Harry Hamm (*Jack Morey*), Walter
Belasco (*Uncle Jeff*), Marcia Moore (*Lynda*), Dixie Carr (*Cora*).

SYNOPSIS
In the years before the Civil War, Lynda was raised by Uncle Jeff, a
slave of Silas Lacey. Lacey believes the girl to be the daughter of a black
woman whom Lacey had raped. In reality, Lynda is the daughter of
Jack Corey and Beth Grant; the secret is being kept by Lynda's sister,
Virginia. Beth died in childbirth and Jack was framed for murder by
Lacey and fled before the child was born. Although Virginia is in love
with Jack's brother, Hugh, she agrees to marry Silas Lacey's son in return for Lynda's freedom. Jack Corey returns in time to stop Virginia
from marrying Lacey's son and exposes Lacey for the murder.

CRITICS' CORNER
Again the old South of the days before the war forms the background
for a drama in which blood runs hot, slaves are mistreated and bloodhounds called into play. . . . This subject because of its sensationalism
will interest a good many people. . . . The cast is entirely acceptable.
Motion Picture News

NOTES
The film's working title was *Love Thine Enemy.*

Tangled Hearts

Bluebird/Universal, 5 reels. *Released:* April 2, 1916. *Picture Code No.:*
1592. *Director:* Joseph de Grasse. *Scenario:* Ida May Park.

CAST

Louise Lovely (*Vera Lane*), Agnes Vernon (*Lucille Seaton*), Lon Chaney (*John Hammond*), Marjorie Ellison (*Enid Hammond*), Hayward Mack (*Montgomery Seaton*), Jay Belasco (*Ernest Courtney*), Georgia French (*Child*), Bud Chase (*John Dalton*).

SYNOPSIS

Mrs. Enid Hammond is but one of several sweethearts of Montgomery Seaton, a married man. Enid tells Seaton that when she was young, she had an affair with a married man and became pregnant. When the nurse who raised the baby dies, Enid begs Seaton to tell her husband it is Seaton's child, born out of wedlock. Mr. Hammond finds a letter that leads him to believe that his wife is having an affair with Seaton. Enraged, he tries to kill Seaton but instead his wife is wounded. When Seaton's wife finds out, Enid admits her past.

CRITICS' CORNER

This is an offering which will interest and hold quite well because the story has some truly tangled situations. . . . As it stands, it will get over, but it falls considerably short of being big. *Wid's Film Daily*

NOTES

The Universal Picture Code Book lists the film's release date as April 13, 1916.[20]

The Gilded Spider

Bluebird/Universal, 5 reels. *Released:* May 8, 1916. *Production Code No.:* 1623. *Director:* Joseph de Grasse. *Scenario:* Ida May Park.

CAST

Louise Lovely (*Leonita/Elisa*), Lon Chaney (*Giovanni*), Lule Warrenton (*Rosa*), Gilmore Hammond (*Cyrus Kirkham*), Marjorie Ellison (*Mrs. Kirkham*), Hayward Mack (*Burton Armitage*), Jay Belasco (*Paul Winston*).

SYNOPSIS

During his visit to Italy, American Cyrus Kirkham meets Leonita, who is married and has a child. He invites her aboard his yacht and attempts to attack her. Rather than submit, Leonita jumps off the boat and drowns. Fifteen years later her husband, Giovanni, and their daughter Elisa arrive in America. Since his wife's death, Giovanni harbors hatred against all Americans, only to become more adamant when his daughter falls in love with an American artist, Paul Winston. Coincidentally,

Cyrus Kirkham sees a painting Paul has done of Elisa and decides to track her down. When he finds her, he invites her to a social party; but her father follows them, intending to kill Kirkham. When Kirkham sees Giovanni, he recognizes him as Leonita's husband and drops dead of shock. Giovanni, in turn, believes his daughter's name has been ruined and kills himself. Elisa and Paul eventually find true love with each other.

CRITICS' CORNER
The theme here presented is familiar but that might pass unnoticed if it were developed after a better fashion. The principal characters are not as well defined as could be. . . . Lon Chaney's Giovanni is a strong piece of character portrayal. *Motion Picture News*

NOTES
The Universal Picture Code Book lists the film's release date as March 8, 1916.[21] The film's working title was *The Full Cup*.

Bobbie of the Ballet

Bluebird/Universal, 5 reels. *Released:* June 12, 1916. *Picture Code No.:* 1705. *Director:* Joseph de Grasse. *Scenario:* Ida May Park, from a story by Grant Carpenter. *Photographer:* George Kull.

CAST
Louise Lovely (*Bobbie Brent*), Lon Chaney (*Hook Hoover*), Jay Belasco (*Jack Stimson*), Jean Hathaway (*Mrs. Stimson*), Gretchen Lederer (*Velma Vrooman*), Gilmore Hammond (*Henry Fox*), Lule Warrenton (*Mrs. Hoover*), Mrs. Louise Emmons (*Woman in Tenement*), John George (*Man in Tenement*).

SYNOPSIS
Raising her younger brother and sister, ballet dancer Bobbie Brent pretends that the two young children are her own and that she is a widow. When her boyfriend, Jack Stimson, learns of this ruse, he breaks up with her. Jack's jealous ex-girlfriend plots to have Bobbie meet a theatrical agent, who tries to take advantage of her. Luckily, Jack intervenes in time and realizes he still loves Bobbie. Later, the court attempts to take Bobbie's brother and sister from her custody. She and Jack marry, and the court allows the two younger siblings to remain with them.

CRITICS' CORNER
The only good thing about this offering is the fact that in a number of places we have some rather pleasing scenes in which the two little kid-

dies figure. . . . Lon Chaney, as the reformed criminal, convinced with his work, but the assembling of the film and the scenario gave him all the worst of it. *Wid's Film Daily*

NOTES

Mrs. Louise Emmons would later appeared with Chaney in *The Blackbird* (1926), *The Unknown* (1927), and *West of Zanzibar* (1928). John George worked with Chaney in *Pay Me* (1917), *Outside the Law* (1921), *The Road to Mandalay* (1926), *The Unknown* (1927), and *The Big City* (1928). He also appears, as an extra, in Chaney's film biography, *Man of a Thousand Faces* (1957).

The Grasp of Greed

Bluebird/Universal, 5 reels. *Released:* July 17, 1916. *Production Code No.:* 1736. *Director:* Joseph de Grasse. *Scenario:* Ida May Park, from the novel *Mr. Meeson's Will* by H. Rider Haggard.

CAST

Louise Lovely (*Alice Gordon*), Lon Chaney (*Jimmie*), Jay Belasco (*Eustace*), C. N. Hammond (*John Meeson*), Gretchen Lederer (*Lady Holmhurst*).

SYNOPSIS

Writer Alice Gordon has an argument with her publisher, John Meeson. John's nephew, Eustace, sides with Alice and is written out of his uncle's will. Alice boards a ship bound for Australia to sign a deal with a new publisher. When Meeson learns of Alice's plans, he takes the same ship in an attempt to change her mind. En route to Australia, the ship encounters a fierce storm, and Meeson and Alice are shipwrecked on a deserted island. Meeson has second thoughts about his nephew, Jimmie, and wants to write a new will but has no paper. The will is tattooed onto Alice's back. They eventually are saved, but Meeson dies shortly thereafter. Alice must expose her back to reveal the will so that Eustace will be named heir. After the hearing, Eustace and Alice marry.

CRITICS' CORNER

Wills have been more or less prominent in motion pictures since their inception. But this is probably the first time a document of such legal importance has been tattooed on the smooth white back of a young lady. This is the most prominent feature of *The Grasp of Greed*. . . . Lon Chaney in a comedy role is excellent. *Motion Picture News*

Mark of Cain

Red Feather/Universal, 5 reels. *Released:* August 7, 1916. *Picture Code No.:* 1790. *Director:* Joseph de Grasse. *Scenario:* Stuart Paton. *Photographer:* King Gray.

CAST

Lon Chaney (*Dick Temple*), Dorothy Phillips (*Doris*), Frank Whitson (*John Graham*), Gilmore Hammond (*Jake*), T. D. Crittenden (*Mr. Wilson*), Gretchen Lederer (*Mrs. Wilson*), Lydia Yeamans Titus (*Dick's Mother*), Mark Fenton (*Dick's Father*), Georgia French (*Baby Wilson*).

SYNOPSIS

Dick Temple goes to jail for the crimes his father has committed to prevent his parents' marriage from crumbling. When he is released, Dick has no job or money and his parents seemed to have disappeared. Despondent, Dick contemplates suicide until he meets Doris and they begin a romance. Doris works as a nursemaid for the wealthy Wilson family, and Dick takes a job with John Graham, a broker of questionable character. John forces Dick to help him rob the Wilson home, while at the same time Doris' Uncle Jake pressures her to let him in to rob the home, as well. The two scheming crooks plan their robberies at the same time, and Dick starts a fight between Graham and Jake. The two men kill each other in the struggle. Dick discovers that his mother is working in the Wilson household, and he and Doris marry.

CRITICS' CORNER

This picture is not up to Red Feather plays. It contains incredible incidents and coincidence plays a very strong part in places. . . . It will please the less critical. *Motion Picture News*

NOTES

The film's working title was *By Fate's Degree*.

If My Country Should Call

Red Feather/Universal, 5 reels. *Released:* September 25, 1916. *Picture Code No.:* 1832. *Director:* Joseph de Grasse. *Scenario:* Ida May Park, from a story by Virginia Terhune Van de Water. *Photographer:* King Gray.

CAST

Dorothy Phillips (*Margaret Ardrath*), Helen Leslie (*Patricia Landon*), Adele Farrington (*Mrs. Landon*), Frank Whitson (*Robert Ogden*), Lon

Chaney (*Dr. George Ardrath*), Albert MacQuarrie (*Col. Belden*), Jack Nelson (*Donald*), Carl Von Schiller (*Zuroff*), Gretchen Lederer (*Mrs. Ardrath*).

SYNOPSIS

Margaret Ardrath's worst fears are realized when her husband, Robert, enlists in England's army at the breakout of World War I. But when her son, Donald, expresses his desire to join the fight on the United States–Mexican border, it is too much for her to bear. Without his knowing it, Margaret gives her son a heart depressant, which prevents him from joining the Army. However, the drug also causes medical problems, because of which his long-time sweetheart leaves him, and Donald eventually becomes an alcoholic. Margaret then receives word that her husband has been killed in battle. Overwhelmed by grief, Margaret takes a drug overdose, only to wake up and discover it was all just a dream.

CRITICS' CORNER

The biggest fault of this offering is the lack of any dominating personality, and there is no character which holds the sympathy perfectly. *Wid's Film Daily*

NOTES

Three of the five reels of this film and a print of *Place Beyond the Winds* (1916), missing its first reel, were found in Dawson City, Canada, during an excavation in 1978. Unfortunately, only reels two, three, and five survive.[22] The existing footage has been preserved and is housed at the National Archives of Canada and the Library of Congress.

Felix on the Job

Victor/Universal, 1 reel. *Released:* October 31, 1916. *Production Code No.:* 1928. *Director:* Joseph de Grasse. *Scenario:* Harry Wielze.

CAST

George Felix (*Felix*), Eva Loring (*His Wife*), Lon Chaney (*Tod*), Lydia Yeamans Titus (*Tod's Wife*).

SYNOPSIS

Felix finally gets to work after taking a forced ride on a moving "dolly." His job is to put a new roof on Tod's home. Naturally, Felix makes a mess of the whole affair and gets into an argument with Tod and his two boys. Felix accidentally sets fire to the house, which collapses into the nearby river. Tod is enraged, and the ever-incompetent Felix tosses Tod into the river.

CRITICS' CORNER
There's no story here, simply a lot of gags which are worked one after another. They are all on practical joke order and while some of them may succeed in getting a laugh, there are too many of them for real enjoyment. *Motion Picture News*

Place Beyond the Winds

Red Feather/Universal, 5 reels. *Released:* November 6, 1916. *Picture Code No.:* 1954. *Director:* Joseph de Grasse. *Scenario:* Ida May Park, from the novel of the same title by Harriet T. Comstock. *Photographer:* King Gray.

CAST
Dorothy Phillips (*Priscilla Glenn*), Jack Mulhall (*Dick Travers*), Lon Chaney (*Jerry Jo*), Joseph de Grasse (*Anton Farwell*), C. Normand Hammond (*Nathan Glenn*), Alice May Youse (*Mrs. Glenn*), Grace Carlyle (*Joan Moss*), Countess Du Cello (*Mrs. Travers*).

SYNOPSIS
Priscilla Glenn is turned away from her home when her strict father, Nathan, finds she has stayed out all night. Priscilla then meets Dick Travers, who came from the city to the mountains for his health, and Anton Farwell, who confesses that he has killed his sweetheart's lover. In the city, Priscilla gets a job as a nurse. Her first patient is Joan Moss, Anton Farwell's sweetheart. Before she dies, Joan tells Priscilla that she forgives Anton for his actions. Eventually Priscilla marries Dick Travers and reconciles with her father.

CRITICS' CORNER
The story is weak. . . . As to the presentation of the story, Mr. De Grasse's work is not so meritorious. *Motion Picture News*

NOTES
This film, with the three reels of *If My Country Should Call* (1916), was found in Dawson City, Canada, in 1978. The first reel is missing, but otherwise *Place Beyond the Winds* is in excellent condition.[23] The remaining footage has been preserved and is housed at the National Archives of Canada and the Library of Congress.

Accusing Evidence

Big U/Universal, 1 Reel. *Released:* November 23, 1916. *Director:* Not credited. *Scenario:* Not credited.

CAST

Lon Chaney, Pauline Bush, Murdock MacQuarrie.

SYNOPSIS

Lon, a member of the Northwest Mounted Police, is in love with a little girl of the woods. He is accused of a breach of duty and, rather than have the morale of the corps suffer, he submits to the false evidence. Later he is vindicated.

NOTES

The Universal Picture Code Book lists the film's release date as November 10, 1916.[24]

There is an interesting debate about this picture since Pauline Bush was no longer working at Universal at the time of the film's release. It's possible that this picture was filmed earlier and its release was delayed for some unexplained reason. Or the movie may have been originally released under a different title, then rereleased as *Accusing Evidence.* There is no review in any of the trade journals for this title.

The Price of Silence

Bluebird/Universal, 5 reels. *Released:* December 11, 1916. *Picture Code No.:* 2066. *Director:* Joseph de Grasse. *Scenario:* Ida May Park, from a short story by W. Carey Wonderly. *Photographer:* King Gray.

CAST

Dorothy Phillips (*Helen Urmy*), Jack Mulhall (*Ralph Kelton*), Lon Chaney (*Edmund Stafford*), Frank Whitson (*Oliver Urmy*), Evelyn Selbie (*Jenny Cupps*), Jay Belasco (*Billy Cupps*), Eddie Brown (*Landlord*).

SYNOPSIS

Helen marries Oliver Urmy but keeps secret from him that she had a child out of wedlock. The only two people who know are her doctor, Edmund Stafford, and his nurse, who raised the baby. Years later, when Helen's legitimate daughter is ready for marriage Dr. Stafford threatens to reveal her secret if he isn't allowed to marry her daughter, Aline, himself. Aline elopes with Billy Cupps, whom Helen believes to be her illegitimate son. Fearing the worst, Helen speaks to Stafford's nurse, who tells her that Helen's son died in infancy. Stafford is killed in an automobile accident, burying Helen's dark secret forever.

CRITICS' CORNER
The Price of Silence is not for that sort of an audience [puritanical]. Which of course doesn't mean that the picture is void of value. Quite the opposite. It is full of value for the exhibitor who caters to a group of people inclined to look for peppers and spices in their entertainment. . . . Lon Chaney is polished as the villain, obviously villainous.
Motion Picture News

CHAPTER FIVE

1917

The Piper's Price

Bluebird/Universal, 5 reels. *Released:* January 8, 1917. *Picture Code No.:* 2162. *Director:* Joseph de Grasse. *Scenario:* Ida May Park, from the short story of the same title by Mrs. Wilson Woodrow. *Photographer:* King Gray.

CAST

Dorothy Phillips (*Amy Hadley*), William Stowell (*Ralph Hadley*), Lon Chaney (*Billy Kilmartin*), Maud George (*Jessica Hadley*), Claire Du Brey (*Jessica's Maid*).

SYNOPSIS

Shortly after his marriage to Amy, Ralph Hadley finds himself falling in love with his first wife, Jessica. They become closer and eventually Amy hears about their affair. Carrying her and Ralph's first child, Amy seeks out Jessica and begs her to give up Ralph for the sake of their marriage and soon-to-be-born child. Jessica understands and ends her fling with Ralph by marrying an old friend, Billy Kilmartin. Ralph is devastated by the quick end to his affair and his thoughts turn to suicide. But the birth of his child rejuvenates him.

CRITICS' CORNER

A well treated domestic drama is *The Piper's Price*, quite conventional when you get down to the bottom of things but original on the surface due to a few new twists. . . . Lon Chaney has the only other part of importance. *Motion Picture News*

Hell Morgan's Girl

Bluebird/Universal, 5 reels. *Released:* March 5, 1917. *Picture Code No.:* 2204. *Director:* Joseph de Grasse. *Scenario:* Ida May Park, from the story

"The Wrong Side of Paradise" by Harvey Gates. *Photographer:* King
Gray. *Cost of Production:* $8,600.

CAST
Dorothy Phillips (*Lola*), William Stowell (*Roger Curwell*), Lon Chaney
(*Sleter Noble*), Lilyan Rosine (*Olga*), Joseph Girard (*Oliver Curwell*), Al-
fred Allen (*"Hell" Morgan*).

SYNOPSIS
Roger Curwell becomes another drunk on San Francisco's Barbary
Coast after he is disowned by his father. He is savagely beaten in Hell
Morgan's saloon one night but is nursed back to health by the saloon
owner's daughter, Lola. Sleter Noble, who covets Lola for himself, is
envious of Curwell. Roger takes a job playing piano in the saloon, then
learns that he has inherited his father's fortune. When Sleter threatens
to kill Roger, Lola, to save Roger's life, agrees to go with him. When
her father hears her screams, he kills Sleter just as the 1906 earthquake
occurs. Lola and her father meet Roger in a park, and she and Roger
make plans for a happy life together.

CRITICS' CORNER
It is no exaggeration to place *Hell Morgan's Girl* among the best five-
reel melodramatic photoplays of the year. The action is fast and
furious. . . . If an exhibitor wishes to have a thrilling melodrama he
could not do much better than book *Hell Morgan's Girl*. *New York Dramatic Mirror*
    As a characterization study this will rank very high. Being an under-
world theme, it will be exceptionally interesting to many. *Wid's Film
Daily*

NOTES
The film earned a $450,000 profit.[25]

The Mask of Love

Laemmle/Universal, 1 reel. *Released:* March 29, 1917. *Director:* Joseph
de Grasse. *Scenario:* Not credited.

CAST
Pauline Bush (*Carlotta*), Lon Chaney (*Marino*).

SYNOPSIS
Carlotta and her elderly father, struggling to make ends meet, are befriended by Marino, a hardened character of the underworld. Under

the guise of friendship, he attempts to take advantage of Carlotta. She is rescued by Peter, an old friend. When Carlotta's father hears of Marino's actions, he seeks out the criminal, and a fight follows. Marino is about to stab the old man when Peter subdues him. Peter and Carlotta then marry and make plans for a happy future.

The Girl in the Checkered Coat

Bluebird/Universal, 5 reels. *Released:* April 23, 1917. *Picture Code No.:* 2280. *Director:* Joseph de Grasse. *Scenario:* Ida May Park, from a story by E. M. Ingleton. *Photographer:* King Gray.

CAST

Dorothy Phillips (*Mary Graham/"Flash Fan"*), William Stowell (*David Norman*), Lon Chaney (*Hector Maitland*), Mrs. A. E. Witting (*Ann Maitland*), David Kirby (*Jim*), Jane Bernoudy (*Sally*), Nellie Allen (*Hector's lady friend*), Countess Du Cello (*Landlady*).

SYNOPSIS

After the death of their mother, Mary and Fannie Graham are left with their father, who is a criminal. Mary leaves home while Fannie follows in her father's footsteps. Years later, they meet again when Fannie, now known as "Flash Fan," is being pursued by police for a purse snatching. Fannie sneaks into Mary's apartment and leaves behind her checkered coat before escaping. When the police find the coat in Mary's room, she is jailed. Attorney David Norman establishes her innocence and Mary is freed. David introduces her to wealthy Ann Maitland, who makes Mary her ward. This angers Hector, Mrs. Maitland's nephew, who was hoping to inherit his aunt's entire fortune. After catching Fannie trying to pick his pockets, Hector enlists her help to oust Mary. He secures her a job as a servant and plots that she is to steal some jewelry and place it on Mary. David exposes the plan, and he and Mary then plan their wedding.

CRITICS' CORNER

In its dramatic substance it is rather lean. . . . A fine production has been tendered by director Joseph De Grasse. *Motion Picture News*

The Flashlight

Bluebird/Universal, 5 reels. *Released:* May 21, 1917. *Picture Code No.:* 2355. *Director and Scenario:* Ida May Park, from a short story "The Flash-Light" by Albert M. Treynore. *Photographer:* King Gray.

CAST
Dorothy Phillips (*Delice*), William Stowell (*Jack Lane*), Lon Chaney
(*Henry Norton/Porter Brixton*), Alfred Allen (*John Peterson*), George Bur-
rell (*Barclay*), Evelyn Selbie (*Mrs. Barclay*), Clyde Benson (*Deputy*), O. C.
Jackson (*Howard, Lane's servant*), Mark Fenton (*Judge*).

SYNOPSIS
Nature photographer Jack Lane takes his new experiment to the mountains for a test. He has invented a flashlight process that will automati-
cally take a picture of any animal or bird that passes by. While camping
in the mountains, he is awakened by gunshots and discovers his camera
has taken a picture of a woman running by, carrying a shotgun. He
later goes to the cabin of the murdered man, Porter Brixton, and is
arrested for the crime. Jack escapes and meets Delice, the woman in
the photo. Jack is recaptured and brought to trial. Henry Norton, the
dead man's half-brother, admits during the courtroom proceedings
that he, not Jack, killed Brixton in self-defense.

CRITICS' CORNER
A picture of merit in rank with some of the best picturizations of dra-
matic narrative and will stand as one of the best efforts yet of
Bluebird. . . . Lon Chaney in support is convincing. *Motion Picture News*

NOTES
The film's working title was *The Flashlight Girl*. This marked the directorial debut of Ida May Park (Mrs. Joseph de Grasse).

A Doll's House

Bluebird/Universal, 5 reels. *Released:* June 11, 1917. *Picture Code No.:*
2410. *Director and Scenario:* Joseph de Grasse, based on the play by Henrik Ibsen. *Photographer:* King Gray.

CAST
Dorothy Phillips (*Nora Helmer*), William Stowell (*Torvald Helmer*), Lon
Chaney (*Nils Krogstad*), Sidney Dean (*Dr. Rank*), Miriam Shelby (*Chris-
tina Linden*), Helen Wright (*Anna*).

SYNOPSIS
Nora Helmer has been living a life of ignorance with her selfish husband, Torvald. He becomes ill, and she forges her dead father's signa-
ture to a check in order to raise money to send her husband to Italy for
treatment. She uses a moneylender named Krogstad to accomplish this

illegal transaction. Some time later, Torvald is managing a bank that employs Krogstad. He dismisses Krogstad after finding him making illegal transactions. Krogstad sends a letter to Torvald revealing his wife's past crime. Regardless of the fact that Nora committed the crime for his benefit, Torvald is still furious over the incident. Nora leaves him in hopes of finding better treatment elsewhere.

CRITICS' CORNER

Bluebird's production of Henrik Ibsen's play *A Doll's House*. . . . turns out to be a dramatically fine piece of work in every respect. . . . *A Doll's House* is more likely to win new audiences than to swell the old ones. *Motion Picture News*

Fires of Rebellion

Bluebird/Universal, 5 reels. *Released:* July 2, 1917. *Picture Code No.:* 2475. *Director and Scenario:* Ida May Park, from her own story. *Photographer:* King Gray.

CAST

Dorothy Phillips (*Madge Garvey*), William Stowell (*John Blake*), Lon Chaney (*Russell Hanlon*), Belle Bennett (*Helen Mallory*), Golda Madden (*Cora Hayes*), Alice May Youse (*Mrs. Garvey*), Edward Brady (*Dan Mallory*), Richard La Reno (*Joe Garvey*).

SYNOPSIS

Madge Garvey is tired of the dreary life that she imagines lies before her by marrying factory foreman John Blake. In a rebellious move, she heads to the big city and takes a job modeling undergarments. However, she is shocked by the minimal amount of material she must wear and the implications of what is expected of her beyond the job. Blake arrives in the nick of time to save her from the advances of Russell Hanlon. She and John return to their normal life and marry.

CRITICS' CORNER

There's not a shadow of doubt that the characters in *Fires of Rebellion* are taken from life. . . . The production is satisfactory. *Moving Picture World*

The Rescue

Bluebird/Universal, 5 reels. *Released:* July 23, 1917. *Picture Code No.:* 2499. *Director and Scenario:* Ida May Park, from a story by Hugh Kahler. *Photographer:* King Gray.

CAST
Dorothy Phillips (*Anne Wetherall*), William Stowell (*Kent Wetherall*), Lon
Chaney (*Thomas Holland*), Gretchen Lederer (*Nell Jerrold*), Molly Malone (*Betty Jerrold*), Claire Du Brey (*Henriette*), Gertrude Astor (*Mrs. Hendricks*).

SYNOPSIS
Actress Anne Wetherall returns to her profession after her divorce from
her husband, Kent. Her childhood friend, Nell Jerrold, begs her to in-
tervene in her daughter's desires to marry Kent. Anne realizes that the
only plan that will work is to enthrall her ex-husband and win him back.
A battle between the two women develops, pitting Betty's youth and
beauty against Anne's charm and talent. In the end, Anne wins out and
realizes that she still loves her husband.

CRITICS' CORNER
A plot of considerable spice which however never grows offensive,
pretty scenes, pretty and capable actresses and a surprise ending unite
to make *The Rescue* a most entertaining piece of pictorial storytelling.
Motion Picture News

Triumph

Bluebird/Universal, 5 reels. *Released:* September 3, 1917. *Picture Code
No.:* 2540. *Director:* Joseph de Grasse. *Scenario:* Fred Myton, from the
story of the same title by Samuel Hopkins Adams.

CAST
Dorothy Phillips (*Nell Baxter*), Lon Chaney (*Paul Neihoff*), William Stowell (*Dudley Weyman*), William J. Dryer (*David Montieth*), Claire Du Brey
(*Lillian Du Pont*), Clyde Benson (*Rupert Vincent*), Helen Wright (*Character Woman*), Ruth Elder (*Second Woman*).

SYNOPSIS
While waiting for her train to take her to Broadway, Nell Baxter makes
the acquaintance of the leading man of a theatrical repertory troupe.
In New York City, she catches the eye of David Montieth, a stage manager. He promises her the leading role in a play provided that she return the favor in a physical way. Nell falls for Paul Neihoff, a playwright,
and the day the show is to open, Nell learns that Montieth has found
out about her love affair with Neihoff and cancels the play. He agrees
to let the show proceed in return for Nell's affections. When he attempts to take advantage of her, she stabs him to death. Nell runs to

Neihoff's apartment and confesses. Neihoff instructs her to go to the theatre and perform in the play as if nothing has happened. During the second act, Nell learns that Neihoff has confessed to the crime. In the last act of the play, she substitutes a real dagger for the prop one and kills herself. In the end, we learn that this was all a story concocted by the leading man to impress upon Nell that a life in front of the footlights isn't all glamour.

CRITICS' CORNER
This is a picture of stage life and possesses more than the usual attraction of such productions due to its artistic and tasteful direction. . . . The production is realistic from start to last. *Motion Picture News*

Pay Me

Jewel/Universal, 5 reels. *Released:* September 1, 1917. *Picture Code No.:* 2480. *Director:* Joseph de Grasse. *Scenario:* Bess Meredyth, from a story by Joseph de Grasse. *Photographer:* King Gray.

CAST
Lon Chaney (*Joe Lawson*), Dorothy Phillips (*Marta*), William Stowell (*Bill the Boss*), Ed Brown (*Martin*), William Clifford (*Hal Curtis*), Evelyn Selbie (*Hilda Hendricks*), Tom Wilson (*"Mac" Jepson*), Claire Du Brey (*Nita*), John George (*Bar Patron*).

SYNOPSIS
Years ago, Joe Lawson, owner of the Nugget dance hall, accidentally killed his ex-mining partner's wife. Lawson then abandoned his family and ran off with the saloon keeper's daughter. They raised the dead woman's child, now known as Marta, as their own. Now a grown woman, Marta is in love with a young lumberjack, Mac Jepson. One day, Lawson's ex-partner shows up in the Nugget and Lawson orders him killed. Mac, however, saves him from certain death. Finally the two ex-partners shoot it out and, on his death bed, Lawson learns that Mac is the son he abandoned years earlier but he does not reveal the truth.

CRITICS' CORNER
Pay Me is a strong, virile drama. It smacks of the melodramatic in its every scene. There is action in every line. The exhibitor can book this picture without a hesitancy. His patrons will be satisfied. . . . The climax reached is well conceived and put over with a punch. *Motion Picture News*

NOTES
The Universal Picture Code Book lists the film's release date as June 21, 1917.[26] The film's working title was *The Vengeance of the West*.

The Empty Gun

Gold Seal/Universal, 3 reels. *Released:* September 4, 1917. *Production Code No.:* 2579. *Director:* Joseph de Grasse. *Scenario:* J. Grubb Alexander and Fred Myton.

CAST
Lon Chaney (*Frank*), Claire McDowell (*Mary*), Sam de Grasse (*Jim*).

SYNOPSIS
Frank cannot get his gold shipped because a storm causes the train to be delayed. He returns home to his wife, Mary, who regrets having married him instead of her true love, Jim. Frank leaves Mary alone in their shack during the violent storm. When she hears a knock on the door, she fingers the gun on the table. The visitor turns out to be Jim. Mary confess to him that she should never have married Frank and recounts his abuse of her. Angry, Jim goes to find Frank and settle the score. Meanwhile, Frank has been attacked by a robber who saw his gold shipment. Frank defeats the robber and, to hide from further attack, he exchanges clothes with the criminal. When Frank returns to the shack in disguise, Mary confronts him with the gun, not knowing who he is. A fight ensues between them, and Jim returns to help her. Mary shoots the man she believes to be a stranger, killing him. She and Jim remove the dead man's mask and discover he is Frank. Solemnly, Jim says, "It is the judgment of the Highest Court."

Bondage

Bluebird/Universal, 5 reels. *Released:* October 17, 1917. *Picture Code No.:* 2580. *Director and Scenario:* Ida May Park, from a story by Edna Kenton. *Photographer:* King Gray.

CAST
Dorothy Phillips (*Elinor Crawford*), William Stowell (*Evan Kilvert*), Lon Chaney (*The Seducer*), Gertrude Astor (*Eugenia Darth*), J. B. McLaughlin (*Bertie Vawtry*), Jean Porter (*Jean*), Eugene Owen (*James*).

SYNOPSIS
Elinor Crawford is a reporter for a New York scandal sheet. She encounters Evan Kilvert, who hails from her hometown. He is somewhat

shocked at her unconventional lifestyle, and she turns her affections to Bertie Vawtry. He pledges his love to her but soon tires of her and marries someone else. Elinor is heartbroken and disappears. Kilvert finds her living in poverty and rescues her, and they are married. Later, when Elinor comes across Bertie, she finds out that his wife has died and rejects his advances towards her. Kilvert confronts his wife with his suspicion that she is being unfaithful, and she leaves him. When he learns the truth, he begs Elinor to return. He then finds her seducer and gives him a beating.

CRITICS' CORNER
She [Ida May Park] has turned out a most skillful piece of work in every department. *Bondage* has more than the usual share of dramatic moments. It is told clearly and concisely. *Motion Picture News*

NOTES
The Universal Picture Code Book lists the film's release date as October 15, 1917.[27]

Anything Once
Bluebird/Universal, 5 reels. *Released:* October 8, 1917. *Production Code No.:* 2623. *Director:* Joseph de Grasse. *Scenario:* William Parker, from a story by Izola Forrester and Mann Page. *Photographer:* Jack MacKenzie.

CAST
Franklyn Farnum (*Theodore Crosby*), Claire Du Brey (*Señorita Dolores*), Lon Chaney (*Waught Mohr*), Marjory Lawrence (*Dorothy Stuart*), Mary St. John (*Mrs. Stuart*), Sam de Grasse (*Sir Mortimer Beggs*), H. M. Thurston (*Getting Mohr*), Raymond Wells (*"Horned Toad" Smith*), William Dyer (*Jethro Quail*), Frank Tokunaga (*Algeron*).

SYNOPSIS
When his father is killed in a dispute over land rights, New Yorker Theodore Crosby inherits his father's ranch with the provision that he take possession and marry Dorothy Stuart within six months. Unfamiliar with the ways of the West, he boards a train for Arizona. On the way he meets "Horned Toad" Smith, his father's assassin, and they become friends, not knowing each other's identities. When Dorothy is abducted by Horned Toad, Theodore attempts to rescue her, only to be taken captive. Dorothy escapes and returns with the ranch cowboys, who find that Theodore has taken all of Horned Toad's clothing and his ranch

in a game of poker. Theodore and Dorothy are married within the will's allotted time.

CRITICS' CORNER
Nothing is to be taken seriously in *Anything Once*. . . . everything goes with a slap and a dash and not the slightest heed taken of such a thing as probability. *Moving Picture World*

NOTES
The film's working title was *The Maverick*.

The Scarlet Car

Bluebird/Universal, 5 reels. *Released:* December 24, 1917. *Picture Code No.:* 2760. *Director:* Joseph de Grasse. *Scenario:* William Parker, from the novel by Richard Harding Davis. *Photographer:* King Gray.

CAST
Franklyn Farnum (*Billy Winthrop*), Al Filson (*Samuel Winthrop*), Lon Chaney (*Paul Revere Forbes*), Edith Johnson (*Beatrice Forbes*), Sam de Grasse (*Ernest Peabody*), Howard Crampton (*Cyrus Peabody*), William Lloyd (*Jim Pettit*).

SYNOPSIS
After nearly driving his father into bankruptcy, Billy Winthrop vows to reform. He is in love with Beatrice Forbes, the daughter of Paul Revere Forbes, who is a cashier at the local bank. Forbes has discovered that Peabody, the bank president, has lost $35,000 of bank funds to speculation. When Forbes confronts Peabody, the two men struggle, and Forbes is apparently killed in the fight. Peabody places Forbes' body in a car and causes an accident; however, by morning Forbes' body has disappeared. Beatrice is pressured into agreeing to marry Peabody's son, but Billy rescues her. They take shelter in an abandoned cabin in which Forbes has also taken refuge. His mind is gone; he thinks himself to be a messenger for his famous relative, Paul Revere. The missing funds have been discovered, and Peabody claims that it was Billy who stole the money. He leads an angry mob to the cabin, where they confront Billy. The young man produces a document Forbes has been holding onto that implicates Peabody in the crime. The mob tars and feathers both of the Peabodys, and Beatrice and Billy are reunited.

CRITICS' CORNER
The Scarlet Car presents a melodrama of considerable interest. . . . The manner in which Billy clears himself is unusual and leads up to a climax of the true melodramatic type. *Motion Picture News*

NOTES

Prints of *The Scarlet Car* can be found at the Library of Congress and in several private film collections. Kino International included clips from this film in their videotape documentary, *Lon Chaney: Behind the Mask* (1995).

CHAPTER SIX

1918

Broadway Love

Bluebird/Universal, 5 reels. *Released:* January 21, 1918. *Picture Code No.:* 2775. *Director and Scenario:* Ida May Park, from the novelette by W. Carey Wonderly. *Photographer:* King Gray.

CAST

Dorothy Phillips (*Midge O'Hara*), William Stowell (*Henry Rockwell*), Lon Chaney (*Elmer Watkins*), Juanita Hansen (*Cherry Blow*), Harry Von Meter (*Jack Chalvey*), Gladys Tennyson (*Mrs. Watkins*), Eve Southern (*Drina*).

SYNOPSIS

Midge O'Hara is a Broadway chorus girl. She attends a party one night at the home of the chorus queen, Cherry Blow. Midge tries to convince Cherry that she should be nicer to Jack Chalvey, Cherry's sweetheart. The party becomes too wild for Midge's liking, so Henry Rockwell escorts her from the event. On the way to her apartment, Rockwell attempts to embrace Midge in the cab. Struggling, Midge falls out of the cab and is injured. Rockwell takes her to the hospital and later follows her to Atlantic City, where he professes his love for her. She accepts his proposal and also learns that Cherry has acknowledged Jack's love.

CRITICS' CORNER

This is another one of the stories that is supposed to depict life as it is along the gay white lane. It doesn't do that, but as a feature picture it is better the usual run of Bluebirds. . . . Lon Chaney carried the "heavy" along nicely, although there was too much comedy in his early make-up. *Wid's Film Daily*

The Grand Passion

Jewel/Universal, 7 reels. *Released:* February 1, 1918. *Picture Code No.:* 2640. *Director and Scenario:* Ida May Park, from the novel *The Boss of*

Powderville by Thomas Addison. *Photographer:* King Gray. *Technical Director:* Milton Moore.

CAST
Dorothy Phillips (*Viola Argos*), Jack Mulhall (*Jack Ripley*), Lon Chaney (*Paul Argos*), William Stowell (*Dick Evans*), Bert Appling (*Red Pete Jackson*), Evelyn Selbie (*Boston Kate*), Alfred Allen (*Ben Mackey*).

SYNOPSIS
In the rough-and-tumble munitions town of Powderville, Dick Evans is the corrupt leader. He puts his best friend, Jack Ripley, in charge of the town's newspaper, and soon Jack's editorials on cleaning up the town have an effect on Evans. When Viola Argos is kidnapped and locked in a brothel by Red Pete Jackson, the two men come to her rescue. Red Pete's gang follows and a huge fight erupts, which causes a fire that destroys much of the town around them. Jack implores Evans and Viola to escape to safety, but Viola returns to Jack, realizing she loves him, only to have him die in her arms.

CRITICS' CORNER
If gun play, mob stuff and exceptional lighting were the principal ingredients of motion pictures, then *The Grand Passion*, the latest Jewel production, would rank with the highest for these ingredients. . . . Dorothy Phillips, William Stowell, Lon Chaney and Jack Mulhall do their best with roles that have not been properly characterized by the scenarist. *Motion Picture News*

NOTES
The Universal Picture Code Book lists the film's release date as February 25, 1918.[28]

The film's working title was *The Boss of Powderville*. Jack Mulhall later appeared with Chaney in *Danger—Go Slow* (1918) and *Flesh and Blood* (1922).

The Kaiser, The Beast of Berlin

Jewel/Universal, 7 reels. *Released:* March 9, 1918. *Picture Code No.:* 2812. *Producer and Director:* Rupert Julian. *Scenario:* Elliott J. Clawson and Rupert Julian. *Photographer:* Edward Kull.

CAST
Rupert Julian (*The Kaiser*), Nigel de Brulier (*Capt. Von Neigle*), Lon Chaney (*Bethmann-Hollweg*), Harry Von Meter (*Capt. Von Hancke*), Harry

Carter (*General Von Kluck*), Joseph Girard (*Ambassador Gerard*), H. Barrows (*General Haig*), Alfred Allen (*General Pershing*), Harry Holden (*General Joffre*), Elmo Lincoln (*Marcas, the Blacksmith*), Ruth Clifford (*Gabrielle*), Betty Carpenter (*Bride*), Ruby Lafayette (*Grandmother Marcas*), Zoe Rae (*Gretel*), Mark Fenton (*Admiral Von Tirpitz*), Jay Smith (*Marshal Von Hindenburg*), Jack MacDonald (*King Albert*), Allan Sears (*Capt. Von Wohlbold*), W. H. Bainbridge (*Col. Schmiedcke*), Walter Belasco (*Admiral Von Pliscott*), Pedro Sose (*General Diaz*), Orlo Eastman (*President Wilson*), Georgie Hupp (*Little Jean*), Winter Hall (*Dr. Von Gressler*), Frank Lee (*Hansel*).

SYNOPSIS

Kaiser Wilhelm II is an egotistical ruler anxious for conquest. During the invasion of Belgium in World War I, Marcas, a local blacksmith, is wounded but is able to save his daughter from the German army. After the United States enters the war, the kaiser is caught and handed over to the king of Belgium. In prison, the kaiser is confronted by his jailer, Marcas the blacksmith.

CRITICS' CORNER

The Kaiser dramatizes patriotism more intensely than any other picture the writer has seen. It combines a wonderful characterization of the Kaiser rendered by Rupert Julian and an intimate drama of one family who suffered when the German hordes swept through Belgium. *Motion Picture News*

NOTES

The Kaiser, The Beast of Berlin was a huge hit for Universal. At one point the film was playing in two Broadway theaters simultaneously owned by Marcus Loew and William Fox. Universal's publicity department boasted that the long lines to see the movie "blocked traffic on Broadway."[29]

Rupert Julian would later direct Chaney in *Phantom of the Opera* (1925). Scenarist Elliott J. Clawson wrote the screenplays for Chaney's *Phantom of the Opera, The Road to Mandalay* (1926) and *West of Zanzibar* (1928).

Fast Company

Bluebird/Universal, 5 reels. *Released:* April 1, 1918. *Production Code No.:* 2822. *Director:* Lynn F. Reynolds. *Scenario:* Eugene B. Lewis and Waldemar Young, from a story by John McDermott. *Photographer:* Edward Ullman.

CAST
Franklyn Farnum (*Lawrence Percival Van Huyler*), Fred Montague (*Peter Van Huyler*), Katherine Griffith (*Mrs. Van Huyler*), Lon Chaney (*Dan Mc-Carty*), Juanita Hansen (*Alicia Vanderveldt*), Edward Cecil (*Richard Barnaby*).

SYNOPSIS
Blue-blooded Lawrence Percival Van Huyler finds out during his family's estate renovation that his family patriarch, Richard Barnaby, is an Irishman of lowly birth who made his fortune as a pirate on the high seas. Knowing this, Lawrence gets a job doing construction work. When he learns that Richard Barnaby's much-talked-about exploits were lifted from a book, however, he exposes the phony for what he was and wins back the love of his sweetheart, Alicia.

CRITICS' CORNER
This is a light, clean comedy-drama possessing considerable heart interest that will please any audience. . . . Supporting cast is good, except Lon Chaney who overacts. *Motion Picture News*

NOTES
Waldemar Young, who coauthored the scenario, would later write several of Chaney and Tod Browning's films at M-G-M, including *The Unholy Three* (1925), *The Blackbird* (1926) and *The Unknown* (1927).

A Broadway Scandal

Bluebird/Universal, 5 reels. 4,400 ft. *Released:* June 1, 1918. *Picture Code No.:* 2873. *Director:* Joseph de Grasse. *Scenario:* Harvey Gates. *Photographer:* Edward Ullman.

CAST
Carmel Myers (*Nanette Bisson*), W. H. Bainbridge (*Dr. Kendall*), Edwin August (*David Kendall*), Lon Chaney (*"Kink" Colby*), Andrew Robson (*Armande Bisson*), S. K. Shilling (*Paul Caval*), Frederick Gamble (*Falkner*).

SYNOPSIS
Nanette Bisson works in her father's French restaurant in New York. One night she takes a joy ride with "Kink" Colby in a stolen car. During a police pursuit, Nanette is shot in the shoulder. Kink leaves the girl at the offices of Dr. David Kendall, who treats her. She falls in love with the young doctor, but he does not return her affections, thinking all

French women are frivolous. Her parents also shun her because of her involvement with Colby, but Nanette goes on to become a big success on the stage. Kendall serves in World War I and, while stationed in France, learns to appreciate the bravery of the French women. On his return, he is reunited with Nanette and he helps her to reconcile with her parents.

CRITICS' CORNER

The plot, in spite of its unpromising title, is thoroughly enjoyable and moves swiftly through its course to a pleasing conclusion. *Moving Picture World*

NOTES

The Universal Picture Code Book lists the film's release date as May 27, 1918.[30] This was the last film Chaney made with director Joseph de Grasse.

Riddle Gawne

Paramount-Artcraft, 5 reels. 4,757 ft. *Released:* August 19, 1918. *In Production:* June 14, 1918 to early July 1918. *Supervisor:* Thomas H. Ince. *Director:* Lambert Hillyer. *Scenario:* Charles Alden Seltzer, from his novel *The Vengeance of Jefferson Gawne*. *Photographer:* Joe August. *Art Director:* G. Harold Percival.

CAST

William S. Hart (*Jefferson "Riddle" Gawne*), Katherine MacDonald (*Kathleen Harkness*), Lon Chaney (*Hame Bozzam*), Gretchen Lederer (*Blanche Dillon*), Gertrude Short (*Jane Gawne*), Leon Kent (*Jess Cass*), Milton Ross (*Reb Butler*), E. B. Tilton (*Col. Harkness*).

SYNOPSIS

Seeking revenge on the man who killed his brother and kidnapped his sister-in-law, Jefferson "Riddle" Gawne spends years searching for the killer. Finally he settles down on his own ranch and falls for the lovely Kathleen Harkness, the daughter of a cattle rustler who is part of Hame Bozzam's gang. Hame Bozzam wants Kathleen for himself and has Gawne shot. Gawne recovers and, fed up with the gang, gets rid of the sheriff, who is in Bozzam's pocket, then leads a group of cowboys against the Bozzam gang. Gawne learns that Bozzam has kidnapped Kathleen and rides to her rescue. In a shootout, Gawne is seriously wounded and overhears Bozzam claim that he killed Gawne's brother years ago. Gawne gathers all his strength and manages to throw Bozzam off the cliff to his death. Gawne recovers, thanks to the care of Kathleen.

CRITICS' CORNER

The nature of the story and the typical Hart role that has been given the star to interpret crowds its way right up to the front lines and retains its position as one of Hart's best. *Motion Picture News*

Well, Bill is as quick on the trigger as ever and puts this over with a wallop. This has all the typical Hart elements with Bill standing off a whole gang. . . . Lon Chaney was an effective willun. *Wid's Film Daily*

NOTES

Portions of the film were shot on location in the Santa Monica Mountains and in Chatsworth, California. A western ranchero set was built on a dairy farm, and was later burned to the ground for a scene in the movie.[31]

Contrary to William S. Hart's account in his autobiography, it was director Lambert Hillyer who had to sell the idea of hiring Chaney as the villain to Hart. It was Hart who felt Chaney was too short to play the role of Hame Bozzam, not the director.[32] It marked Chaney's first freelancing role after leaving Universal over a salary increase.

Only two reels of *Riddle Gawne* exist and are housed at the Russian film archive, Gosfilmofond, in Moscow. It is uncertain whether Chaney appears in those reels.

That Devil, Bateese

Bluebird/Universal, 5 reels. *Released:* September 2, 1918. *Picture Code No.:* 2949. *Director:* William Wolbert. *Scenario:* Bernard McConville, from a story by Bess Meredyth. *Photographer:* Charles Seeling.

CAST

Monroe Salisbury (*Bateese Latour*), Ada Gleason (*Kathleen St. John*), Lamar Johnstone (*Martin Stuart*), Lon Chaney (*Louis Courteau*), Andrew Robson (*Father Pierre*).

SYNOPSIS

Kathleen St. John arrives in the village of Montrouge to teach school. Leaving the train station, she gets lost on her way to town and is attacked by Louis Courteau. Bateese Latour, a lumberjack, steps in to save Kathleen. He soon falls in love with her and swears off drinking so that he might marry her. When Kathleen's ex-lover, Martin, shows up in town, Bateese is sure that she still loves Martin and therefore plans to kill himself by going over the falls in his canoe. Louis Courteau's sister still wears the wedding dress she had on when her groom jilted her. She recognizes Martin as her former groom, and when Kathleen learns of Martin's actions, she goes to find Bateese. Her true love is hurt but alive. She helps him return home, and they plan for a future together.

CRITICS' CORNER
Step out and get this Bluebird! I don't remember when I've seen a production where a one characterization stands out. . . . The superb natural scenic backgrounds in the offering are remarkably beautiful throughout. . . . Lon Chaney did a very effective bit of character work as the 'willun'. *Wid's Film Daily*

NOTES
That Devil, Bateese marked Chaney's return to Universal as a freelance actor. The film's working title was *The Devil Baptistie*.

The Talk of the Town

Bluebird/Universal, 6 reels. *Released:* September 28, 1918. *Production Code No.:* 2871. *Director and Scenario:* Allen Holubar, from the novelette "Discipline and Genevra" by Harold Vickers. *Photographer:* Fred Granville.

CAST
Dorothy Phillips (*Genevra French*), George Fawcett (*Major French*), Clarissa Selwynne (*Aunt Harriet*), William Stowell (*Lawrence Tabor*), Lon Chaney (*Jack Langhorne*), Gloria Jay (*Genevra at age 5*), Una Fleming (*Dancer*).

SYNOPSIS
Brought up in a strict household, Genevra French longs for freedom. After reading a book on how to attract the opposite sex, she tries the material out on her father's friend, Lawrence Tabor. He falls for the young woman and quickly agrees to her proposal of marriage. However, he soon discovers that marrying him was the girl's way of getting out from under her father's rule. When Genevra asks her new husband to introduce her to handsome Jack Langhorne, a man with a questionable reputation, he refuses, so she pursues the man on her own, meeting him in secret. Langhorne and Genevra meet for dinner at an inn, where he tries to attack her, but Lawrence shows up in time to save her. The following day, Lawrence gives Jack a check for helping to change

his wife's wildness, but Jack refuses the money, saying that he is joining the army.

CRITICS' CORNER
This is going to register with a bang with most folks. It gets nearly naughty several times, and some incidents have been rather broadly dealt with. *Wid's Film Daily*

Danger—Go Slow

Universal Special/Universal, 6 reels. *Released:* December 16, 1918. *Production Code No.:* 2860. *In Production:* late March 1918 to late April 1918. *Director:* Robert Z. Leonard. *Scenario:* Robert Z. Leonard and Mae Murray. *Photographer:* Allan Siegler.

CAST
Mae Murray (*Muggsy Mulane*), Jack Mulhall (*Jimmy, the Eel*), Lon Chaney (*Bud*), Lydia Knott (*Aunt Sarah*), Joseph Girard (*Judge Cotton*).

SYNOPSIS
With the arrest of Jimmy, the Eel, leader of the gang, Muggsy Mulane hops a freight train headed for the country. Landing in Cottonville, she befriends Aunt Sarah, who turns out to be Jimmy's mother. Learning that Judge Cotton has planned to foreclose on Aunt Sarah's property, Muggsy threatens to blackmail him and he backs down. Muggsy then sells a portion of Aunt Sarah's property for a large sum of money and finally convinces Jimmy to come home and live a life without crime.

CRITICS' CORNER
Here is a feature that starts like a whale, but when it is about half finished takes a header into the briny and stays there. If the picture had held the pace that it hit during the first reel and a half it would have either developed into a *Alias Jimmy Valentine* or a *Turn to the Right*. *Variety*

CHAPTER SEVEN

1919

The Wicked Darling

Universal, 6 reels. *Released:* February 3, 1919. *Production Code No.:* 3014. *In Production:* December 7, 1918 to early January 1919. *Director:* Tod Browning. *Scenario:* Harvey Gates, from a story by Evelyn Campbell. *Photographer:* Alfred Gosden.

CAST

Priscilla Dean (*Mary Stevens*), Wellington Playter (*Kent Mortimer*), Lon Chaney (*Stoop Connors*), Spottiswoode Aitken (*Fadem*), Gertrude Astor (*Adele Hoyt*), Kalla Pasha (*Bartender*).

SYNOPSIS

Mary Stevens has learned the fine art of picking pockets from her guardian, Fadem, a bartender. Together with Stoop Connors, they commit crimes against the wealthy. While waiting outside a reception for their next victims, Mary encounters Kent Mortimer. Kent has recently been thrown over by his sweetheart, Adele, because she learned he is no longer rich. In a fit of rage, Adele threw out the pearl necklace Kent had given her. Mary retrieves the necklace and shortly after renounces her life of crime. She takes a job as a waitress, and a romance with Kent blooms. When Kent cannot pay his back rent, Mary pawns two of the pearls to Fadem, who then engages Stoop to find the rest of the necklace. Stoop tells Kent that Mary stole the pearl necklace, condemning her for the act. But Kent has second thoughts and tracks Mary down to Fadem's, where he intervenes in a fight between Mary and Stoop. Mary seeks the aid of the burly bartender to stop Stoop from killing Kent. The two lovers are reunited and head west to buy a farm.

CRITICS' CORNER

This new six-part Universal offering, *The Wicked Darling*, is an exceptional tale of slum life in the city. . . . Despite its picturing of the seamy side of life, the picture is full of human sympathy and marks a long step ahead for this type of photoplay. *Moving Picture World*

This is a remarkable film, and more than that it is a genuinely interesting one for those who like crook stories with a liberal element of romance. . . . When it comes to a crook role, Lon Chaney, as you may recall from his previous interpretations, is excellent. *Wid's Film Daily*

This last offering should be a success in every way. The story is strong and interesting, the situations good, and it impresses in its apparent reality. Particularly commendable is the work of Lon Chaney as "Stoop," a crook. . . . The entire picture carries itself along clear with lucidity. *Variety*

NOTES
The Universal Picture Code Book lists the film's release date as February 24, 1919.[33]

The film's various working titles were *The Gutter Rose, The Rose of the Dark,* and *The Rose of the Night.*

This was the first picture Chaney made with director Tod Browning. Chaney would play opposite Priscilla Dean in *Paid In Advance* (1919) and *Outside the Law* (1921); Spottiswoode Aitken in *Nomads of the North* (1920); and, Kalla Pasha in *West of Zanzibar* (1928).

A print of *The Wicked Darling*, with Dutch inter-titles, is housed at the Netherlands Filmmuseum in Amsterdam.

Daredevil Jack

Pathe Pictures, 15-episode serial. *Released:* February 15, 1919. *Director:* W. S. Van Dyke. *Scenario:* Jack Cunningham, from a story by Frederic Chapin and Harry Hoyt. *Episode 1:* The Mysterious Bracelets; *Episode 2:* The Ball of Death; *Episode 3:* Wheels of Fate; *Episode 4:* Shanghaied; *Episode 5:* Race for Glory; *Episode 6:* A Skirmish of Wits; *Episode 7:* A Glow in the Dark; *Episode 8:* Blinding Hate; *Episode 9:* Phantoms of Treachery; *Episode 10:* Paths of Destruction; *Episode 11:* Flames of Wrath; *Episode 12:* The Unseen Menace; *Episode 13:* Baiting a Trap; *Episode 14:* A Terrible Vengeance; *Episode 15:* The Triple Chase.

CAST
Jack Dempsey, Josie Sedgewick, Lon Chaney, Spike Robinson, Ruth Langston, Hershall Mayall, Fred Starr, Frank Lanning, Albert Cody, Al Kaufman.

SYNOPSIS
Jack Derry is both working his way through an eastern college and supporting his mother. His father has been sent to prison, wrongly accused

of a crime he did not commit. In the town lives Billings, an unscrupulous man, with a son, Edgar, and a stepdaughter, Glory. Glory possesses
a mysterious bracelet, given to her years before by her father, that bears
one half the directions to an underground oil lake. The other half, with
the remainder of the directions, is in the possession of Meeney, a crook
who sends his gang to steal Glory's bracelet. When her stepfather learns
of the bracelet's significance, he also plans to steal it. Glory is abducted
but Jack saves her and learns that Glory's stepfather is responsible for
his father's imprisonment. With this knowledge, Jack has a double motive for pitting his strength against Billings.

CRITICS' CORNER
Still another kind of serial. Not exactly subtle, this one, but if you are a
small boy of any age, you'll enjoy Jack Dempsey, who can certainly with-
stand an awful lot of punishment. *Photoplay*

NOTES
Chaney applied Jack Dempsey's make-up in this film. The fighter said
Chaney had a feather-like touch compared with others, who had ap-
plied make-up to his face much like a boxing opponent.[34]

The False Faces

Paramount-Artcraft, 7 reels. 6,940 ft. *Released:* February 16, 1919. *Presented by:* Thomas H. Ince. *Director and Scenario:* Irvin V. Willat, from
the novel by Louis Joseph Vance. *Photographers:* Edwin W. Willat and
Paul Eagler.

CAST
Henry B. Walthall (*Michael Lanyard, "The Lone Wolf"*), Mary Anderson
(*Cecilia Brooke*), Lon Chaney (*Karl Ekstrom*), Milton Ross (*Ralph Crane*),
Thornton Edwards (*Lt. Thackeray*), William Bowman (*Capt. Osborne*),
Garry McGarry (*Submarine Lieutenant*), Ernest Pasque (*Blensop*).

SYNOPSIS
During World War I, Michael Lanyard, a notorious thief known as "The
Lone Wolf," crosses no-man's land to reach the British side. Once
there, he encounters Captain Osborne, a former agent of the British
Secret Service, who sends him on a secret mission to the United States.
Crossing the Atlantic by ship, Lanyard meets Cecilia Brooke, who gives
him a secret message. Also on board is Karl Ekstrom, Lanyard's long-
time enemy and a German agent. Ekstrom gets a signal to the Germans, and the ship is torpedoed. Lanyard is thrown overboard and,

picked up by a German U-boat, passes himself off as Ekstrom. The U-boat lands near Martha's Vineyard, where Lanyard destroys the German submarine and heads for New York City. He discovers that the Germans have a secret headquarters and have taken Cecilia captive. Lanyard breaks into the headquarters and has a fight to the death with Ekstrom. With Cecilia's help, Lanyard exposes the German spy ring and delivers the secret message to the authorities.

CRITICS' CORNER

A secret service melodrama of the war, *The False Faces* is derived from one of the best stories of its kind. It is also one of the best of its kind released by the Paramount-Artcraft. . . . *The False Faces* will hold closely the attention of any audience. *Moving Picture World*

It's a sure 'nuff thriller from the beginning to end, with a mystery plot that introduces a succession of surprises and a lot of situations that will get any crowd by reason of their novelty and dramatic strength. . . . Lon Chaney is the personification of villainy as Ekstrom. *Wid's Film Daily*

NOTES

The film's working title was *The Lone Wolf*. In one sequence, Chaney dons a false beard, the only time Chaney was photographed in moving pictures applying make-up to his face.

Jane Daly, who under the name Jacqueline Daly later played Chaney's wife in *West of Zanzibar* (1928), appeared as a haunting vision to the German U-boat captain. Chaney applied her make-up to give the appearance of a sea corpse.[35]

The July 13, 1918 issue of *Motion Picture News* announced that producer Thomas H. Ince had purchased the rights to the Louis Joseph Vance novel. Irvin Willat and Jerome Storm were announced as co-directors of the production, which was scheduled to begin principal photography the third week in August.[36] Production was delayed until October 1918, and Willat was given credit as sole director.

Prints of *The False Faces* can be found at the George Eastman House in Rochester, New York, the Turner Film Library, and in several private film collections.

A Man's Country

Robertson-Cole Co., 5 reels. *Released:* July 13, 1919. *Director:* Henry Kolker. *Scenario:* E. Richard Schayer, from a story by John Lynch. *Photographer:* Robert Newhard.

CAST

Alma Rubens (*Kate Carewe*), Albert Roscoe (*Ralph Bowen*), Lon Chaney ("*Three Card*" *Duncan*), Joseph Dowling (*Marshall Leland*), Edna May Wilson (*Ruth Kemp*), Alfred Hollingsworth (*Oliver Kemp*), Phil Gastrock (*Connell*).

SYNOPSIS

The town of Huxley's Gulch is like many others during the 1849 gold rush. Kate Carewe is the town's favorite saloon dancer. The Reverend Ralph Bowen urges the wild crowd to change their ways and drive sin from the town, but he is generally ignored by the townspeople. Kate is particularly scornful of the preacher because he assumes she is immoral. When "Three Card" Duncan kills the owner of the saloon where Kate works, she hatches a plan to win the place back. Challenging Duncan to a poker game, Kate agrees that if she loses, she will marry Duncan. Luckily, Kate wins the game, but Duncan swears revenge. A deadly plague sweeps through the town, and everyone flees except Kate and the minister. His opinion of her changes when he sees her taking care of the sick children. Duncan returns for his vengeance but the reverend rescues Kate, only to face death himself until Marshall Leland kills Duncan. Kate promises to help the reverend with his work and gives up the dance hall.

CRITICS' CORNER

Alma Rubens is seen in the stellar role and the story closely follows the rules laid down for western drama. . . . Lon Chaney is a brutal villain. *Exhibitors Trade Review*

There is not a great deal of merit in the Robertson-Cole production *A Man's Country*, if viewed from the critics corner. . . . As presented, the outline of the plot is not clear. *Moving Picture World*

NOTES

Scenarist E. Richard Schayer would later write Chaney's *Tell It to the Marines* (1927).

Paid In Advance

Jewel/Universal, 6 reels. 5,565 ft. *Released:* July 7, 1919. *Production Code No.:* 2790. *Director and Scenario:* Allen Holubar, based on a story by James Oliver Curwood. *Photographer:* King Gray. *Film Editor:* Grant Whytock.

CAST
Dorothy Phillips (*Joan Gray*), Joseph Girard (*John Gray*), Lon Chaney
(*Bateese Le Blanc*), Priscilla Dean (*Marie*), William Stowell (*Jim Blood*),
Frank Brownlee (*Gold Dust Barker*), Bill Burress (*Regan*), Harry De More
(*Flapjack*).

SYNOPSIS
Joan Gray finds herself the object of two men's affections: Bateese Le
Blanc and one known as "The Beast." Le Blanc kills "The Beast" in a
fight over Joan, but Joan and her father leave to investigate a business
offer in Dawson City. Joan arrives in the city by herself because her
father has died along the way. To her horror, she learns that the business offer was merely a ruse to bring her to Gold Dust Barker's saloon.
Joan is given the choice of being Barker's mistress or becoming one of
his cheap dancehall girls. Joan agrees to be married to the highest bidder, who turns out to be Jim Blood, a drunken miner. Jim is the highest
bidder for Joan's hand until Barker forges an I.O.U. The two men fight
and Jim kills Barker. Jim and Joan are separated as they leave Dawson
City but are reunited a year later in Montreal, where they realize they
love each other.

CRITICS' CORNER
Dance hall meller that misses because of story weaknesses and ancient
situations. . . . Lon Chaney good. *Wid's Film Daily*

    A splendid dramatic success is achieved in this six-reel Universal-
Jewel production. . . . The cast, so far as the principals are concerned,
is made up entirely of screen favorites, and so excellent is the team
work of these tried players that the numerous tense situations are raised
to extreme dramatic heights. *Moving Picture World*

NOTES
The Universal Picture Code Book lists the film's release date as September 1, 1919.[37]

    Priscilla Dean said that she learned of Lon's thoroughness in apply-
ing a wig the hard way. The two were supposed to have a heated argument and she was to grab at his hair. The only thing that gave, as Lon
pulled away, was Ms. Dean's fingernails, which pulled completely out
of her fingers![38]

    A print of *Paid In Advance* is housed at the Narodni Filmovy Archive
in Czechoslovakia. The film contains Czech inter-titles and, as of this
writing, is on a nitrate film stock.

The Miracle Man

Paramount-Artcraft, 8 reels. *Released:* August 31, 1919. *Picture Code No.:* A 88. *Producer, Director and Scenario:* George Loane Tucker, from the novel by Frank L. Packard and the play by George M. Cohan. *Photographers:* Philip Rosen and Ernest Palmer. *Assistant Directors:* Chester L. Roberts and Alfred A. Grasso.

CAST

Thomas Meighan (*Tom Burke*), Betty Compson (*Rose*), Lon Chaney (*The Frog*), J. M. Dumont (*The Dope*), Joseph Dowling (*The Patriarch*), W. Lawson Butt (*Richard King*), Elinor Fair (*Claire King*), F. A. Turner (*Mr. Higgins*), Lucille Hutton (*Ruth Higgins*), Frankie Lee (*Little Boy*), Thomas Kurihara (*The Jap*).

SYNOPSIS

A gang of four criminals in New York's Chinatown section use their "tricks" to sucker contributions from the sightseers. The Frog is able to contort his limbs to appear as a cripple, begging for money. The Dope is a drug addict who steals, while Rose poses as the abused wife of the Dope. Tom Burke is the leader of the group and has big plans for himself and his colleagues. He announces his plans after reading a newspaper clipping that describes the work of a blind man known as the Patriarch. Rose poses as his long-lost niece, and the Frog will arrive and crawl up to the Patriarch and pretend to be healed. The amount of money they intend to haul in seems unlimited and the plan, foolproof. The Frog causes quite a stir among the passengers on the train by discussing his journey to see this "Miracle Man." A large crowd follows him to the feet of the Patriarch, where he seems to be cured. The crook's plan, however, does not include the faith of a young crippled boy who, after seeing the Frog "healed," drops his crutches and runs up to the Miracle Man. Crowds and cures continue and the money increases, but the goodness of the Patriarch rubs off on all four criminals. The Frog becomes the adopted son of a widow; the Dope gives up his drugs and falls in love. But it takes the death of the Patriarch to make Rose and Tom renounce their past and realize their love for each other.

CRITICS' CORNER

It's time to rejoice. *The Miracle Man* is the most exceptionally entertaining and tremendously appealing dramatic production I have ever seen. You can bet your red shirt that this will hold your audience every minute and send them out boosting more enthusiastically than they ever had in the past, and you will find a very large percentage of them coming back to see it, bringing some friend or some other part of the family with them. . . . Lon Chaney, in an exceptional characterization, will be remembered forever by everyone who sees this film. *Wid's Film Daily*

Lon Chaney, as the deformed cripple, the Frog, does some of the best work of his career. As the ghastly deformed mass of flesh and bones faked for the purpose of exciting pity and then as the loveable adopted son of a lonely old lady, Mr. Chaney offers a bit of character study that will entrench him firmly in the ranks of film players. . . . George Loane Tucker has given the screen a masterpiece. It is a story that will remain long in the minds of those who witness it. Its advent has produced another miracle—a miracle of the screen. *Exhibitors Trade Review*

Unusually good work is done by Thomas Meighan, Betty Compson and Lon Chaney in a picture which will please all movie enthusiasts and convert a few more. *New York Times*

Upon one scene alone depends the amazing sentimental success unquestionably achieved by the picture version of *The Miracle Man*, which opened Tuesday night at the George M. Cohan Theatre before an audience that, like a single person, lost its breath in a sob at a certain point. Unfortunately for the cumulative dramatic value of this offering, that scene occurs in the forepart of the picture. Nothing that follows can touch it. . . . Commercially, this is a picture that will coin money. Artistically, it marks hopes triumphant over experience. *Variety*

NOTES

Studio interiors were shot at the Robert Brunton Studios on Melrose Avenue in Hollywood. Alfred A. Grasso, who was Tucker's assistant director, later worked as Chaney's business manager.

The movie was chosen as one of the year's top ten by the *New York Times*.

The Miracle Man was remade by Paramount in 1932, with John Wray playing the role of the Frog.

The healing sequence and another brief portion of the film were incorporated in an early 1930s newsreel called *Movie Memories*. It featured clips from several silent films produced by Paramount. This newsreel can be found in several private film collections. Kino International include *The Miracle Man* clips in their videotape documentary, *Lon Chaney: Behind the Mask* (1995).

When Bearcat Went Dry

C. R. Macauley Photoplays, 6 reels. *Released:* November 2, 1919. *In Production:* early March to late June 1919. *Director:* Ollie L. Sellers. Based on the novel by Charles Neville Buck. *Photographer:* Jack MacKenzie. *Assistant Director:* Justin McCloskey.

CAST

Vangie Valentine (*Blossom Fulkerson*), Walt Whitman (*Joel Fulkerson*), Bernard Durning (*Turner Stacy, "Bearcat"*), Winter Hall (*Lone Stacy*), Ed Brady (*Rattler Webb*), Millard K. Wilson (*Jerry Henderson*), Lon Chaney (*Kindard Powers*). *Others in the cast:* Gordon Russell, John Lynch.

SYNOPSIS

Turner Stacy, known as "Bearcat," is in love with Blossom Fulkerson, the daughter of a missionary in the Kentucky Cumberland Mountains. Bearcat's father, Lone Stacy, is arrested for running a still. Jerry Henderson is a railroad surveyor but is suspected by many to be a revenue man. Henderson takes refuge in Blossom's house after a run-in with Kindard Powers and his gang. Meanwhile, Bearcat has fled to Virginia to avoid testifying against his father. When he returns, he learns that Blossom and Henderson are engaged. When Henderson is wounded by Powers' gang, Bearcat takes him to Blossom to be married, but he dies shortly after the ceremony. Bearcat vows to destroy Powers' gang, but Blossom's father talks him out of it. Instead, Bearcat destroys all the stills in the area, and when his father is freed, he kills Powers, whose gang disbands. Blossom returns to the area to teach, and she and Bearcat marry.

CRITICS' CORNER

Besides being remarkably well directed, produced and acted, this is a picture with a big, red-blooded theme. . . . Walt Whitman, Ed. Brady, and Lon Chaney portray difficult character parts with remarkable art. . . . For a picture which unfolds life in the American mountain country to the world, and supplies tension and enjoyment at the same time, this is it. *Exhibitors Trade Review*

The production is replete with the atmosphere of the southern mountains, and presents interesting types of men. . . . impersonated by a competent cast. *Moving Picture World*

NOTES

Portions of this film were shot on location in Marlin, Kentucky.[39]

A print of *When Bearcat Went Dry* is housed at the Netherlands Film-museum in Amsterdam. The print contains Dutch inter-titles and is missing some titles in the first reel.

Another print was donated to the American Film Institute in September 1996 by retired projectionist Bill Buffum, who had a copy of the film in his private collection for many years.[40]

Victory

Paramount-Artcraft, 5 reels. 4,735 ft. *Released:* December 7, 1919. *In Production:* July 1919. *Picture Code No.:* A-98. *Presented and Directed by:* Maurice Tourneur. *Scenario:* Stephen Fox, from the novel by Joseph Conrad. *Photographer:* Rene Guissart. *Art Director:* Ben Carre and Floyd Mueller.

CAST

Jack Holt (*Axel Heyst*), Seena Owen (*Alma*), Lon Chaney (*Ricardo*), Wallace Beery (*Schomberg*), Ben Deely (*Mr. Jones*), Laura Winston (*Mrs. Schomberg*), Bull Montana (*Pedro*), George Nicholls (*Capt. Davidson*).

SYNOPSIS

Seeking a life of solitude, Axel Heyst lives on a South Seas island. While traveling to a neighboring island on business, he encounters Alma, who is being abused by Schomberg, the owner of the local hotel. Heyst offers to take Alma to his island to escape the abusive Schomberg, but when Schomberg learns of Alma's disappearance, he sends three criminals after them; Mr. Jones, Ricardo, and Pedro. They go with the belief that there is hidden treasure on the island. Ricardo attempts to attack Alma but is killed by Heyst. Mr. Jones meets the same fate he dealt to Pedro's brother years earlier, being thrown into a fire. Alma and Heyst realize their love for each other and live happily on the island.

CRITICS' CORNER

If you are looking for the unusual you will find it in *Victory*. . . . The characterization of Lon Chaney as Ricardo and that of Bull Montana as Pedro were especially well handled. *Wid's Film Daily*

The vividly vicious work of Lon Chaney, as Ricardo, deserves more than passing mention. His impersonation of this singularly unlovable character is a wonderful bit of pantomime. . . . In fact, Mr. Chaney may be said in slang phrase to "run away with the play" at certain stages, completely overshadowing his contemporaries. *Exhibitors Trade Review*

Maurice Tourneur has created a moving and effective picture drama for Paramount. . . . Probably the eagle eye of the censor is responsible for cutting the fight between Alma and Ricardo, but it is well cut. Of the latter character, Lon Chaney gave a visualization that was very effective. *Variety*

NOTES

Interior scenes were shot at Maurice Tourneur's studio in Culver City. The film was chosen as one of the year's top ten by the *New York Times*. Prints of *Victory* are housed at the Library of Congress and in several private film collections.

Two other film versions of Conrad's novel were produced by Paramount Pictures, *Dangerous Paradise* (1930) and *Victory* (1940).

CHAPTER EIGHT

1920

Treasure Island

Paramount-Artcraft, 6 reels. *Released:* April 4, 1920. *Picture Code No.:* A 97. *Presented by and Director:* Maurice Tourneur. *Scenario:* Stephen Fox, from the novel by Robert Louis Stevenson. *Photographer:* Rene Guissart. *Art Director:* Floyd Mueller.

CAST

Shirley Mason (*Jim Hawkins*), Charles Ogle (*Long John Silver*), Sydney Dean (*Squire Trelawney*), Charles Hill Mailes (*Dr. Livesey*), Lon Chaney (*Pew*), Lon Chaney (*Merry*), Jose Melville (*Mrs. Hawkins*), Al Filson (*Bill Bones*), Wilton Taylor (*Black Dog*), Joseph Singleton (*Israel Hands*), Bull Montana (*Morgan*), Harry Holden (*Capt. Smollet*).

SYNOPSIS

Jim Hawkins helps his mother run the Admiral Benbow Inn on the coast of England. Jim finds the map of former pirate Billy Bones, who was killed at the inn by other pirates seeking the map to the lost treasure of Captain Flint. Jim turns the map over to his mother's friends, Dr. Livesey and Squire Trelawney, who form an expedition to find the treasure. Jim stows away on the ship, whose crew has been chosen by Long John Silver, a one-legged pirate posing as a cook. Silver's mutiny plans are discovered by Jim, who tells Livesey and Trelawney. They hold the pirates at bay until they arrive at the island, where they take refuge with Jim and other loyal crew members. A battle between the pirates eventually results in the turning over of the map to Long John Silver and his group. However, the pirates are eventually defeated, and Jim, Livesey, Trelawney, and others find Flint's treasure and return to England.

CRITICS' CORNER

Treasure Island is a fine picture and one which will probably stand with the unusual money-makers of the season. . . . Innumerable fine pirate types, headed by those two sterling character actors, Lon Chaney and Charles Ogle, add the finishing touch of Stevenson's atmosphere. *Wid's Film Daily*

In this production, Maurice Tourneur has given the screen actual touches of something a part of boyhood days. . . . Under the able leadership of Maurice Tourneur this production is worthy of everything said in its favor. *Exhibitors Trade Review*

It is to the credit of this director's artistic perceptions that he has been able to catch the charm and atmosphere of the memorable story even though the scenario is not a faithful adaptation—Lon Chaney gives another of his vivid character studies as one of the pirate cutthroats or two. *Motion Picture News*

NOTES

The film was chosen as one of the top forty pictures of the year by the National Board of Review. The first film version of Stevenson's novel was made in 1917 by Fox Film Corp. but released in 1918. Five versions have been produced since the Tourneur film, including a 1996 version featuring Jim Henson's Muppet characters.

The September 13, 1919, issue of *Moving Picture World* announced that Jack Holt and Wallace Beery had been cast as Long John Silver and Israel Hands, respectively. Charles Ogle and Joseph Singleton eventually played the roles.

The ship used in the film was an abandoned barkentine called the *Fremont*. It had an interesting background, having been used to transport slaves from Africa. The ship was later seized by the United States government for participating in illegal activities. When the production company found the ship, it was in a terrible state of disrepair.[41]

The Gift Supreme

C. R. Macauley Productions, 6 reels. *Released:* May 9, 1920. *Director:* Ollie L. Sellers. Based on the novel by George Allan England. *Photographer:* Jack MacKenzie. *Assistant Director:* Justin H. McCloskey.

CAST

Bernard Durning (*Bradford Chandler Vinton*), Seena Owen (*Sylvia Alden*), Melbourne McDowell (*Eliot Vinton*), Tully Marshall (*Irving Stagg*), Lon Chaney (*Merney Stagg*), Eugenie Besserer (*Martha Vinton*), Jack Curtis (*Rev. Ebenezer Crowley Boggs*), Dick Morris (*Dopey Dan*), Anna Dodge (*Mrs. Wesson*), Claire McDowell (*Lalia Graun*).

SYNOPSIS

Bradford Vinton is the son of wealthy Eliot Vinton, who ventures into the slums of the city to gather material for a book. There he meets a missionary, Sylvia Alden, and falls in love with her. His father is furious at his son's interest in a girl from a lower class and threatens to disown Bradford if he continues his relationship with Sylvia. Eliot Vinton has the girl framed for charges of prostitution, and she quickly disappears. Bradford, however, does not believe the accusations and remains loyal to the girl. He opens a cheap restaurant to feed the poor and has a run-in with Merney Stagg, who it turns out framed Sylvia at the direction of Eliot Vinton. Bradford is stabbed by Stagg and is rushed to the hospital for treatment, where he encounters Sylvia working as a nurse. Bradford is in need of blood to save his life and Sylvia offers to donate hers to save her lover. When Bradford's father learns of this gesture, he forgives his son and approves of the couple's relationship.

CRITICS' CORNER

The story, adapted from the original by George Allan England, is interpreted by a cast of well-known and capable players. . . . Lon Chaney and Tully Marshall play up to the standard of former triumphs. *Moving Picture World*

As an underworld melodrama *The Gift Supreme* passes average muster. It would have been possible, with the material in the story, to make a much stronger picture had the director hung his sequences together more compactly and dramatically. . . . Tully Marshall, Lon Chaney and Jack Curtis are the principal figures in the corps of assisting players and the work that each does stands out through sheer skill. *Wid's Film Daily*

The production is in six reels and runs a trifle too long. . . . Of the character actors Chaney takes all the honors. *Variety*

NOTES

A partial print of *The Gift Supreme* can be found in several private film collections. Kino International included a brief clip from *The Gift Supreme* in their videotape documentary, *Lon Chaney: Behind the Mask* (1995).

Nomads of the North

Associated First National, 6 reels. *Released:* October 11, 1920. *Presented by:* James Oliver Curwood. *Director:* David M. Hartford. *Scenario:* David

M. Hartford and James Oliver Curwood, from the novel by James Oliver Curwood. *Photographer:* Walter Griffin.

CAST
Betty Blythe (*Nanette Roland*), Lon Chaney (*Raoul Challoner*), Lewis S. Stone (*Cpl. O'Connor*), Melbourne MacDonald (*Duncan McDougall*), Spottiswoode Aitken (*Old Roland*), Francis MacDonald (*Buck McDougall*), Gordon Muller (*Black Marat*), Charles H. Simly (*Father Beauvais*).

SYNOPSIS
Nanette Roland refuses the advances of Buck McDougall while awaiting the arrival of her long-absent lover, Raoul Challoner. Buck forges evidence that Raoul is dead, and Nanette grudgingly accepts Buck's offer of marriage. Raoul arrives in town just as the wedding ceremony is about to begin and a fight between Raoul and Buck ensues, during which Raoul accidently kills another man. Raoul is arrested. Nanette helps him to escape into the wilderness after they are quickly married. Cpl. O'Connor of the Northwest Mounted Police is assigned to bring in Raoul, and three years later, Raoul is arrested by O'Connor, who is accompanied by Buck. A forest fire erupts and traps Raoul and his family as well as O'Connor and Buck. O'Connor is injured by a fallen tree and Raoul saves him from certain death. Buck dies in the fire but Raoul, his family, and O'Connor are safe. The mountie feels a debt of gratitude to Raoul and, saying that he will claim Raoul perished in the fire, heads back to civilization, leaving Raoul and Nanette to their happiness.

CRITICS' CORNER
It's truly an audience picture, for it holds the attention all the way through and at the end leaves you thoroughly satisfied and thrilled by its gripping climax. . . . Lon Chaney and Lewis S. Stone do very well. *Wid's Film Daily*

Emphasis on beauty in the Northwoods, a capable cast and generally intelligent direction, cause *Nomads of the North*, as shown at the Strand Theatre, to be valued as good entertainment. *Moving Picture World*

The dramatic burden is carried by Lon Chaney and Betty Blythe, and the humor of it is strengthened by the antics of a pet cub bear and a small dog who have many experiences by flood and fire. A good family picture, this one. *Photoplay*

NOTES
In 1961, Walt Disney Pictures released *Nikki, Wild Dog of the North*, based on Curwood's novel.[42] The plot is not similar to the Chaney film.

Prints of *Nomads of the North* were sold for many years on the film collectors' market by Blackhawk Films. Prints also are housed at National Film Archives of Canada and the Archivo Nacional de la Imagen in Montevideo, Uruguay. Kino International released a print to the videotape market in 1995.

The Penalty

Goldwyn Pictures, 7 reels. *Released:* November 21, 1920. *In Production:* February 7, 1920 to April 2, 1920; 49 days. *Picture Code No.:* 98. *Presented by:* Samuel Goldwyn and Rex Beach. *Director:* Wallace Worsley. *Scenario:* Charles Kenyon and Philip Lonergan, from the novel by Gouverneur Morris. *Photographer:* Dan Short. *Film Editor:* Frank S. Hall and J. G. Hawks. *Cost of Production:* $88,868.

CAST

Lon Chaney (*Blizzard*), Ethel Grey Terry (*Rose*), Charles Clary (*Dr. Ferris*), Claire Adams (*Barbara Ferris*), Kenneth Harlan (*Dr. Wilmont*), James Mason (*Frisco Pete*), Edouard Trebaol (*Bubbles*), Milton Ross (*Lichtenstein*), Wilson Hummel (*One of Blizzard's Men*), Cesare Gravina (*Sculpting Instructor*).

SYNOPSIS

Maimed as a child by an inexperienced doctor, Blizzard grows up to become the ruler of San Francisco's underworld. His criminal activities are driven by his plan for revenge against Dr. Ferris, whose bungling caused Blizzard's legs to be amputated above the knees. Blizzard plans to use the doctor's daughter, Barbara, as part of his plot by posing for her sculpture of "Satan, After the Fall." Slowly she falls under the criminal's spell, ignoring her fiance's wishes to stay away from the crime boss. Rose, a government agent working undercover in Blizzard's warehouse, soon becomes the mastermind's favorite and learns of his plan to loot the city with the help of disgruntled foreigners. His plan for revenge against the doctor becomes more clear when Blizzard kidnaps Barbara's fiance, Dr. Wilmont, and holds him hostage. Dr. Ferris is summoned by Blizzard, who demands that he graft Wilmont's legs onto his own stumps. The doctor agrees, but instead of carrying out that gruesome task, he performs an operation to relieve pressure on Blizzard's brain, eliminating his evil motives. Rose and other government agents arrive to learn of the successful operation, and Dr. Ferris urges them to let Blizzard lead a normal life so that he can be of use to society. Rose and Blizzard marry and, with Dr. Ferris, plan to do great things together. However, their happiness is cut short when Blizzard's former gang, believing they will be turned in, kill him while he is playing his piano.

CRITICS' CORNER

Hats off to Lon Chaney! As "Blizzard," the deformed ruler of the Barbary Coast's underworld, he gives one of the screen's greatest performances. . . . However, up to almost the very conclusion the gripping melodramatic incidents hold securely and Chaney's work is so unusually fine that it will probably hold the production for all that is necessary. *Wid's Film Daily*

Lon Chaney, whose work in *The Miracle Man* won so much praise, portrays a role that might have been written for him. . . . He is wicked and cunning, but in the end he wins sympathy and applause. Chaney makes splendid use of every opportunity. *Moving Picture World*

One of the striking things about the picture is the remarkable characterization given by Lon Chaney. . . . Rarely has the screen seen a better piece of acting. *Exhibitors Trade Review*

Here is a picture that is about as cheerful as a hanging—and as interesting. . . . It is a remarkably good performance this actor [Chaney] gives. . . . Wallace Worsley's direction helps the picture a lot. *Photoplay*

NOTES

Portions of *The Penalty* were shot on location in San Francisco, California. The film was rereleased in 1926 by M-G-M.

Goldwyn Pictures announced in the November 11, 1919, issue of *Motion Picture News* that they had purchased the rights to Morris' novel. There was no mention of Chaney being associated with the production. When the film was originally released, producers inserted a scene at the end showing Lon Chaney walking down a flight of stairs (on his own legs) and smiling at the camera. The reason behind this insertion was to prove that Chaney was not doubled, nor was he an amputee.[43] This sequence does not exist in any surviving prints.

Chaney's leather stumps, crutches, and costume from the film were donated to the Natural History Museum in Los Angeles in 1931. They are occasionally placed on display, along with Chaney's make-up case.

This was the first of five films (the others being *Ace of Hearts* [1921], *Voices of the City* [1922], *A Blind Bargain* [1922], and *The Hunchback of Notre Dame* [1923]) Chaney would make with director Wallace Worsley.

Prints of *The Penalty* can be found at the Museum of Modern Art in New York City, the George Eastman House in Rochester, New York, the Turner Film Library, and in several private film collections. Kino International released a print to the videotape market in 1998.

CHAPTER NINE

1921

Outside the Law

Universal-Jewel, 8 reels. 7,754 ft. *Released:* January 6, 1921. *Picture Code No.:* 3341. *Presented by:* Carl Laemmle. *Director:* Tod Browning. *Scenario:* Lucien Hubbard, from a story by Tod Browning. *Titles:* Lewis Lipton and Fred Archer. *Photographer:* William Fildew. *Art Director:* E. E. Sheeley. *Assistant Director:* Leo McCarey.

CAST

Priscilla Dean (*Molly Madden, "Silky Moll"*), Wheeler Oakman (*"Dapper Bill" Ballard*), Lon Chaney (*"Black Mike" Sylva*), Ralph Lewis (*Silent Madden*), E. A. Warren (*Chang Low*), Lon Chaney (*Ah Wing*), Stanley Goethals (*"That Kid Across the Hall"*), Melbourne McDowell (*Morgan Spencer*), Wilton Taylor (*Inspector*), John George (*Humpy*).

SYNOPSIS

Silent Madden and his daughter, Molly, are criminals. Their friend Chang Low preaches to them of the teachings of Confucius in an attempt to turn the two from lives of crime. He is fairly successful until Silent Madden is framed for murder by "Black Mike" Sylva and his gang. Resentful over her father's arrest and prison sentence, Molly joins up with Black Mike and "Dapper Bill" Ballard to pull a jewel heist during a society party. Bill confesses to Molly that it is all a set-up, and they turn the tables on Black Mike by stealing the jewels and getting away before the police arrive. Molly and Bill hide out in a tiny apartment in San Francisco, which begins to grate on their nerves after awhile. But the affection and innocence of the little boy across the hall soften Molly and Bill, and they decide to return the jewels and go straight. Black Mike finds them and a fight ensues between Bill and Mike. Molly and Bill manage to escape to Chang Low's store, where there is a bloody battle between Silent Madden's gang and Black Mike's. During the confrontation, Chang Low's assistant, Ah Wing, kills

Black Mike. When the police arrive, Molly and Bill return the jewels; and, through Chang Low's influence, they and her father are set free.

CRITICS' CORNER
Tod Browning, who wrote and directed the feature, has made it thoroughly attractive to the eye and it is also exceptionally fine from a photographic standpoint. *Exhibitors Trade Review*

Tod Browning's promise as evidenced in *The Virgin of Stamboul* with Priscilla Dean is justified in the production he has given Universal with Miss Dean again as star. . . . It is a mighty good picture. . . . One of the best casts ever assembled. Lon Chaney mighty fine in dual role. *Wid's Film Daily*

Outside the Law is a Tod Browning picture all the way, written, directed and produced by him. Mr. Browning did the job well, very well, in all particulars, turning out a Universal that can stand up on the billing, most unusual for the U. . . . Chaney though makes his "Blackie" sneaky role so vicious he throws the house right into the young couple's laps. *Variety*

Outside the Law is one of the most powerful melodramas seen on the screen. It is strong, but free from brutal or depressing situations; and yet, one of the fiercest fights ever staged on the screen takes place in it. . . . It is a clean picture. *Harrison's Reports*

NOTES
Portions of the film were shot on location in San Francisco's Nob Hill, waterfront, and Chinatown areas. The film was rereleased in 1926 by Universal.

Leo McCarey, who would later go on to direct some of Laurel and Hardy's finest silent comedies as well as *Going My Way* and *An Affair to Remember*, recalled one night when he was allowed to direct part of the film:

> Browning was ill so the studio sent me to direct Chaney. At night a thousand people gathered in the street to watch me direct him. I walked back and forth, like a little De Mille . . . I went over and said, "Lon at least give the appearance of listening to me." We had a little conference and I suggested he light a cigarette or something, which was nothing since he knew exactly what to do. But I gave the appearance of directing him for three nights in a row, and made a big impression on the crowds.[44]

According to the January 15, 1921, issue of *Motion Picture News*, the climatic fight sequence, which lasts only a few minutes on screen, took two weeks to film. Six rooms of a brick building were constructed of two-by-four studding and covered by lathing plaster, with a phony brick wall facade to give it realism. Each wall was built as a separate unit so that it could either be lifted or rolled aside to accommodate the camera.

This marked Chaney's first interpretation of a Chinese character. According to the February 5, 1921, issue of *Motion Picture News*, the role of Ah Wing was listed as Joe Wang, and Chaney's billing was simply "Guess Who?" All other reviews referred to the character as Ah Wing and gave Chaney his proper credit.

The film was given an advance screening at the Superba Theatre in Los Angeles during Christmas week in 1920.[45] On January 16, 1921 *Outside the Law* opened in four Broadway theaters (the Astor, the Longacre, the Lyric, and the George M. Cohan) as a special premiere for one day.[46]

A print of this film was found in Yugoslavia in the early 1970s. It was restored and sold to private film collectors by Blackhawk Films. Kino International released a print to the videotape market in 1995. A print is also housed at the Library of Congress.

Bits of Life

Associated First National, 6 reels. 6,339 ft. *Released:* September 4, 1921. *Presented by and Director:* Marshall Neilan. *Scenario:* Lucita Squier. Additional story by Marshall Neilan. *Photographer:* David Kesson. *Assistant Directors:* James Flood and William Scully.

CAST

Wesley Barry (*Tom Levitt, as a boy*), Rockliffe Fellowes (*Tom Levitt*), Lon Chaney (*Chin Gow*), Noah Beery (*Hindoo*), Anna May Wong (*Chin Gow's Wife*), John Bowers (*Reginald Vanderbrook*). *Others in the cast:* Dorothy Mackaill, Edythe Chapman, Frederick Burton, James Bradbury, Jr., Teddy Sampson, Tammany Young, Harriet Hammond, James Neill, Scott Welsh.

SYNOPSIS

First Story: Tom Levitt was the victim of childhood brutality that, in turn, led to his life of crime. He encounters a friend who announces that since his release from prison, he plans to go straight, and so asks Tom for money to help him leave town. Tom takes a wallet from a young pickpocket who has just stolen it and gives his friend the money. Later, Tom overhears the sermon of a street preacher, who relates the story of the Good Samaritan. When Tom crosses paths with a man who has been assaulted, he comes to his aid and summons the police. The police find the stolen wallet on Tom and he is arrested. Facing a ten-year sentence, Tom reflects that his downfall was caused by trying to be a "Good Samaritan."

Second Story: Ed Johnson is a deaf barber who believes that his wife loves him and that, despite his handicap, life isn't so bad after all. When he inherits a device that allows him to hear, he learns that his wife has been unfaithful and that he cannot trust his friends. Rather than confront the disappointments, Ed smashes the device, deciding instead to return to his deaf world.

Third Story: Chin Gow has been raised to believe that a first-born girl-child is unacceptable in Chinese culture. When his wife, Toy Sing, bears him a baby girl, he beats his wife unmercifully and swears to slay the child. After he leaves, his wife's friend brings her a crucifix sent by a local priest. As she nails it into the wall with a long spike, it penetrates the skull of Chin Gow, who is lying on a bunk in the next room, killing him.

Fourth Story: Reginald Vanderbrook meets a beautiful woman on an island during his yachting trip around the world. He overhears her being called "Princess" and sees her following an East Indian into a temple. When he follows, he finds himself surrounded by Hindus who are about to kill him. But then he awakens to find himself in a dentist's chair, having a tooth extracted.

CRITICS' CORNER

Director Marshall Neilan introduces a decided novelty to the screen in this film, made up of four short stories, which he explains in a foreword subtitle, were all too good to lose, but none of sufficient length to make a full feature in itself. . . . Lon Chaney [gives] one of his wonderfully artistic character sketches as Chin Gow. *Exhibitors Trade Review*

Marshall Neilan has given a novelty to the screen in *Bits of Life*, which might well prove the forerunner of more entertainment of this description. . . . Lon Chaney gives one of his own special kind of bits which has made him so prominent in character work. *Film Daily*

Marshall Neilan has put over a real novelty in his individual idea of making a full-length feature out of a succession of detached stories, all of the utmost compactness and "punch." Here are six reels of picture drama that fairly vibrate with action, suspense and surprise. . . . Lon Chaney here plays another of those sensational roles of villainy. *Variety*

NOTES

Interior scenes were filmed at the Goldwyn Studios and location scenes were shot in San Francisco. According to the June 25, 1921, issue of

Motion Picture News, director Marshall Neilan appeared in the film, but this is unsubstantiated.

Bits of Life had its world premiere at the Raymond Theatre in Pasadena, California, on Tuesday, August 9, 1921. Charles Chaplin, Buster Keaton, Marshall Neilan, Allen Holubar, and Charles Ray were in attendance. These celebrities had their films released through Associated First National. There was no mention of Lon Chaney attending the event.

Ace of Hearts

Goldwyn Pictures, 6 reels. 5,883 ft. *Released:* November 21, 1921. *Picture Code No.:* 151. *In Production:* mid-March through early May 1921. *Director:* Wallace Worsley. *Scenario:* Ruth Wightman, from the novel by Gouverneur Morris. *Photographer:* Don Short.

CAST

Leatrice Joy (*Lilith*), John Bowers (*Forrest*), Lon Chaney (*Farralone*), Hardee Kirkland (*Morgridge*), Raymond Hatton (*The Menace*), Roy Laidlaw (*Doorkeeper*), Edwin Wallock (*Chemist*).

SYNOPSIS

The members of a radical secret society meet to ponder the fate of a person whom they believe does no good for society and must be eliminated. In order to determine which of them must carry out the deed, cards are dealt, and the one who draws the Ace of Hearts is the chosen one. This card, and thus the act itself, is dealt to Forrest. He and Farralone are both infatuated with Lilith, the female member of the group. She, however, is only committed to "the cause." But because Forrest has drawn the Ace of Hearts and will probably meet his death in his attempt to carry out the fateful deed, she agrees to marry him. Farralone is overcome with jealousy and depression because she and Forrest will marry. The morning following their wedding, Lilith discovers that she truly loves Forrest and asks him to abandon his plan. When he refuses, Lilith seeks out Farralone, begging him to stop Forrest before he can set off the bomb; but it is too late. Lilith is relieved when Forrest returns, bringing back the bomb and confessing that he couldn't go through with it. Forrest and Lilith are ordered to leave so that the remaining members of the society can discuss their fate. Farralone sets off the bomb, killing himself and the rest of the group. Forrest and Lilith flee the city, and arriving in another town, learn of Farralone's sacrifice for them.

CRITICS' CORNER

Ace of Hearts is far from being a cheerful picture, although its prevailing tone of gloom and murderous atmosphere is partly atoned for by a climax which leaves the hero and heroine safe and happy. . . . The work of Lon Chaney as Farralone is excellent. Chaney is always at his best in roles requiring such powerful character delineation and in the present instance he fully lives up to his reputation. *Exhibitors Trade Review*

The motives that prompt the characters to action in this production are certainly not made clear in this pathological production. . . . Lon Chaney does well in a difficult and improbable character. *Film Daily*

This is a recent release by Goldwyn, an excellent product from many angles. . . . The picture is done in splendid, dignified style and has as its featured actor, Lon Chaney, whose work ever since his playing of "The Frog" in *Miracle Man* has added to his reputation as an actor of utmost sincerity and skill. *Variety*

NOTES

The original ending, in which Morgridge, the leader of the group, confronts Lilith and Forrest at their mountain cabin, was filmed in Pine Crest, California.[47] The ending was later reshot.

Ace of Hearts went into production after *The Night Rose* (working title for *Voices of the City* [1922]) was completed.[48] Chaney's character was originally named Radovitch.

Prints of *Ace of Hearts* can be found at the George Eastman House in Rochester, New York, the Turner Film Library, and in several private film collections.

For Those We Love

Goldwyn Pictures/Betty Compson Productions, 6 reels. 5,752 ft. *Released:* December 9, 1921. *Producer:* Betty Compson. *Director and Scenario:* Arthur Rosson, from a story by Perley Poore Sheehan. *Production Supervisor:* Alfred Grasso.

CAST

Betty Compson (*Bernice Arnold*), Richard Rosson (*Jimmy Arnold*), Lon Chaney (*Trix Ulner*), Camille Astor (*Vida*), Bert Woodruff (*Dr. Bailee*), Harry Duffield (*George Arnold*), Walter Morosco (*Johnny Fletcher*), George Cooper (*Bert*), Frank Campeau (*Frank*).

SYNOPSIS

Bernice Arnold takes care of her father and younger brother, Jimmy. She discovers that Jimmy is involved in gambling and has stolen money from his father to pay off gambling debts. Bernice enlists the aid of Trix Ulner in recovering the money. Her association with Trix, a notorious gambler, causes gossip and scandal. She begs Frank, to whom Jimmy lost the money, to return the money Jimmy stole, but is turned down. Trix plans to replace the money by stealing it from Frank's house. During the robbery, Jimmy is shot by Frank and dies. Trix threatens to turn him in for murder unless he returns the money and swears that Jimmy was killed while protecting Frank. Bernice eventually marries her sweetheart, Johnny Fletcher.

CRITICS' CORNER
It is without doubt one of the most incoherent stories that has been screened in a long, long time. . . . Miss Compson has a corking company supporting her, which includes Lon Chaney and others of equal note, but even they cannot pull the picture through. . . . This is a good one to pass up, except when one can make use of the Compson name at a price for a double feature bill. *Variety*

Among other good characterizations is that of Lon Chaney as the gambler, who in the event of reformation would have an easy chance to over-act, but who cleverly avoids this. . . . The picture should make money for the exhibitor. *Moving Picture World*

There's just enough variety of situation and climax to this melodrama to carry it away from conventional channels. . . . This actor's [Chaney] gift for pathos is keenly emphasized. When he rescues the girl from various dangers he inspires the greatest sympathy. *Motion Picture News*

NOTES
Scenarist Arthur Rosson worked in several films with Chaney during the actor's early years at Universal. Perley Poore Sheehan later adapted the scenario for *The Hunchback of Notre Dame*.

CHAPTER TEN

1922

The Trap

Universal/Jewel, 6 reels. 5,481 ft. *Released:* May 9, 1922. *Picture Code No.:* 3678. *In Production:* August 22 to September 16, 1921. *Director:* Robert Thornby. *Scenario:* George C. Hull, from a story by Lon Chaney, Lucien Hubbard, Robert Thornby, and Irving Thalberg. *Photographer:* Virgil Miller.

CAST

Lon Chaney (*Gaspard*), Alan Hale (*Benson*), Dagmar Godowsky (*Thalie*), Stanley Goethals (*The Boy*), Irene Rich (*The Teacher*), Spottiswoode Aitken (*The Factor*), Herbert Standing (*The Priest*), Frank Campeau (*The Police Sergeant*).

SYNOPSIS

Benson steals Gaspard's mine and the man's sweetheart, Thalie. Gaspard's good nature turns vengeful and he incites a fight between Benson and Pierre, during which Benson shoots Pierre in self-defense. Gaspard refuses to testify that Benson acted in self-defense, and his enemy is sent to prison. While Benson is in prison, Thalie dies and Gaspard takes her young son to live with him. He grows to love the young boy as his own, and when the young boy goes to school, Gaspard is befriended by the school teacher. When Benson is freed, Gaspard fears he will lose the boy and prepares for the worst. He captures a wolf and constructs a cage connecting to his shack. He then leaves the half-starved animal inside his shack so that when Benson returns and opens the door, he will fall victim to the wolf. Unfortunately, the young boy arrives first, and Gaspard must then rescue the child. Benson arrives to find Gaspard wounded but alive, and the two former enemies make amends. When Benson takes his son with him, Gaspard is consoled by the school teacher and the promise of romance in his future.

CRITICS' CORNER

Judged from the double standpoint of artistic achievement and commercial value, *The Trap* registers 100 per cent. . . . Lon Chaney's splendid dramatic talents were never demonstrated to better effect than in his portrayal of the simple-minded, joyous Gaspard, whose all-embracing love of mankind is temporarily turned to hate by the cruel strokes of Fate. His performance is a keen, incisive study in contrasts, which grip one with unfailing power and adds fresh lustre to his already brilliant reputation. *Exhibitors Trade Review*

No one is credited with the authorship of *The Trap*, but after having seen the picture you are convinced that the person responsible for the story is not responsible for the success of the picture, for the plot is a conventional one. . . . The reasons for the film's success are two: first, the splendid direction; and secondly, the acting of Lon Chaney. . . . Chaney vividly depicts every step and does fine work all the time. There are a few too many close-ups of him, however. *Film Daily*

A melodrama of the Canadian Northwest, so powerful that the attention of the spectator is absorbed to the point of making him think that he is witnessing a real-life occurrence. . . . Mr. Chaney, unlike in other pictures in which he has appeared in the past, in this one he [sic] awakens sympathy, although at times he makes the spectator hate him for what he contemplates. . . . It should give excellent satisfaction to those who enjoy strong melodramas. *Harrison's Reports*

NOTES

The Universal Picture Code Book lists the film's release date as May 29, 1922.[49] The film's working titles were *Wolfbreed*, *The Mask*, and *The Heart of a Wolf*. Portions of *The Trap* were shot on location in Yosemite, California. This was the first Chaney film to use the panchromatic film stock, which became popular in the late 1920s. The movie was re-released in 1926 by Universal.

Prints of *The Trap* were sold for many years to film collectors by Blackhawk Films. Prints also are housed at the Cinematheque Royale in Brussels, Belgium, the Cineteca Nazionale in Rome, Italy, and in several private film collections. Kino International included clips from the film in their videotape documentary, *Lon Chaney: Behind the Mask* (1995).

Voices of the City

Goldwyn Pictures, 6 reels. 5,630 ft. *Released:* August 20, 1922. *Picture Code No.:* 143. *In Production:* February through early March 1921. *Direc-*

tor: Wallace Worsley. *Scenario:* Arthur F. Statter, from the novel by Leroy Scott.

CAST

Leatrice Joy (*Georgia Rodman*), Lon Chaney (*O'Rourke*), John Bowers (*Graham*), Cullen Landis (*Jimmy*), Richard Tucker (*Clancy*), Mary Warren (*Mary Rodman*), Edythe Chapman (*Mrs. Rodman*), Betty Schade (*Sally*), Maurice B. Flynn (*Pierson*), Milton Ross (*Courey*), John Cossar (*Garrison*).

SYNOPSIS

At a San Francisco cafe, Jimmy and Georgia witness the killing of a policeman by O'Rourke's gang. O'Rourke befriends the young couple, planning to eliminate them before they can testify for the district attorney. The criminal convinces Georgia that the police are seeking her so she remains hidden during the day, only coming out at night. When O'Rourke lavishes his attentions on her and refers to her as the "Night Rose," his girlfriend Sally becomes enraged. She confides to Georgia O'Rouke's plans to kill them at his ball. Georgia therefore plans to kill O'Rourke at the event, but Sally shoots him first. The two lovers are freed and O'Rourke's criminal flurry is brought to an end.

CRITICS' CORNER

Leroy Scott's story of the underworld couldn't secure the approval of the Censorship Commission when submitted under the title of *The Night Rose*, but with some changes in subtitles and the necessary cuts, plus a new main title, the picture is being shown at the Capitol. . . . Through the process the story has become somewhat disjointed and illogical as well as rather hard to follow. . . . Lon Chaney has done much better things than the role of McGee in this. *Film Daily*

It is not a particularly convincing sort of story and the continuity is rather ragged in spots. . . . Lon Chaney plays his part of the gang chief with his usual energy and ability to invest such roles with a species of sinister fascination. *Exhibitors Trade Review*

Interesting underworld melodrama with intricate plotting and counter-plotting by a master criminal and an abundance of gun play. . . . Lon Chaney, as always, gets the utmost out of the role of a powerful leader of law breakers. He has a gift for quiet emphasis in pantomime which fits nicely into this lurid tale. *Variety*

NOTES

The film's working titles were *The Night Rose* and *Flowers of Darkness*. Chaney's character was originally named McGee. The film was in production before *Ace of Hearts* (1921), but was released almost nine months the after completion and release of that film. A possible reason for the delay may have been the "suggestive" title, which would have caused problems with state censor boards.

For the ball sequence, the production hired 300 couples and the dances were introduced by the Marion Morgan dancers. Five days were required to film the ball sequence.[50]

Flesh and Blood

Western Pictures Exploitation, 6 reels. 5,300 ft. *Released:* August 27, 1922. *In Production:* April 17 to May 13, 1922. *Presented by and Director:* Irving Cummings. *Scenario:* Louis Duryea Lighton.

CAST

Lon Chaney (*David Webster*), Edith Roberts (*The Angel Lady*), Noah Beery (*Li Fang*), De Witt Jennings (*Detective Doyle*), Ralph Lewis (*Fletcher Burton*), Jack Mulhall (*Ted Burton*), Togo Yamamoto (*The Prince*), Kate Price (*The Landlady*), Wilfred Lucas (*The Policeman*).

SYNOPSIS

Escaping from prison with the help of his long-time friend Li Fang, David Webster hopes to find his wife and daughter. He learns, however, that his wife has died and his daughter is now known as the Angel Lady because of her work in a local mission. To get past the police dragnet, Webster disguises himself as a cripple and goes to the mission, where he is able to meet his daughter without revealing his identity. He learns that she is engaged to marry Ted Burton, the son of Fletcher Burton, the man who framed him and sent him to prison. When the elder Burton tells the young woman she cannot marry his son, Webster goes to see the man who framed him. He reveals documents that prove the elder Burton framed him and forces him to sign a confession, then offers not to reveal the incriminating evidence on the condition that Burton allow his daughter to marry Ted. When Burton agrees, Webster tears up the confession and returns to prison, taking solace in the fact that his daughter's happiness is assured.

CRITICS' CORNER

While the story is full of incident and character it contains very little action. To make up for this you have melodrama and some nice bits of characterization. . . . [Chaney] does good work as a cripple. *Film Daily*

There is a bit of inserted action, illustrating a tale related to the impatient Webster by the philosophical Li Fang, which is told in color with Chinese players. . . . *Flesh and Blood* ought to go well anywhere, and strongly if reasonably exploited. And in the latter event there will be no complaints on the part of patrons—they will be entirely satisfied. *Exhibitors Trade Review*

Flesh and Blood gives Lon Chaney opportunity to show why he is called one of the most gifted character actors on the screen. . . . Chaney can bring out pathos so that mawkish sentiment never intrudes. The picture is a good audience number. *Motion Picture News*

NOTES

The film's working titles were *Fires of Vengeance* and *Prison*. Interior sequences were shot at Universal Studios. *Flesh and Blood* was rereleased in 1927.

The sequence shot in color with Chinese players does not exist in any known prints today.

Prints of *Flesh and Blood* were sold for many years to film collectors by Blackhawk Films. A print can also be found at the George Eastman House in Rochester, New York. Kino International included clips from the movie in their documentary, *Lon Chaney: Behind the Mask* (1995).

The Light in the Dark

Associated First National, 7 reels. 5,600 ft. *Released:* September 3, 1922. *Director:* Clarence Brown. *Scenario:* William Dudley Pelley and Clarence Brown, based on the story "White Faith" by William Dudley Pelley. *Photographer:* Alfred Ortlieb.

CAST

Hope Hampton (*Bessie MacGregor*), E. K. Lincoln (*J. Warburton Ashe*), Lon Chaney (*Tony Pantelli*), Theresa Maxwell Conover (*Mrs. Templeton Orrin*), Dorothy Walters (*Mrs. Callerty*), Charles Mused (*Detective Braenders*), Edgar Norton (*Peters*), Dore Davidson (*Jerusalem Mike*), Joe Bonomo (*Stunt Double for Chaney*).

SYNOPSIS

Bessie MacGregor is struck by an automobile driven by Mrs. Orrin, who takes pity on her and takes her in. Bessie proceeds to fall in love with Mrs. Orrin's brother, J. Warburton Ashe, but is crushed when she later sees him kissing another woman, so she leaves the Orrin household and goes to a tenement house. Later, weak from starvation, Bessie falls down a flight of stairs and is rescued by Tony Pantelli, a small-time thief, who takes an interest in her. When Bessie tells Tony of how she was struck by Mrs. Orrin's car, he goes to Mrs. Orrin in an unsuccessful attempt to obtain money for the sick girl. He and Bessie read how Ashe has found a cup in Europe that is believed to be the Holy Grail. Knowing of the Grail's healing powers, Tony steals the cup and has Bessie drink from it. She quickly recovers, but Tony is arrested for the theft. In the courtroom, Tony is acquitted, and Bessie and Ashe are reunited.

CRITICS' CORNER

The Light In The Dark, otherwise Faith, is by odds, the best story, and certainly is better handled by Hope Hampton than anything she has ever done. . . . Lon Chaney, excellent actor that he is, does splendid work as an Italian who in a simple way loves the heroine. His work is very good. *Film Daily*

By all odds the best picture in which Hope Hampton has appeared, *The Light in the Dark*, has A-1 merits as a box-office attraction. . . . Lon Chaney is, as always, the crook par excellence and adds another striking portrait to his gallery of characters. *Exhibitors Trade Review*

It has a penetrating theme and symbolic beauty that has been emphasized just enough to keep the picture within easy understanding of all. . . . Lon Chaney has the type of role in which he has proven exceptionally skillful. His is a real sympathetic contribution. *Moving Picture World*

NOTES

The Light in the Dark was filmed on location in New York City in December 1921. Interiors were filmed in Fort Lee, New Jersey. The world premiere was held at the Strand Theatre in Niagara Falls, New York.

Prints of *The Light in the Dark* are housed at the George Eastman House in Rochester, New York, and the Library of Congress. The print at the George Eastman House contains foreign titles. A condensed version, entitled *Light of Faith*, was sold for many years to film collectors by Blackhawk Films. Kino International released a print to the videotape market in 1995.

Shadows

Preferred Pictures, 7 reels. 7,040 ft. *Released:* November 5, 1922. *Picture Code No.:* F 1. *Presented by:* B. P. Schulberg. *Director:* Tom Forman. *Scenario:* Eve Unsell and Hope Loring, from the story "Ching, Ching, Chinaman" by Wilbur Daniel Steele. *Photographer:* Harry Perry.

CAST

Lon Chaney (*Yen Sin*), Marguerite De La Motte (*Sympathy Gibbs*), Harrison Ford (*John Malden*), John Sainpolis (*Nate Snow*), Walter Long (*Daniel Gibbs*), Buddy Messenger ("*Mister Bad Boy*"), Priscilla Bonner (*Mary Brent*), Frances Raymond (*Emsy Nickerson*).

SYNOPSIS

During a rescue attempt of a ship, Sympathy Gibbs' husband, Daniel, is lost at sea. Yen Sin, a Chinese from the ship, is the only survivor and experiences racial and religious intolerance from the local New Englanders. Sympathy falls in love with the new minister, John Malden, and they marry. John receives a blackmail note revealing that Sympathy's husband is alive and that his wife will be exposed as a bigamist unless he pays money. Yen Sin learns of the young minister's problem and helps him by revealing that it was Nate Snow who wrote the letter and that Sympathy's husband is indeed dead. When, on his deathbed, Yen Sin witnesses Malden's forgiveness of Nate Snow for the man's crime against his family, the Chinese decides to accept the Christian faith. Then, as a fierce storm erupts on the sea, Yen Sin cuts the moorings of his houseboat and disappears into the storm.

CRITICS' CORNER

It is excellently done in the main and tells a powerful story of how a Chinaman in his bland, naive, simple way proves a better Christian than either the minister of the gospel or the deacon of the church. . . . Lon Chaney gives probably the most superior performance of his long and important career. *Film Daily*

Now and then a picture is produced that stands out above others, just as the Woolworth building stands out above all buildings that surround it. It is such pictures as these that prove beyond any doubt that picture-making is an art. Such a one is *Shadows*—a picture that stands out above the others. . . . The acting of Mr. Chaney, who assumes the role of the Chinaman, is remarkable. Better acting he has never done in his life. *Harrison's Reports*

Mr. Chaney has been seen in a number of great characterizations. . . . Yet it must be borne in mind that the role assigned to him in the present instance is one of unusual difficulty; and because of that fact his triumph will be conceded to be all the greater. *Exhibitors Trade Review*

An idea of delicacy and charm has been translated with great care to the screen; and the result is a good picture. . . . The central figure, the oriental laundry man remarkably acted by Lon Chaney, is a fine and true conception. *Photoplay*

NOTES

The film's working title was *Ching, Ching, Chinaman*. Portions of it were shot on location in Balboa and Del Monte, California. Studio interiors were filmed at the Louis B. Mayer Studios.[51]

Shadows was chosen by film critic Robert Sherwood as one of the best films of the year and as one of the year's top forty pictures by the National Board of Review. Marguerite De La Motte (Sympathy Gibbs) was briefly considered by Chaney for the role of Esmeralda in *The Hunchback of Notre Dame* (1923).

Prints of *Shadows* were sold for many years on the film collectors' market by Blackhawk Films. Prints can also be found at the Library of Congress and the Cineteca Nazionale in Rome, Italy. Kino International released a print to the videotape market in 1995.

Oliver Twist

Associated First National/Jackie Coogan Productions, 8 reels. 7,761 ft. *Released:* November 5, 1922. *Presented by:* Sol Lesser. *Supervisor:* Jack Coogan, Sr. *Director:* Frank Lloyd. *Scenario:* Frank Lloyd and Harry Weil, from the novel by Charles Dickens. *Photographers:* Glen McWilliams and Robert Martin. *Titles:* Walter Anthony. *Art Director:* Stephen Goosson. *Film Editor:* Irene Morra. *Costumes:* Walter J. Israel. *Cost of Production:* $400,000.

CAST

Jackie Coogan (*Oliver Twist*), Lon Chaney (*Fagin*), Gladys Brockwell (*Nancy Sikes*), George Siegmann (*Bill Sikes*), James Marcus (*Mr. Bumble*), Aggie Herring (*The Widow Corney*), Lionel Belmore (*Mr. Brownlow*), Edouard Trebaol (*The Artful Dodger*), Taylor Graves (*Charley Bates*), Carl Stockdale (*Mr. Monks*), Lewis Sargent (*Noah Claypool*), Joan Standing (*Charlotte*), Nelson McDowell (*Mr. Sowerberry*), Joseph H. Hazelton (*Mr. Grimwig*), Eddie Boland (*Toby Crackit*), Florence Hale (*Mrs. Bedwin*), Esther Ralston (*Rose Maylie*), Gertrude Claire (*Mrs. Maylie*).

SYNOPSIS

Young Oliver Twist is tossed out of an English orphanage after having the audacity to ask for more gruel. The orphanage apprentices him to an undertaker, but Oliver runs away to London. There he is befriended by the Artful Dodger, who introduces him to Fagin. Staying with Fagin and his group of boys, Oliver learns to pick pockets. Caught during his first attempt at thievery, Oliver is taken to court but is released into the custody of kindly Mr. Brownlow and lives a happy life. Fearing Oliver might implicate them in his crime, Bill Sikes and the Dodger kidnap the boy. Nancy Sikes attempts to help Oliver escape and return to Mr. Brownlow, but she is caught by Bill and beaten to death. Oliver is forced to help Sikes in a robbery that goes wrong, and Sikes is killed by the mob and the police. Fagin and his boys are arrested, and Oliver is reunited with Mr. Brownlow, who turns out to be his grandfather.

CRITICS' CORNER

Charming, delightful, thoroughly Dickens. . . . They're there from Fagin—at times too theatrically portrayed by Lon Chaney. . . . This is a picture that the entire industry can well be proud of. *Film Daily*

The result is a motion picture thoroughly worthwhile and of very definite appeal. . . . Lon Chaney, who these days is adding rapidly to his fame as a real character genius, makes Fagin one of the most impressive of his gallery of portraits. *Exhibitors Trade Review*

All things considered, they've done a good job, an excellent job, with Dickens in the picturized *Oliver Twist*, which is at the Strand this week, and destined to keep the house full, if the crowds that packed the place yesterday mean anything. But whether it is Mr. Dickens or little Jackie Coogan that is drawing them in, of course, is a question. . . . There's Fagin, too, vividly present in the person of Lon Chaney. *New York Times*

NOTES

Studio interiors were filmed at the Robert Brunton Studios in Hollywood. *Oliver Twist* was chosen as one of the year's best pictures by *New York Times*, *Film Daily*, *Life*, *Chicago Tribune*, and *Los Angeles Times*.

The Charles Dickens novel had been adapted in three earlier filmed versions, the first a 1909 Vitagraph short. The two others released before the Jackie Coogan version were produced in 1912 and 1916, with Nat C. Goodwin and Tully Marshall respectively playing Fagin. Other versions include a 1933 Monogram production, the 1948 David Lean film, and the 1968 musical, *Oliver!*[52]

For years, *Oliver Twist* had been considered lost until a print surfaced in the early 1970s in Yugoslavia. Producer Sol Lesser and Jackie Coogan worked with Blackhawk Films to reconstruct the title cards in English. The restored *Oliver Twist* had a special screening at Filmex in Los Angeles in 1975.[53]

The film was available for years to collectors through Blackhawk Films. Prints of *Oliver Twist* can also be found at the UCLA Film and Television Archive and the Library of Congress. Kino International released a print to the videotape market in 1995.

Quincy Adams Sawyer

Metro Pictures, 8 reels. 7,895 ft. *Released:* December 4, 1922. *Picture Code No.:* 136. *Presented by:* Arthur H. Sawyer and Herbert Lubin. *Director:* Clarence Badger. *Scenario:* Bernard McConville, from the novel by Charles Felton Pidgin. *Photographer:* Rudolph Berquist. *Assistant Director:* Charles Hunt.

CAST

John Bowers (*Quincy Adams Sawyer*), Blanche Sweet (*Alice Pettengill*), Lon Chaney (*Obadiah Strout*), Barbara La Marr (*Lindy Putnam*), Elmo Lincoln (*Abner Stiles*), Louise Fazenda (*Mandy Skinner*), Joseph Dowling (*Nathaniel Sawyer*), Claire McDowell (*Mrs. Putnam*), Edward Connelly (*Deacon Pettengill*), June Elvidge (*Betsy Ann Ross*), Victor Potel (*Hiram Maxwell*), Gale Henry (*Samanthy*), Hank Mann (*Ben Bates*), Kate Lester (*Mrs. Sawyer*), Billy Franey (*Bob Wood*), Harry Depp and Taylor Graves (*Cobb Twins*).

SYNOPSIS

Quincy Adams Sawyer, a young lawyer from Boston, is sent by his father to Mason's Corner to assist Mrs. Lindy Putnam in the probate of her late husband's will. Obadiah Strout, the village lawyer, is suspected of holding back some bonds belonging to the widow. Lindy Putnam is thrilled to have the young lawyer staying in her home and makes every attempt to charm him. Strout, who would like to have Lindy for himself, takes an immediate dislike to Quincy and solicits the help of the local blacksmith, Stiles, to rid the town of Quincy by spreading a malicious rumor about him and Lindy. Quincy quickly moves out of the Putnam house and takes up residence in Deacon Pettengill's home, where he meets the Deacon's blind daughter, Alice. They become fast friends and a romance blossoms. Lindy is furious because of this relationship and decides to join Strout to get revenge. They plan to do away with the blind girl, and Strout secretly hopes to get rid of Quincy at the same time so that he can have Lindy to himself. Their plan fails when Quincy rescues Alice from the nearby rushing river. The shock of the accident restores her sight, and they live happily ever after.

CRITICS' CORNER

If *Quincy Adams Sawyer* doesn't start a new era of smashing box office records there is something wrong, because boys, this has got it all. . . . Then there is Lon Chaney, who adds another to his long list of splendid characterizations as the village attorney with his special haircut for the party and his elaborate use of facial expression. He practically steals this picture. *Film Daily*

There are comparatively few pictures that can boast of a cast containing any more well known players assembled than in *Quincy Adams Sawyer*. . . . It holds good interest and many unexpected thrills occur as the story progresses. Lon Chaney, Elmo Lincoln, Louise Fazenda and Barbara La Marr are also excellent in their character parts. *Exhibitors Trade Review*

An excellent picture of its kind, with the "homey" atmosphere accentuated. But in the long run the thing which marks it from the rest is that it contains more hokum than every other picture produced this year. . . . Lon Chaney and Elmo Lincoln do good work as the villains. *Variety*

NOTES

Portions of *Quincy Adams Sawyer* were filmed along the Columbia River in Washington state. The film was chosen as one of the year's top ten pictures by *Harrison's Reports*. Hank Mann, who played Ben Bates in the film, would later play a comedy waiter in Chaney's film biography, *Man of a Thousand Faces* (1957).

This was very popular book, selling over a million and a half copies. It also enjoyed a successful run as a play. Puritan Special Features Company produced a version of the novel in 1912. The public so enjoyed the characters that author Charles Felton Pidgin penned two sequels, *The Further Adventures of Quincy Adams Sawyer* and *The Chronicles of Quincy Adams Sawyer, Detective*.

A Blind Bargain

Goldwyn Pictures, 5 reels. 4,473 ft. *Released:* December 10, 1922. *Picture Code No.:* 165. *In Production:* early October 1921 through early November 1921. *Director:* Wallace Worsley. *Scenario:* J. G. Hawks, from the novel *Octave of Claudius* by Barry Pain. *Photographer:* Norbert Brodin.

CAST

Lon Chaney (*Dr. Lamb/Ape-Man*), Raymond McKee (*Robert Sandell*), Jacqueline Logan (*Angela*), Virginia True Boardman (*Mrs. Sandell, Robert's Mother*), Fontaine La Rue (*Mrs. Lamb*), Aggie Herring (*Bessie*), Virginia Madison (*Angela's Mother*).

SYNOPSIS

Robert, despondent over his ill luck as a novelist and his mother's declining health, attempts to rob a theatregoer. His victim turns out to be Dr. Lamb, a fanatical surgeon living in the suburbs of New York. When

Robert tells him why he needs the money, the doctor agrees to perform the needed operation on Robert's mother, with one condition—that after eight days, Robert deliver himself to Dr. Lamb to do with as he will for experimental purposes. Desperate, Robert agrees. Both Robert and his mother take up residence at the Lamb estate and are watched carefully by the doctor and his wife as well as a grotesque ape-man whom Robert later learns is the result of one of the doctor's experiments. The doctor also arranges for Robert's book to be published through the Wytcherly Publishing Company. Robert meets and falls in love with Wytcherly's daughter, Angela. As the time draws near for Robert's bargain to be fulfilled, the ape-man shows him what is in store. He reveals, in several cages in the basement, various half-human, half-animal creatures, and Robert understands that he is destined for the same fate. The doctor discovers the two and realizes that Robert knows the truth. The ape-man then releases one of the doctor's failed experiments, which kills Dr. Lamb. Robert is set free from his bargain and, with the success of his book, he is able to help his mother and pursue a romance with Angela.

CRITICS' CORNER
A theme that is thoroughly appropriate and suitable for Lon Chaney, providing him with two distinct roles in which he is given plenty of opportunities to live up to his reputation as "a man with a thousand faces." Chaney displays his ability to handle grotesque characterization. Those who like his particular type of portrayal will find plenty to satisfy them. *Film Daily*

One merely has to say "Lon Chaney" and mention next director Wallace Worsley. The former has given the picture its greatest power to interest the spectator and the director has contrived many scenes of photographic distinction and dramatic effect. . . . Mr. Chaney essays the dual role assigned to him with that fine assurance which marks all his work. His make-up is of course wonderful and one marvels at the contrast between the Doctor with his erect and distinguished carriage and the deformed little man victimized by the surgical experiments. *Exhibitors Trade Review*

Lon Chaney attains perfection in make-up with the character of a half-monkey in this picture. As the doctor, for he plays a double part, he is not so good. Lon as a grotesque mistake of nature is far more thrilling than Lon in a frock coat and a vandyke beard. There are many thrills—illogical, perhaps, but now and then breath taking. *Photoplay*

NOTES

Claims that Wallace Beery appeared in an uncredited role as one of Dr. Lamb's experiments have never been proven. Chaney was signed for this production in late September 1921 while completing *The Trap* (1922).[54] This is one of the few true horror films Lon Chaney appeared in.

One reason for the year-long delay between completion of filming and release may have been the subject matter of the film. The theme of the doctor creating artificial life, no matter how insane he may be, was akin to attempting to play God. This would surely have sent the censors and church groups into a frenzy and may explain why the movie was cut from six to five reels and why four different versions of title cards were written.[55] *A Blind Bargain* was chosen as one of the year's top forty films by the National Board of Review.

Outside the Law (1921). Wheeler Oakman, Lon (as Black Mike), and Priscilla Dean.

Outside the Law (1921). Priscilla Dean, Ralph Lewis, Lon (as Ah Wing), and E. A. Warren.

For Those We Love (1921). Lon and Betty Compson.

Bits of Life (1921). Lon and Anna May Wong.

Ace of Hearts (1921). Lon, Leatrice Joy, and John Bowers.

The Trap (1922). Lon and Irene Rich.

Voices of the City (1922). Lon and John Bowers.

Flesh and Blood (1922). Lon and Edith Roberts.

The Light In the Dark (1922). Lon and Dore Davidson.

Shadows (1922). Lon and John Sainpolis.

Oliver Twist (1922). Lewis Sargent, Lon, and Joan Standing.

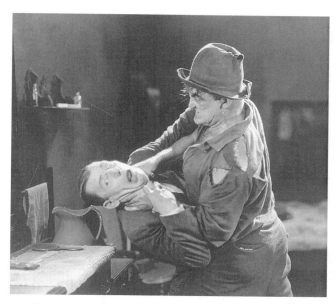

Quincy Adams Sawyer (1922). Lon and Elmo Lincoln.

A Blind Bargain (1922). Lon (as Dr. Lamb) and Raymond McKee.

A Blind Bargain (1922). Aggie Herring, Lon (as the ape-man), and Fontaine La Rue.

All the Brothers Were Valiant (1923). Malcolm McGregor, an unidentified player, Robert McKim, Lon, and William V. Mong.

While Paris Sleeps (1923). Lon and Mildred Manning.

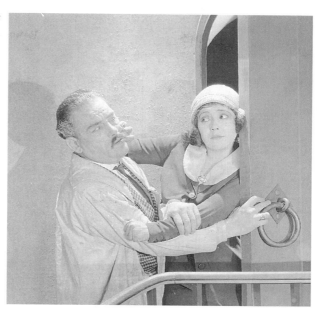

The Shock (1923). Lon and Christine Mayo.

The Hunchback of Notre Dame (1923).

The Hunchback of Notre Dame (1923). Lon and Nigel De Brulier.

The Hunchback of Notre Dame (1923). Raymond Hatton and Lon.

The Next Corner (1924). Lon and Dorothy Mackaill.

He Who Gets Slapped (1924).

He Who Gets Slapped (1924). Ruth King, Lon (as the scientist), and Marc McDermott.

He Who Gets Slapped (1924). John Gilbert, Norma Shearer, and Lon.

The Monster (1925). George Austin, Lon, Johnny Arthur, and Walter James.

The Monster (1925). George Austin, Lon, Walter James, Johnny Arthur, Hallam Cooley, Gertrude Olmsted, and Knute Erickson.

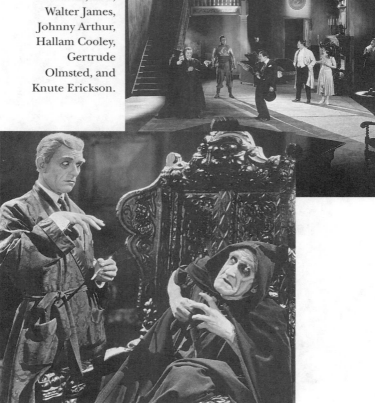

The Monster (1925). Lon and George Austin.

The Unholy Three (1925). Harry Earles, Lon, Matthew Betz, and Victor McLaglen.

The Unholy Three (1925). A. E. Warren, Lon, and Edward Connelly.

The Unholy Three (1925). Lon, Harry Earles, and Victor McLaglen.

The Phantom of the Opera (1925). Lon stands patiently as his wardrobe receives a final adjustment on the Grand Staircase set. Director Rupert Julian (left, standing next to his wife) coaches the extras for the scene.

The Phantom of the Opera (1925). Lon and Mary Philbin.

The Phantom of the Opera (1925). Arthur Edmund Carewe (lying on floor), Norman Kerry, Mary Philbin, and Lon.

Tower of Lies (1925). Lon and Claire McDowell. Chaney's character ages over thirty years in this film. In this picture the character is at his youngest age.

Tower of Lies (1925). Lon (in middle-age makeup), Norma Shearer, and William Haines.

Tower of Lies (1925). At this point in the film, the character of Jan is over sixty years old.

The Blackbird (1926). Lon as the Limehouse criminal, the Blackbird.

The Blackbird (1926). Lon (as the crippled bishop) and Owen Moore.

The Blackbird (1926). Lon and Renee Adoree.

The Road To Mandalay (1926).

The Road To Mandalay (1926). Lon and Owen Moore.

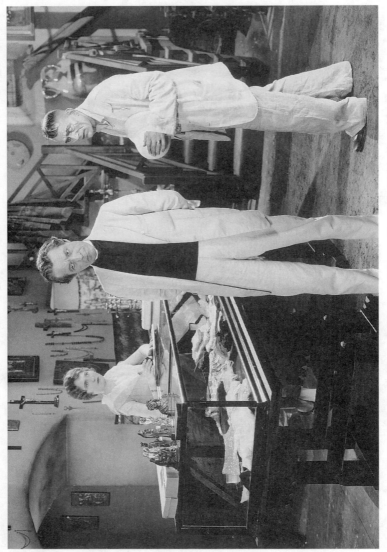

The Road To Mandalay (1926). Lois Moran, Henry B. Walthall, and Lon.

LON CHANEY
The Man of 1000 faces

IT was M-G-M who developed Lon Chaney into the great Lon Chaney. "He Who Gets Slapped," "The Unholy Three," "The Blackbird," "The Road to Mandalay," "Tell It to the Marines," "Mr. Wu," "The Unknown." Everyone outstanding, all money pictures.

In 1927-1928 Lon Chaney will first appear in "The Hypnotist," a role which tells a story in itself.

A page from a 1927–28 theatre exhibitors book distributed by M-G-M. These books were sent to various theatre owners to promote the studio's stars and their upcoming releases.

LON CHANEY

CHAPTER ELEVEN

1923

All the Brothers Were Valiant

Metro Pictures, 7 reels. 6,265 ft. *Released:* January 15, 1923. *Picture Code No.:* 140. *In Production:* late September 1922 to October 30, 1922. *Director:* Irvin V. Willat. *Scenario:* Julien Josephson, from the novel by Ben Ames Williams. *Photographer:* Robert Kurrle.

CAST

Malcolm McGregor (*Joel Shore*), Billie Dove (*Priscilla Holt*), Lon Chaney (*Mark Shore*), William H. Orlamond (*Aaron Burnham*), Robert McKim (*Finch*), Robert Kortman (*Varde*), Otto Brower (*Morrell*), Curt Rehfeld (*Hooper*), William V. Mong (*Cook*), Leo Willis (*Tom*), Shannon Day (*The Brown Girl*).

SYNOPSIS

Mark Shore, the elder brother of Joel, is captain of a whaling schooner, but when the ship returns to port, the captain is missing. Joel, who has been working on another ship, asks to be transferred to his brother's ship to find him. Joel's request is granted, and he is given his brother's place as captain. Before sailing, Joel marries his sweetheart, Priscilla, and takes her with him. She believes that her husband, unlike the other male members of the Shore family, is a coward. They find Mark when the ship comes upon some islands, and he tells them of his experiences. When he boards his old ship, he tries to convince his brother to alter his course to go to another island, where he is sure to find pearls. When Joel refuses, Mark incites a mutiny. Joel puts down the mutiny but is eventually overpowered. Mark realizes his mistake and stops the mutiny, but in doing so, he is hit over the head and falls overboard. Joel attempts to rescue him, but Mark has disappeared. Joel returns the ship safely to port, and Priscilla sees that her husband does not fall below the heroism of his forefathers.

CRITICS' CORNER

Here is a story that will send real thrills up and down the spine. . . . It is one of the best sea pictures that has come on the screen recently and should give entire satisfaction wherever shown. . . . Lon Chaney is excellent as Mark Shore the elder brother. *Exhibitors Trade Review*

A delightful, adventurous tale of the water that contains all the elements of popular appeal. . . . The picture is a first rate entertainment of its kind and should please a great many. . . . Lon Chaney gives his usual splendid performance. *Film Daily*

We might try to be funny and say that this is a whaling good story, though over long. Most of the action is on board ship, and there is some good saltwater atmosphere. It is curious how many tales of the sea are suddenly taking to celluloid. Both the brothers are valiant. One of them, Malcolm McGregor, is a likable hero. And the other, Lon Chaney, is most villainous! *Photoplay*

NOTES

Portions of *All the Brothers Were Valiant* were shot on location in San Francisco. The film employed the use of two whaling ships located in San Francisco, the 65-foot *Port Saunders* and the 165-foot *Carolyn Frances*.[56]

Chaney apparently had little respect for some of his costars. In a letter to his business manager, Alfred Grasso, he described Malcolm McGregor as "a dumb bell" and called Billie Dove "one of those 'Blah' sort that has all beauty and no brains."[57]

In 1953 M-G-M remade *All the Brothers Were Valiant* under the same title with Stewart Granger playing Chaney's role.

While Paris Sleeps

W. W. Hodkinson Corp./Maurice Tourneur Productions, 6 reels. 4,850 ft. *Released:* January 21, 1923. *Picture Code No.:* H-134. *Director:* Maurice Tourneur. Based on the story "The Glory of Love" by Pan. *Photographer:* Rene Guissart. *Scenic Effects:* Floyd Mueller.

CAST

Lon Chaney (*Henri Santodos*), Mildred Manning (*Bebe Larvache*), John Gilbert (*Dennis O'Keefe*), Hardee Kirkland (*Dennis's Father*), Jack MacDonald (*Father Marionette*), J. Farrell MacDonald (*George Morier*).

SYNOPSIS

Henri Santodos is a sculptor in the Latin quarter of Paris. He bears an unrequited love for his young model, Bebe, who has fallen in love with an American tourist named Dennis O'Keefe. Dennis' father pleads with Bebe to give up his son, and she agrees provided that she may have one evening of happiness with him during the Mardi Gras festival. Santodos' jealousy rages and he seeks the aid of a crazed owner of a wax museum to help him kill the young American. Dennis is kidnapped and tortured before he is freed. Santodos is killed and the two lovers are reunited.

CRITICS' CORNER

It is quite apparent that Tourneur made the picture before Chaney came to the fore as a "man of a thousand faces." . . . Just to think what Chaney could have done with the madman character certainly detracts greatly from the role he does portray. *Film Daily*

It is hard to believe Maurice Tourneur directed this film. . . . Lon Chaney is miscast. *Photoplay*

There is in *While Paris Sleeps* nothing to lift it out of the class of ordinary pictures. . . . The settings, whose reproductions of the French Latin Quarter are correct to the smallest detail, are worthy of note; but settings do not make a picture any more than the proverbial swallow makes a summer. . . . The French atmosphere plus the Chamber of Horrors background may appeal to a certain type of picture-goer. *Harrison's Reports*

NOTES

While Paris Sleeps had been shot in 1920 under the title *The Glory of Love*. The reason for the three-year delay in releasing the film remains unknown.

The Shock

Universal/Jewel, 7 reels. 6,738 ft. *Released:* June 10, 1923. *Picture Code No.:* 3817. *Director:* Lambert Hillyer. *Scenario:* Arthur Statter and Charles Kenyon, from the story "The Pit of the Golden Dragon" by William Dudley Pelley. *Photographer:* Dwight Warren.

CAST

Lon Chaney (*Wilse Dilling*), Virginia Valli (*Gertrude Hadley*), Jack Mower (*Jack Cooper*), William Welsh (*Mischa Hadley*), Henry Barrows (*John Cooper, Sr.*), Christine Mayo (*Anne Vincent, "The Dragon Lady"*), Harry Devere (*Olaf Wismer*), John Beck (*Bill*), Walter Long (*The Captain*), Robert Kortman (*Henchman*), Togo Yamamoto (*Messenger at Restaurant*).

SYNOPSIS

Wilse Dilling, a crippled member of a gang of crooks run by Anne Vincent, is sent to the small town of Fallbrook to spy on Mischa Hadley. Hadley has been victimized by Anne to such a degree that he has resorted to embezzling from the bank where he works. Dilling meets and falls in love with Hadley's daughter, Gertrude. He vows to free her father from the grip of Anne Vincent by blowing up the vault that contains the evidence of embezzlement. Gertrude happens by the bank at the moment of the explosion, and it cripples her. Dilling pays for the operation that cures her, but she is kidnapped by Anne Vincent's gang and held for ransom. Dilling returns to San Francisco to confront Vincent in a Chinese restaurant. He attempts to rescue Gertrude but fails. Just then the great San Francisco earthquake of 1906 hits, killing Vincent and her gang. Both Dilling and Gertrude survive, and Dilling regains the use of his legs. A promising future for the two lies ahead.

CRITICS' CORNER

An uncommonly realistic, well directed story of the underworld, *The Shock* registers as a melodrama of compelling interest. . . . Lon Chaney's work in the role of the crippled crook, Wilse Dilling, stands out as a really astonishing performance. *Exhibitors Trade Review*

An excellent vehicle for the exploitation of Lon Chaney, whose ability to handle the role of a cripple is little short of uncanny. His portrayal of Wilse Dilling. . . . is interesting and for the most part convincing. *Film Daily*

Lon Chaney gives another of his hideously distorted, and uncannily clever, characterizations. *Photoplay*

NOTES

The Universal Picture Code Book lists the film's release date as July 2, 1923.[58] The film's working title was *Bittersweet*. It was originally scheduled for release in February 1923.

Lambert Hillyer had previously directed Chaney in *Riddle Gawne*. Scenarist Charles Kenyon coauthored the script of *The Penalty*.

Prints of *The Shock* were sold for many years on the film collectors' market by Blackhawk Films. Prints can also be found at the Library of Congress, the National Film and Television Archive in London, and the Cineteca del Comune dei Bologna in Bologna, Italy. Kino International released a print to the videotape market in 1995.

The Hunchback of Notre Dame

Universal/Super Jewel, 12 reels. 12,000 ft. *Released:* September 6, 1923. *Picture Code No.:* 3874 (The number was changed to 4847 for the 1928 reissue). *In Production:* December 16, 1922 to June 3, 1923, 146 Days. *Presented by:* Carl Laemmle. *Director:* Wallace Worsley. *Scenario:* Edward T. Lowe, Jr. from the novel by Victor Hugo. *Adapted by:* Perley Poore Sheehan. *Photographers:* Robert Newhard and Tony Kornman. *Film Editors:* Sidney Singerman, Maurice Pivar, and Edward Curtiss. *Art Directors:* Elmer E. Sheeley and Sidney Ullman. *Costume Supervision:* Col. Gordon McGee. *Lighting Director:* Harry D. Brown. *Additional Photographers:* Virgil Miller, Charles Stumar, and Stephen S. Norton. *Assistant Directors:* Jack Sullivan, James Dugan, and William Wyler. *Cost of Production:* $1,250,000.

CAST

Lon Chaney (*Quasimodo*), Ernest Torrance (*Clopin*), Patsy Ruth Miller (*Esmeralda*), Norman Kerry (*Phoebus*), Kate Lester (*Madame de Gondelaurier*), Brandon Hurst (*Jehan*), Raymond Hatton (*Gringoire*), Tully Marshall (*King Louis XI*), Nigel De Brulier (*Dom Claude*), Harry Van Meter (*Monsieur Neufchatel*), Gladys Brockwell (*Godule*), Eulalie Jensen (*Marie*), Winifred Bryson (*Fleur de Lis*), Nick De Ruiz (*Monsieur le Torteru*), Edwin Wallock (*King's Chamberlain*), W. Ray Meyers (*Charmolou's Assistant*), John Cossar (*Judge of Court*), William Parke, Sr. (*Josephus*), Roy Laidlaw (*Charmolu*), Robert Kortman (*Hook-Hand*), Harry Holman (*Fat Man*), John Gough (*Prisoner in Torture Chamber*), Joe Bonomo and Harvey Perry (*Stunt Doubles for Lon Chaney*). *Others in the Cast:* Ethan Laidlaw, Al Ferguson, John George, George MacQuarrie, Albert MacQuarrie, Jay Hunt, Harrison DeVere, Pearl Tupper, Eva Lewis, Jane Sherman, Helen Brunneau, Gladys Johnston, Lydia Yeamans Titus, Alex Manuel, Arthur Hurni, Rene Traveletti.

SYNOPSIS

In Paris, during the rein of King Louis XI, there lives a freak of nature who is known as the Hunchback of Notre Dame. Blind in one eye, deaf, and cursed with a horrible visage, Quasimodo lives in the towers of the Catholic cathedral of Notre Dame. Although the church's large bells have deafened him, they are his only love. He is subservient to Jehan, a former priest who desires more than the church offers. Quasimodo is bewitched by the beauty of Esmeralda, the daughter of Clopin, King of the Gypsies. Phoebus, the Captain of the King's Guard, is also taken by the beauty of the girl. One night, Jehan sends Quasimodo to kidnap Esmeralda, but the hunchback is caught by the King's Guard, who happen by. Phoebus takes the gypsy girl to a tavern and they fall in love. Quasimodo is tried for his crimes and sentenced to the whipping wheel located in the center of the square. Esmeralda answers his call for water and, at that moment, he becomes her loyal friend. Later, Phoebus and Esmeralda meet in the garden of the church, where he is stabbed by Jehan. She is wrongly sentenced to hang for the crime and, while doing penance at the steps of Notre Dame, is rescued by Quasimodo. Jehan lies to Clopin that Esmeralda will be handed over to the authorities despite the law of sanctuary. Hearing this, Clopin arouses his band of thieves to storm the great cathedral and save the girl. Gringoire takes the news to Phoebus that Esmeralda's safety is at risk. The captain summons his guard to descend upon the church. As the large group of gypsies surround the cathedral, Quasimodo launches a counterattack upon those storming his beloved cathedral. The King's Guard arrives and quickly puts an end to the uprising. During the commotion, Esmeralda is dragged away by Jehan, who attempts to attack her. Quasimodo confronts Jehan, and hoists him above his head, while Jehan drives a knife into Quasimodo's back. Mortally wounded, Quasimodo throws his attacker over the balcony to his death. Dying himself, the hunchback sees Esmeralda and Phoebus embracing and he nods, understanding that she has found her true love. He staggers to his bell tower, where he rings his beloved bells for the last time.

CRITICS' CORNER

Here, then, is a picture that will live forever. Lon Chaney's portrayal of Quasimodo, the hunchback, is superb, not only a marvel of make-up such as is seldom seen upon the screen and stage, but a marvel of sympathetic acting. . . . Chaney, in some miraculous way, awakens within us a profound feeling of sympathy and admiration for this most unfortunate and physically revolting human being. *Motion Picture World*

A stupendous production! In these days of super-films the hapless reviewer is likely to run out of adjectives to meet the description of magnificent sets, photography deluxe and general gorgeousness. And the weakness of his vocabulary is never more apparent than when gazing upon the splendors of *The Hunchback of Notre Dame*. The Quasimodo of Lon Chaney is a creature of horror, a weird monstrosity of ape-like ugliness, such a fantastically effective makeup as the screen has never known and in all human probability will never know again. Add to this the wonderful agility and terribly intense pantomimic ability of his impersonator, and you face a Quasimodo such as can only be imagined under the stress of a peculiarity vindictive nightmare. *Exhibitors Trade Review*

In spite of the liberties taken with the Victor Hugo novel, this picture is a superb and remarkably impressive spectacle. The Hugo story is pure melodrama, and the picture is just that, with the addition of some of the most stupendous and interesting settings ever shown. . . . The picture is very much worth while because of the acting of Lon Chaney in the title role. His performance transcends anything he has ever done, both in his make-up and in his spiritual realization of the character. He is weird, almost repellent at times, but always fascinating. He falls short, perhaps, in creating the sympathy which is due of the *Hunchback*, but he more than atones for this by the wonderful acting. . . . This picture should be placed on your list and not missed by any means. *Photoplay*

This picture is a legitimate example of movie elephantiasis. . . . All this was done on the Gargantuan scale of which only cinema directors can conceive. All this would have been futile, as it so often is with spectacle productions, if the story had not furnished it with backbone and if Lon Chaney had not provided a singularly fine performance in the title role. *Time*

The Hunchback of Notre Dame is a two-hour nightmare. It's murderous, hideous and repulsive. . . . Mr. Chaney's performance as a performance entitles him to starring honors. . . . Produced as it is, *The Hunchback of Notre Dame* may become a detriment to the box office it plays for. *Variety*

What makes this production a piece of art, however, is the work of Mr. Chaney; the Cathedral, the characters, the King of the Beggars, the mob scenes, the love story—all impress one, but the one thing that stands out in one's memory is Quasimodo. . . . Mr. Chaney's work will live in the memory when all else will have faded away. *The Hunchback of Notre Dame* is an accomplishment of which any producer should feel proud. *Harrison's Reports*

NOTES

Chaney's performance was voted one of the best picks of the month by *Photoplay*. The film was chosen as one of the year's best pictures by the *New York Times, Film Daily, Motion Picture News, Harrison's Reports, Exhibitors Trade Review, Moving Picture World, Film Fun, Life,* and *New York Evening World*. In 1925, movie fans voted the film as one of the ten best in a promotion run by London's *Daily Chronicle*.

The exact amount the film earned at the box office is unknown, although it did make more than $1.5 million. It was shown throughout the 1920s, playing as late as 1929, and is still a popular film at revival screenings.[59]

Hugo's novel had previously been adapted for the screen six times, dating back to a French 1905 ten-minute short titled *Esmeralda*. This version was pirated in the United States and released in 1910 by Vitagraph as *Hunchback* and by Selig as *Hugo the Hunchback*. That same year, Butcher Films of England released a version of Hugo's novel as *The Loves of a Hunchback*. In 1911, Pathe released *Notre Dame de Paris*, while a 1913 version featuring tinted scenes, *Notre Dame*, was made by Patheplay in England. Fox Pictures released *The Darling of Paris* in 1916; Master Pictures of England, *Esmeralda* in 1922; and the German film company Helios, *Hunchback and the Dancer* (1923), directed by F. W. Murnau.[60] *The Hunchback of Notre Dame* was remade as a sound film in America in 1939 by RKO Pictures, with Charles Laughton playing Quasimodo. Anthony Quinn played the hunchback in a 1957 version, as did Anthony Hopkins in a 1982 television special. An animated version was released by Walt Disney Pictures in 1996.

Chaney had optioned the rights to the novel in 1921 and attempted to secure independent financing for the project with several investors, to no avail. Chelsea Pictures Corp. announced in April 1922 that it would produce the picture in Europe with Chaney starring and Alan Crosland directing, but the project collapsed because of monetary problems, and eventually Universal took on the project. Chaney had input on the scenario, director, cast, and editing.[61]

Cinematographer Virgil Miller shot most of Chaney's close-ups and certain special effects. He recalled that Chaney's make-ups were as convincing in person as they were on the screen. He added,

> Lon took an awful lot of time on this stuff [his make-up]. He'd come to the studio sometimes at 3:30 or 4 o'clock in the morning, and we wouldn't be able to shoot him till 8:30 or 9 o'clock. And he'd ask me then: "What would you suggest?"[62]

More than 2,000 extras were used for the large crowd scenes. The filming of night sequences took two months to complete. Officers of the Quarter Master Corp were lent to help feed more than 3,000 people and have them back on the set in thirty minutes. The *Hunchback* set, albeit somewhat altered over the years, appeared in several films, including *The Road Back* (1937) and Chaney's film biography, *Man of a Thousand Faces* (1957). Destroyed in a fire in 1967, the set was located where the "Earthquake" attraction now stands on the Universal lot.

Chaney and his business manager, Alfred A. Grasso, traveled to New York for the premiere of *The Hunchback of Notre Dame* at Carnegie Hall on September 2, 1923. Upon his arrival in New York, Chaney viewed the film one last time. Film editor Sidney Singerman recalled,

I was sent into a projection room to sit with Lon Chaney while he looked at the film. After he got through he said it was a very good job [the editing]. He said, "It's important to me how good the picture is." He was very pleased with what we did and made a few suggestions for some scenes. He knew more about the picture than the producers.[63]

The film's title was parodied in Mack Sennett's 1924 comedy, *The Halfback of Notre Dame*.

Columnist Louella O. Parsons reported in the September 30, 1923 edition of the *New York Morning Telegraph* that Chaney wanted to stage a theatrical production of the Victor Hugo novel. However, in a January 27, 1924 interview with the same paper, Chaney reported he declined an offer to do a stage version because he felt it would not be successful.

The April 5, 1930, issue of *Hollywood Filmograph* announced that Universal planned to remake the movie, but did not mention whether they intended to seek Chaney for the role.

Prints of *The Hunchback of Notre Dame* were sold for many years on the film collectors' market by Blackhawk Films. Prints are also housed at Museum of Modern Art in New York City, the George Eastman House in Rochester, New York, the Netherlands Filmmuseum in Amsterdam, the Cineteca del Friuli in Gemona, Italy, the Cinematheque Royale in Brussels, Belgium, and the Cinemateket-Svenska Filminstitutet in Stockholm, Sweden. Kino International released a print to the videotape market in 1995. A laser disc version was released by Image Entertainment in 1996.

CHAPTER TWELVE

1924

The Next Corner

Paramount Pictures, 7 reels. 7,081 ft. *Released:* February 18, 1924. *Picture Code No.:* 628. *Presented by:* Adolph Zukor and Jesse L. Lasky. *Director:* Sam Wood. *Scenario:* Monte Katterjohn, from the novel and play by Kate Jordan. *Photographer:* Alfred Gilks.

CAST

Conway Tearle (*Robert Maury*), Lon Chaney (*Juan Serafin*), Dorothy Mackaill (*Elsie Maury*), Ricardo Cortez (*Don Arturo*), Louise Dresser (*Nina Race*), Remea Radzina (*Countess Longueval*), Dorothy Cumming (*Paula Vrain*), Mrs. Bertha Feducha (*Julie*), Bernard Seigel (*The Stranger*).

SYNOPSIS

Elsie Maury becomes infatuated with Don Arturo because her husband is too busy to give her attention. She accompanies Arturo to his home outside Paris, but her guilty conscience forces her to write a letter to her husband confessing her indiscretion. Arturo attempts to stop the letter from being mailed, but he is killed by a peasant whose daughter he had betrayed. Elsie flees and awaits the arrival of the letter at her home. When it finally comes, it contains a blank piece of paper, substituted by Arturo. Elsie confesses everything to her husband, who forgives her.

CRITICS' CORNER

An unintentionally funny melodrama, which may amuse but will not impress intelligent audiences. . . . Why Lon Chaney, an actor of rare parts, consented to appear in such a foolish role as that of foster-brother Serafin remains an unsolved problem. *Exhibitors Trade Review*

Nowhere near enough to this story to warrant the footage that has been expended upon it. Slow, draggy development and poor direction generally. . . . Lon Chaney's great ability completely lost in this. *Film Daily*

Just a programme picture, that's all. . . . Conway Tearle and Lon Chaney, who have little to do. *Photoplay*

All the surface elements of a fine picture are here assembled. Still, the production isn't worth the trouble, for the reason it has a silly story. . . . Lon Chaney has a weak part and gets into the fore now and then in subordinate situations where he has little to build on. *Variety*

He Who Gets Slapped

Metro-Goldwyn, 7 reels. 6,614 ft. *Released:* November 2, 1924. *Picture Code No.:* 192. *In Production:* June 17, 1924 to July 28, 1924, 37 days. *Presented by:* Louis B. Mayer. *Producer:* Irving G. Thalberg. *Director:* Victor Seastrom. *Scenario:* Victor Seastrom and Carey Wilson, from the play by Leonid Andreyev. *Photographer:* Milton Moore. *Sets:* Cedric Gibbons. *Film Editor:* Hugh Wynn. *Costumes:* Sophie Wachner. *Assistant Director:* M. K. Wilson. *Production Manager:* David Howard. *Cost of Production:* $172,000. *Profit:* $349,000.

CAST
Lon Chaney (*Paul Beaumont/HE*), Norma Shearer (*Consuelo*), John Gilbert (*Bezano*), Tully Marshall (*Count Mancini*), Marc MacDermott (*Baron Regnard*), Ford Sterling (*Tricaud*), Harvey Clark (*Briquet*), Paulette Duval (*Zinida*), Ruth King (*HE's Wife*), Clyde Cook (*Clown*), Brandon Hurst (*Clown*), George Davis (*Clown*), Erik Stocklassa (*Ringmaster*). *Cut from the Release Print*: Billy Bletcher (*Clown*).

SYNOPSIS
Paul Beaumont's scientific thesis is stolen by his benefactor, Baron Regnard, who has also stolen the affections of Beaumont's wife. Unable to cope, Beaumont joins the circus as a clown known as "HE Who Gets Slapped." In his clown act, HE is slapped by his fellow clowns for saying absurd things. This act becomes tremendously popular with the public. Bezano is a bareback rider in the circus who is teamed up with the beautiful Consuelo, who recently joined the circus to help her financially strapped father, Count Mancini. The two quickly fall in love, but Count Mancini has other plans. With the hope that his daughter might marry into wealth, he introduces her to Baron Regnard, who has recently left HE's wife. During his act, HE spots the baron in the audience and soon learns of Mancini's plans for his daughter. HE loves Consuelo, even after she playfully slaps him when he confesses his love for

her. Determined to keep her away from the baron, HE finds his adversary and Count Mancini in a room backstage. HE places an open lion cage behind the other door to the room. Then, after locking the main door, HE incites the baron into an argument, and his old benefactor recognizes HE. Mancini loses his temper and stabs HE with his cane sword. When they try to escape, they find the door is locked. As they open the other door, the lion attacks and kills both men. Mortally wounded, HE staggers out into the ring to perform his act. The clowns are unaware of HE's condition until HE falls and struggles to get up. HE dies in the arms of Consuelo, knowing she will be happy with Bezano.

CRITICS' CORNER

He Who Gets Slapped is a superb thing—and it lifts Seastrom to the very front rank of directors. . . . It is told clearly and directly in pantomime, as is the right function of the photoplay. True, there are subtitles, but in the main they are philosophic (and well written) comments upon the action. . . . Lon Chaney does the best work of his career. Here his performance has breadth, force and imagination. *Photoplay*

He Who Gets Slapped is undoubtedly a fine moving picture. . . . Unlike a great many movies made from stage plays, this one retains in a large measure the spirit of the original. . . . Lon Chaney puts into this part of the Clown his talent for impersonation. He plays it with all the pathos it calls for. *Liberty Magazine*

In picturizing one of last year's outstanding stage successes, *He Who Gets Slapped*, Victor Seastrom, as is his wont, has turned out an excellent production, but whether or not it will be considered excellent screen entertainment by the masses is another and different question. . . . Lon Chaney gives just the sort of performance one expects from him. *Harrison's Reports*

Occasionally an exceptional picture comes along which makes no attempt to pander to the box office. *He Who Gets Slapped* is one of this sort, an artistic masterpiece. . . . His [Chaney] make-up, as usual, is perfect, and he gives you a magnificent performance, full of pathos that brings a gulp to your throat. . . . and Metro-Goldwyn is to be congratulated because of their willingness to buy stories for their sheer artistry. *Movie Weekly*

Never before have I seen Mr. Lon Chaney perform so faithfully and so knowingly as he does in this part of the tragic clown. . . . Mr. Chaney is not an actor of solitary, grotesque parts. Both as the scientist, and later as the circus clown, he is shown to be abundantly equipped with those essential gifts which make for compelling characterization before the camera. . . . More than once it [the film] relies gloriously upon its audience's sense of perception by suggestion. And still, with all its fineness, I am inclined to think that Mr. Lon Chaney is the real triumph. *New York World*

NOTES
This was the first picture produced by the newly formed Metro-Goldwyn-Mayer Studios. The worldwide box office gross for the film was $881,000.

Chaney's performance was voted as one of the best picks of the month by *Photoplay Magazine*. *He Who Gets Slapped* was chosen as one of the top ten movies of the year by *Photoplay, Movie Monthly, Motion Picture Magazine, Cine Mundial*, the *Boston Post*, the *Los Angeles Times*, the *New York Times*, and the *New York News*. The theatrical version, produced by the Theatre Guild, had premiered at the Garrick Theatre on January 9, 1922. Richard Bennett played the role of HE.

The circus sequences took two weeks to film on the studio's biggest stage. George Davis, a popular European clown, coached Chaney in his clown role.[64] He also appeared as the man who tries to stop Raoul from entering Christine's dressing room in *Phantom of the Opera* (1925). Victor Seastrom called Chaney "the finest actor in the history of the screen or the stage."[65]

The film's title was parodied in Mack Sennett's two-reel comedy, *He Who Gets Smacked* (1925) and Earl Hurd's animated comedy, *He Who Gets Socked* (1925).

Prints of *He Who Gets Slapped* can be found at the George Eastman House in Rochester, New York, the Cineteca del Friuli in Gemona, Italy, the Cinemateket-Svenska Filminstitutet in Stockholm, Sweden, the Turner Film Library, and in several private film collections.

The film has aired frequently on the Turner Classic Movies cable television channel. *He Who Gets Slapped*, along with *The Monster* (1925), *The Unholy Three* (1925 version), and *West of Zanzibar* (1928) were shown on several PBS television stations in the early 1970s.

CHAPTER THIRTEEN

1925

The Monster

Metro-Goldwyn, 7 reels. 6,425 ft. *Released:* February 22, 1925. *Director:* Roland West. *Scenario:* Willard Mack and Albert Kenyon, from the play by Crane Wilbur. *Titles:* C. Gardner Sullivan. *Photographer:* Hal Mohr. *Film Editor:* A. Carle Palm. *Production Manager:* W. L. Heywood.

CAST

Lon Chaney (*Dr. Ziska*), Johnny Arthur (*The Under Clerk*), Gertrude Olmsted (*Betty Watson*), Hallam Cooley (*Watson's Head Clerk*), Charles A. Sellon (*The Constable*), Walter James (*Caliban*), Knute Erickson (*Daffy Dan*), George Austin (*Rigo*), Edward McWade (*Luke Watson*), Ethel Wales (*Mrs. Watson*).

SYNOPSIS

Johnny, the under clerk at Watson's General Store, has recently received his diploma from a detective's correspondence school. He puts his training into practice when his boss mysteriously disappears after an auto accident. The head clerk and Watson's daughter, Betty, are out for an evening drive when they have a car accident. To get out of the rain, they go to the deserted sanitarium up the road, where they find themselves the guests of Dr. Ziska and some of his unusual patients. Johnny happens by at the same time and he, the head clerk, and Betty become the subjects of Dr. Ziska's experiments. The doctor plans to use the brain of the head clerk in an experiment and attempts to strap him into an electric chair, but the man resists and, during the struggle, Ziska himself is strapped into the chair, then accidentally electrocuted by one of his assistants. Johnny manages to escape and bring help. They learn that Ziska and his assistants are actually the patients of the sanitarium who have overpowered the real doctors. Because of his bravery, Johnny wins Betty's love.

CRITICS' CORNER

Spook story that mingles laughs and thrills in rapid succession and includes a quantity of hair-raising stunts. . . . Johnny Arthur's part seems more important than Chaney's. *Film Daily*

The Monster seems to us Lon Chaney's best part of recent years, because his art comes from within and not from without. Let a man be an adept at putting on a papier mache torso, a putty nose and protruding teeth, and everyone is ready to proclaim him a great actor. In *The Monster*, he appears as himself, with no disfiguring make-up. . . . *The Monster* is a thrilling picture. *Movie Weekly*

B-r-r-r-r, this one will give you delicious creeps. . . . A real thriller. *Photoplay*

The starch seems to have been taken out of the pictorial conception of *The Monster*, by the inclusion of too much light comedy. The result is that, although this film possesses a degree of queer entertainment, it is neither fish, fowl nor good red herring. . . . Mr. Chaney looks as if he could have enjoyed a more serious portrayal of the theme. *New York Times*

An entertaining comedy and mystery play. . . . There are situations which make one laugh and which at the same time hold him in breathless suspense. . . . *The Monster* should also please. But it will prove too grewsome for tender-hearted people. *Harrison's Reports*

NOTES

It had always been believed that this picture was made by M-G-M, but was originally produced by Tec-Art and Roland West Productions. M-G-M distributed the film, buying the rights from Roland West in 1927. Tec-Art Studios was located on Melrose Avenue; it still stands today on its original location. The studio is now called Raleigh Studios.

Prints of *The Monster* can be found at the Library of Congress, the Turner Film Library, and in several private film collections. The film has aired frequently on the Turner Classic Movies cable television channel. *The Monster*, along with *He Who Gets Slapped* (1924), *The Unholy Three* (1925 version), and *West of Zanzibar* (1928) were shown on several PBS television stations in the early 1970s.

The Unholy Three

Metro-Goldwyn-Mayer, 7 reels. 6,948 ft. *Released:* August 16, 1925. *Picture Code No.:* 217. *In Production:* December 20, 1924, to January 17, 1925, 25 days. *Presented by:* Louis B. Mayer. *Producer:* Irving G. Thalberg. *Director:* Tod Browning. *Scenario:* Waldemar Young, from the novel by Clarence A. Robbins. *Photographer:* David Kesson. *Sets:* Cedric Gibbons and Joseph Wright. *Film Editor:* Daniel J. Gray. *Cost of Production:* $114,00. *Profit:* $328,000.

CAST

Lon Chaney (*Echo*), Mae Busch (*Rosie*), Matt Moore (*Hector MacDonald*), Victor McLaglen (*Hercules*), Harry Earles (*Tweedledee*), Matthew Betz (*Regan*), Edward Connelly (*Judge*), William Humphreys (*Defense Attorney*), A.E. Warren (*Prosecuting Attorney*), John Merkyl (*Jeweler*), Charles Wellesley (*John Arlington*), Percy Williams (*Butler*), Lou Morrison (*Commissioner of Police*), Walter Perry (*Announcer in Dime Museum*), Alice Julian (*Fat Lady*), Walter P. Cole (*Human Skeleton*), Peter Kortos (*Sword Swallower*), Vera Vance (*Dancer*), Mickey McBan (*Boy Watching Hercules' Act*), Louis Shank (*Newsboy*). *Cut from Release Print*: Violet Crane (*Arlington Baby*), Marjorie Morton (*Mrs. Arlington*).

SYNOPSIS

Tweedledee (a midget), Hercules (a strongman), and Echo (a ventriloquist) perform in a local sideshow, while Rosie, Echo's sweetheart, picks the pockets of unsuspecting patrons. When the sideshow is shut down by the police, the three men form an alliance to commit robberies, calling themselves the Unholy Three. Using a bird store as their front, Echo poses as a kindly old woman who sells talking parrots. Using his skill as a ventriloquist to convince the customer that the birds really talk, he is also ensuring that there will be the expected complaints that the birds don't talk when they are taken home. Disguised as the old woman, Echo then goes to the customer's house pushing Tweedledee, masquerading as a baby in a baby carriage. Echo uses his ventriloquism to make the bird "speak" again, satisfying the customer. The criminals are then able to look over the premises with an eye to returning later to rob the home. They hire naive Hector MacDonald to work in the store, and he falls in love with Rosie. Echo's jealousy gets the better of him when he learns that Rosie loves Hector and has accepted his proposal of marriage. Meanwhile, the trio's crime spree continues successfully until one night the midget and strongman commit a robbery on their own and kill one of the victims. The trio realize that they could be caught, so they plant the jewels on the unsuspecting Hector. Rosie learns of their plan and tries to warn Hector, but she is abducted by the trio, who flee with her to a cabin in the mountains. Hector is brought to trial and faces the death penalty. Rosie pleads with Echo to help Hector, promising to remain faithful to him in return. Echo goes to the courtroom and plants a letter on Hector's defense table, urging him to take the witness stand; when Hector does, Echo throws his voice and tells the story of the Unholy Three. But the prosecuting attorney gets Hector's testimony thrown out. As the jury is about to go into deliberation, Echo stands up in the courtroom and confesses. At the cabin, Tweedledee overhears Hercules tell Rosie about the midget's plan to kill her and Echo. Tweedledee releases Echo's gorilla, but the strongman kills the midget before being killed by the great ape. Rosie escapes. The court releases both Hector and Echo, and the ventriloquist joins another sideshow. Rosie returns to Echo, offering to fulfill her promise, but he realizes that she loves Hector and tells her to stay with Hector.

CRITICS' CORNER
Crowded with action, suspense and thrills, this latest Chaney film of the underworld stands among the foremost melodramas screened for some time. . . . The marvelous characterization and impersonation of Lon Chaney. As the villainous Professor Echo, ventriloquist, he is fine. And his transition to the character of Mother O'Grady once more proves him a master in the art of make-up. *Exhibitors Trade Review*

Powerful story that is as unique as it is big. Something far off the beaten path and gripping all the way, great picture. . . . Chaney again proves himself a master of pantomime. . . . A really great characterization to add to his already large list. *Film Daily*

It was President Wilson who used to read detective stories to ease his mind. He would have liked *The Unholy Three*. . . . The very complicated plot, the murder, the trial and the solution are too intricately contrived for reworking here. *Time*

If you really enjoy good crook melodramas be sure to see this. It is one of the finest pictures ever made, due to the able and clever direction of Tod Browning. . . . Lon Chaney gives a perfect performance as the ventriloquist. *Photoplay*

Not often does one see so powerful a photodrama as *The Unholy Three*. . . . It is a stirring story stocked with original twists and situations, a picture that teems with surprises and one in which the suspense is kept as taut as the string of a bow. . . . Mr. Chaney gives a brilliant, restrained and earnest performance. *New York Times*

NOTES
The worldwide box office gross for *The Unholy Three* was $704,000. The film was chosen as one of the top ten of the year by *Film Mercury*, *Film Daily*, *Photoplay*, *Movie Monthly*, *Motion Picture*, *Screenland*, *Harrison's Re-*

ports, *Motion Picture Bulletin, National Board of Review, New Yorker, Life,* the *New York Times,* and the *Los Angeles Times.* Chaney's performance was voted as one of the best picks of the month by *Photoplay.*

Scenes of Tweedledee choking the Arlington baby and Hercules killing her father were cut from the final release print.

Unlike the Mack Sennett comedies that simply parodied the film title, Hal Roach produced a two-reel comedy, *The Uneasy Three,* starring Charley Chase in 1925. The plot, which featured Bull Montana in the strongman role and Katherine Grant in the Mae Busch role, was very similar to the Chaney film.[66]

Prints of *The Unholy Three* are housed at the Museum of Modern Art in New York City, the George Eastman House in Rochester, New York, the Cinematheque Royale in Brussels, Belgium, the Cinemateket-Svenska in Stockholm, Sweden, the Turner Film Library, and in several private film collections.

The film has aired frequently on the Turner Classic Movies cable television channel. *The Unholy Three,* along with *He Who Gets Slapped* (1924), *The Monster* (1925) and *West of Zanzibar* (1928) were shown on several PBS television stations in the early 1970s.

Phantom of the Opera

Universal/Jewel, 10 reels. 8,464 ft. *Released:* September 6, 1925. *Picture Code No.:* 4159 (the number was changed to 5019 for the 1929 reissue). *In Production:* October 29, 1924, to early January 1925. Originally released with Technicolor sequences. *Presented by:* Carl Laemmle. *Director:* Rupert Julian. *Supplemental Director:* Edward Sedgwick. *Scenario:* Elliott Clawson, from the novel by Gaston Leroux. *Titles:* Walter Anthony. *Photographer:* Charles Van Enger, A.S.C., and Milton Bridenbecker. *Art Director:* Charles D. Hall. *Film Editor:* Maurice Pivar. *Assistant Director:* Robert Ross. *Ballet Master:* Ernest Belcher. *Cost of Production:* $632,357. *Profit:* $539,682.

CAST

Lon Chaney (*The Phantom*), Mary Philbin (*Christine Daae*), Norman Kerry (*Raoul de Chagny*), Snitz Edwards (*Florine Papillon*), Gibson Gowland (*Simon Buquet*), Arthur Edmund Carewe (*Ledoux*), John Sainpolis (*Phillippe de Chagny, Raoul's brother*), Virginia Pearson (*Carlotta*), Edith Yorke (*Mama Valerius*), Anton Vaverka (*The Prompter*), Bernard Seigel (*Joseph Buquet*), Olive Ann Alcorn (*La Sorelli*), Edward Cecil (*Faust*), Alexander Bevani (*Mephistopheles*), John Miljan (*Valentine*), Grace Marvin

(*Martha*), George B. Williams (*M. Richard, Manager*), Bruce Covington (*M. Moncharmin, Manager*), Cesare Gravina (*Retiring Manager*), William Tryoler (*Director of Orchestra*), George Davis (*Man at Christine's Dressing Room*). *Cut from Release Print:* Ward Crane (*Count Ruboff*), Chester Conklin (*Orderly*).

SYNOPSIS

Mysterious things have been happening in the famed Opera House of Paris. There are rumors that the Opera House is haunted by a Phantom, which the new owners quickly dismiss. Christine Daae, the understudy for Carlotta, the prima donna, has been vocally trained by what she believes is the Angel of Music sent to her by her deceased father. In truth it is the Phantom, who longs for her love. Christine becomes reunited with her long-ago lover, Raoul, who wants to marry her. The new owners fail to heed the Phantom's letters demanding that Christine perform the lead in *Faust*, so the Phantom releases the massive chandelier above the unsuspecting audience. During the ensuing commotion, the Phantom beckons Christine to come to him through the mirror in her dressing room. She follows this masked man five tiers below the Opera House and across a black lake to his domain. While he plays the organ, Christine rips off his mask to see his face. Her dreams of a handsome mentor are shattered when she sees the face of a living skull. After Christine pleads with him, the Phantom releases her so that she may sing in the Opera once again, but he warns her never to see her lover, Raoul. At the Masquerade Ball in the Opera, Christine and Raoul meet, and she tells him of her experiences. The Phantom, dressed as Red Death, watches them and learns of their plan to flee Paris after tomorrow night's performance. The following night, however, the Phantom kidnaps Christine as the lights in the Opera House go out. Raoul, along with Ledoux of the secret police, follows the Phantom's trail. They fall into the room of many mirrors, an old torture chamber. The Phantom hears their voices and with a flick of a switch, the room of many mirrors radiates intense heat. The two men escape through a trap door that leads them under the Phantom's domain, which is stacked with barrels of dynamite. Christine pleads for the men's freedom, and the Phantom relents. As Christine and Raoul are reunited, the Phantom's anger is distracted by a warning device. He sees a large mob, led by Simon Buquet, seeking revenge for his brother's death. The Phantom grabs Christine and seizes the waiting carriage. In a mad frenzy, the Phantom drives wildly through the streets of Paris until Christine falls out of the carriage. The Phantom stops, but the mob is close behind. They chase the Phantom to the bank of the Seine River, where the Phantom holds them at bay, pretending he has a bomb. When he reveals he has nothing in his hands, the mob kills him.

CRITICS' CORNER

A marvelous money getting picture. Chaney's make-up and character, while repulsive to perhaps some, is a great piece of work. *Film Daily*

A super ghost story has been made into a really great picture. It will thrill and chill audiences with its fascinating horror. And they'll like it. . . . Chaney is wonderfully effective in the title role. His much heralded make-up for the part is sufficiently repellent to satisfy the greatest cravings. . . . He is indeed a forceful villain and at all times dominates the action. *Exhibitors Trade Review*

It is something of a pleasure to be able to sit back and hurl the word horrible at a motion picture star and still realize that the fellow is getting a dandy notice. . . . If this boy [Chaney] doesn't thrill you with his underground-kidnapping of the beautiful Parisian opera singer he will positively, and I guarantee it, send you home determined to leave the lights burning all night long. *New York World*

Universal has turned out another horror. . . . Lon Chaney is again the "goat" in the matter, no matter if it is another tribute to his character acting. . . . It is impossible to believe there are a majority of picturegoers who prefer this revolting sort of a tale on the screen. It is better for any exhibitor to pass up this film or 100 like it than to have one patron pass up his theatre through it. *Variety*

The Phantom of the Opera is entertainment, no doubt about that. Entertainment of the most shuddery, gruesome kind. There are spectral, ominous sets, a coffin, horrors a'plenty. But, as a whole, it disappointed us. . . . Chaney is, as usual, amazing and wonderful. *Movie Magazine*

If you have been looking for a thriller, the kind that will make your patrons' hair stand on end, *The Phantom of the Opera* is the one. . . . Mr. Lon Chaney's role is terrible; the make-up of his face is hideous; but he is fascinating. *Harrison's Reports*

The Phantom of the Opera is an ultra fantastic melodrama, an ambitious production in which there is much to marvel at in the scenic effects. . . . The narrative could have been fashioned in a more subtle manner and would then have been more interesting to the few. . . . Lon Chaney impersonates the Phantom. It is a role suited to his liking, and one which he handles with a certain skill, a little exaggerated at times, but none the less compelling. *New York Times*

NOTES

Phantom of the Opera was chosen as one of the top ten movies of the year by *Film Daily, Photoplay, Movie Monthly, Screenland, Motion Picture News, Moving Picture World, Exhibitors Trade Review, Reel Journal, Motion Picture Bulletin, Film Mercury,* and *National Board of Review*. Chaney's performance was one of the best picks of the month by *Photoplay*.

Chaney had optioned the rights to the novel in November 1923. During a meeting in New York in January 1924, Universal wanted him to make the film for $100,000. Relaying this to his business manager, Alfred Grasso, Chaney asked whether the film could be produced for that amount. In a reply telegram, Grasso stated:

> Read *Phantom [of the] Opera*. Do not think advisable attempt producing it without $200,000 available.[67]

Ed Wolff, who later appeared in such films *The Colossus of New York* and *The Return of the Fly*, played one of the mob members who, after the foot chase, was to grab the Phantom and throw him into the Seine River. Apparently, in his eagerness to grab Chaney, he mangled the star's make-up, which caused a delay in filming. Chaney went out of his way to make Wolff feel at ease, even inviting him into his dressing room as he touched up his make-up.[68]

After completion of the film, it was previewed in Los Angeles. The audience felt there was too much suspense in the picture and suggested adding some comedy to "lighten up" the film. Universal promptly recut *Phantom of the Opera*, canceling the February New York premiere. After filming of additional scenes, including the climatic carriage chase, the movie was premiered in San Francisco at the Curran Theatre. Unfortunately, *Phantom of the Opera* did not perform well and, after a four-week run, the picture was pulled and reedited. It premiered at the Astor Theatre in New York on September 6, 1925, to mixed reviews. The final budget, because of the many retakes, was $632,357.[69]

A recut *Phantom of the Opera* was reissued with sound effects, musical score, and talking sequences. The Universal Picture Code Book lists the reissue release date as December 15, 1929. Chaney did not speak in this version.

The film was shown on the Sony JumboTron Screen in Times Square in New York City on October 31, 1993, by special arrangement with Kino International. It marked the first time a full-length film was shown on the large-screen television.[70]

Universal remade *Phantom of the Opera* in 1943 and 1962 with Claude Rains and Herbert Lom playing the title role, respectively. The Gaston

Leroux novel was sent before the cameras three more times: in 1983, with Maximilian Schell as the Phantom; a 1990 version with Charles Dance as the title character and Burt Lancaster as his father!; and a gory and no crashing chandelier version featuring Robert Englund. Director Brian DePalma made a parody of the film in 1974, a rock-and-roll version entitled *Phantom of the Paradise*. Another variation of the Leroux novel is a 1974 television movie, *Phantom of Hollywood*. The story centered on a former movie star, played by Jack Cassidy, who is badly disfigured in an accident on a movie set and haunts his old back lot. He wreaks havoc with those who are tearing down his "home," and like his namesakes in the other versions, meets his demise at the end of the story. The highlight of the TV movie was footage of many sets from the M-G-M lot being razed to make way for a housing development.

Numerous prints of both the 1925 and 1929 versions can be found in private film collections. Other prints are housed at the UCLA Film and Television Archive, the George Eastman House in Rochester, New York, the Museum of Modern Art in New York City, the Library of Congress, the Netherlands Filmmuseum in Amsterdam, the National Archives of Canada, the Cineteca del Friuli in Gemona, Italy, and the Cinematheque Royale in Brussels, Belgium.

Phantom of the Opera was also released on laser disc by Image Entertainment and Lumavision, and Kino Video released a print to the videotape market in 1995.

Tower of Lies

Metro-Goldwyn-Mayer, 7 reels. 6,753 ft. *Released:* October 11, 1925. *Picture Code No.:* 235. *In Production:* May 5, 1925, to July 2, 1925, 53 days. *Producer:* Irving G. Thalberg. *Director:* Victor Seastrom. *Scenario:* Agnes Christine Johnson, from the novel *The Emperor of Portugallia* by Selma Lagerlof. *Titles:* Marian Ainslee and Ruth Cummings. *Photographer:* Percy Hilburn. *Sets:* Cedric Gibbons and James Basevi. *Cost of Production:* $185,000. *Profit:* $271,000.

CAST

Norma Shearer (*Goldie*), Lon Chaney (*Jan*), Ian Keith (*Lars*), Claire McDowell (*Katrina*), William Haines (*August*), David Torrance (*Eric*), Anne Schaffer (*Helma*), Leo White (*Peddler*), Bodil Rosing (*Midwife*), Mary Jane Irving (*Little Girl*), Adele Watson (*Farmer's Wife*), Edward Connelly (*Curate*).

SYNOPSIS

Until the birth of his daughter, Goldie, Jan knew nothing but hard work. He becomes a doting father, often playing a game with Goldie in which he imagines he is the emperor of a fictional kingdom. Goldie grows up to become a beautiful woman and is the object of the affections of August and Lars. When Lars' uncle is killed by a falling tree, Lars inherits his estate, which contains the lease on many farms, including Jan's property. Lars demands payment on all notes immediately. To prevent her parents' eviction, Goldie goes to the city to earn money, but she is followed by Lars. The money arrives, allowing Jan to keep his property, but his daughter fails to return. Jan keeps hoping for his daughter's return but eventually loses his sanity. He plays the old childhood game with the village children, pretending to be the mythical emperor. When Goldie finally returns, gossip surrounds her virtue because of her fine clothes. When it is suspected that Lars may have led her into prostitution, Goldie can no longer stand the gossip and prepares to return to the city. She leaves for the steamship, with Jan following her. He falls off the pier and drowns. When the ship is quickly shifted into reverse to save Jan, Lars loses his balance and falls to his death. August, who has remained loyal to Goldie, pledges his love for her and they marry.

CRITICS' CORNER

If the director had been as concerned with telling the story as he was with thinking up symbolic scenes, this would have been a great picture. . . . The emotions are those of the theatre, not of life, in spite of the fact that both Lon Chaney and Norma Shearer might have made them real. . . . Heartily recommended for those who think most movies too flippant. *Photoplay*

Another of those really distinctive and rare artistic achievements. A very worthy effort and yet probably not the best box office. . . . Lon Chaney passes by his usual grotesque characterization and does something just a bit different. Excellent as the man who can see no wrong. *Film Daily*

To those who believe Lon Chaney needs the aid of unusual make-up to put his role over, *The Tower of Lies* will certainly prove a revelation. He does not resort to the grotesque—but from the first sequences, where he appears as the tiller of the soil who neither loves nor hates, just works, until the coming of a daughter who brings him a realization of love, to the last when he becomes a demented, old man, his interpretation is pathetically convincing. *Movie Magazine*

Mr. Chaney's entire performance struck me as being a notable one. . . . I feared that he [Chaney] was destined to be the Richard Bennett of the screen—a skilled impersonator, a master of technique, but without that final touch of the actor's art that turns an impersonation into a characterization, that breathes real feeling into what is otherwise cold mechanics of acting. But, toward the close of the film, Chaney is far more than a mere artificer. He really is Jan, the gnarled, mad old peasant. *New York Tribune*

Some picture-goers may like this picture very well; others will not. It is a picture that will create a difference of opinion, for the reason that though Mr. Seastrom's direction and the acting of the players are masterful, the theme is not very pleasant. . . . Mr. Chaney does excellent work; he awakens warm sympathy in a role that is the exact opposite in nature to those he has been given in pictures lately. *Harrison's Reports*

NOTES

Portions of the film were shot on location in the Sacramento River Delta, Lake Arrowhead, and in the Laurel Canyon area of Los Angeles, California. The film's working title was *The Emperor of Portugallia*, the title of the novel, which had been published in Sweden in 1915. The rights to the story were purchased in 1922 by Metro Pictures.

The Tower of Lies was chosen as one of the top ten movie of the year by *Photoplay, Film Mercury,* the *New York Post,* and the *New York Morning Telegraph.* Chaney's performance was voted one of the year's best by *Film Mercury.*

It took Chaney three hours to complete his old-age make-up as Jan.[71] In spite of Chaney's films proving to be a huge success at the box office, Norma Shearer received billing over him in all the posters, lobby cards, and newspaper ads.

The worldwide box office gross for the film was $653,000. This is one of three films Chaney made for M-G-M that is considered lost.

1926

The Blackbird

Metro-Goldwyn-Mayer. 7 reels. 5,437 ft. *Released:* January 11, 1926. *Picture Code No.:* 249. *In Production:* 26 days. *Producer:* Irving G. Thalberg. *Director:* Tod Browning. *Scenario:* Waldemar Young, from "The Mockingbird" a story by Tod Browning. *Titles:* Joseph Farnham. *Photographer:* Percy Hilburn. *Film Editor:* Errol Taggart. *Sets:* Cedric Gibbons and Arnold Gillespie. *Wardrobe:* Kathleen Kay, Maude Marsh, and Andre-Ani. *Set Musicians:* Sam and Jack Feinberg. *Cost of Production:* $166,000. *Profit:* $263,000.

CAST

Lon Chaney (*Dan Tate, The Blackbird/The Bishop*), Renee Adoree (*Fifi*), Owen Moore (*West End Bertie*), Doris Lloyd (*Limehouse Polly*), Andy Mac-Lennon (*The Shadow*), William Weston (*Red*), Eric Mayne (*A Sightseer*), Sidney Bracy (*Bertie's No. 1 Man*), Ernie S. Adams (*Bertie's No. 2 Man*), Cecil Holland (*Old Man at Mission*), Eddie Sturgis (*The Bartender*), Willie Fung (*Chinese Man*), Mrs. Louise Emmons (*Old Lady at Mission*), Polly Moran (*Flower Lady*), Frank Norcross (*Music Hall Announcer*).

SYNOPSIS

The Blackbird is a notorious thief of London's Limehouse district. He disguises himself as the Bishop, the Blackbird's crippled brother, who runs a mission. This disguise serves as a perfect alibi from the police. The Blackbird is in love with Fifi, a local music hall favorite. His boorish manner is completely opposite that of West End Bertie's, another thief, who maintains a refined demeanor, and the two soon find themselves competing for the affections of Fifi. The rivalry becomes so intense for the Blackbird that he kills a Scotland Yard man and frames Bertie for the crime. Both Fifi and Bertie seek the advice of the Bishop, who offers to hide Bertie in his mission. When the two lovers are separated, the Bishop seizes the opportunity to alienate them from each other and proceeds to win the affections of Fifi. Polly, the Blackbird's former wife, informs him that the police know he, not Bertie, killed the Scotland Yard. Fifi becomes enraged when she learns this. Polly's jealousy leads her to bring the police to the mission. The Blackbird quickly runs into the Bishop's room and starts to change into his alter ego, faking an argument between the Bishop and the Blackbird while the police try to knock down the door. As the Bishop is about to open the door, the police come through, knocking him down, breaking his back. Polly comes to his aid and realizes that both the Blackbird and the Bishop are the same man. He refuses medical help, knowing it would reveal his identity, and dies in bed as members of the mission come to pay their respects to the man who helped them. Bertie and Fifi are now free to marry.

CRITICS' CORNER

Chaney in another masterful performance with crook story background that is both novel and interesting. Great suspense and dramatic action. . . . Chaney reaches his customary heights for unusual characterization. *Film Daily*

This is one of the finest characterizations to Chaney's credit. He doesn't resort to heavy make-up to put over his character. . . . As clever as Chaney is, Tod Browning's direction is just as remarkable. . . . Excellent entertainment and so mystifying that we'll wager you'll like to see it again. *Photoplay*

The Blackbird is a perfectly fine melodrama of London's Limehouse district, that convenient locale where we can always find crooks of the better sort. It was directed by Tod Browning, who directed *The Unholy Three*, and though I didn't find it as absorbing a tale as that unusual film, it was quite thrilling enough. When Lon Chaney takes to playing a double role, you may be sure that he will come to no good end. . . . it's a marvelous part for Chaney; he enjoys his villainy so. *Picture Play*

Chaney handles his two parts well and Waldemar Young's scenario has been so constructed that the unique dual role is plausible at all times. . . . *The Blackbird* is an okey picture—good for the first runs in the smaller houses. What's more remarkable about it is that Chaney who has recently had a great run of pictures (with a corresponding rise in fame), sticks to his more or less old line with outstanding success. *Variety*

Mr. Chaney's acting is wonderful, but the story is weak. . . . The attempt to produce another *The Unholy Three* success, therefore, has missed fire. The last part interests fairly well. Mr. Chaney assumes a Dr.

Jekyll and Mr. Hyde role. . . . In the "cripple" part, his acting is superb. . . . NOTE: At the opening at the Capitol last Sunday large lines were formed, even though the weather condition was very bad. It is evident that the picture will draw. *Harrison's Reports*

NOTES

The film's original working title was *The Mockingbird*. The worldwide box office gross for *The Blackbird* was $656,000. It was voted one of the best picks of the month by *Photoplay*.

Cecil Holland, who played one of the old men at the mission, was also in charge of the make-up department at M-G-M for many years.

Eddie Sturgis, who appears briefly as the bartender, appeared in two other Chaney-Browning films, *The Road To Mandalay* (1926) and *The Big City* (1928), as well as in *While the City Sleeps* (1928). Willie Fung, who plays the Chinese man with the young white girl, appeared in several other Chaney films including, *The Road To Mandalay, Tell It to the Marines* (1927) and *Where East Is East* (1929).

Prints of *The Blackbird* can be found at the George Eastman House in Rochester, New York, the Turner Film Library, and in several private film collections.

The Road to Mandalay

Metro-Goldwyn-Mayer, 7 reels. 6,641 ft. *Released:* June 28, 1926. *Picture Code No.:* 275. *In Production:* March 29, 1926, to April 29, 1926, 28 days. *Producer:* Irving G. Thalberg. *Director:* Tod Browning. *Scenario:* Elliott Clawson, from a story by Tod Browning and Herman Mankiewicz. *Titles:* Joseph Farnham. *Photographer:* Merritt Gerstad. *Art Director:* Cedric Gibbons and Arnold Gillespie. *Film Editor:* Errol Taggart. *Set Musicians:* Sam and Jack Feinberg. *Cost of Production:* $209,000. *Profit:* $267,000.

CAST

Lon Chaney (*Singapore Joe*), Henry B. Walthall (*Father James*), Owen Moore (*The Admiral*), Lois Moran (*Joe's Daughter*), Kamiyama Sojin (*English Charlie Wing*), Rose Langdon (*Pansy*), John George (*Servant*), Willie Fung (*Chinese Man in Bar*), Eddie Sturgis (*Bartender*).

SYNOPSIS

When his wife dies giving birth to their daughter, Joe sends the baby to live with his brother, Father James, a priest. Through the years, Joe has engaged in shady dealings and runs a notorious dive in Singapore. His face is scarred from a long-ago fight, and one of his eyes has gone blind. He secretly visits his daughter, who is unaware that he is her father, at a religious curio shop she runs in Mandalay. Joe promises his brother that he will soon quit his criminal dealings, obtain corrective facial surgery, and take his daughter away. One of Joe's associates, the Admiral, meets and falls in love with Joe's daughter. When Joe learns of the impending marriage of his daughter and the Admiral, he pleads with his brother not to marry them. When this fails, he kidnaps the Admiral just before the wedding and they return to Singapore. Joe's daughter pursues them to his dive in Singapore, followed by Father James. While waiting for Joe, she is almost assaulted by English Charlie Wing, a lecherous Chinese and an enemy of Joe. Joe intervenes and during a fight with the Admiral, his daughter stabs him. Learning of Joe's condition, English Charlie Wing tries to take the girl away from Joe, but he holds the Chinaman off until the Admiral and his daughter escape. Joe dies knowing his daughter has found happiness with the Admiral.

Critics' Corner

Not so much as a story, but lifted to melodramatic interest by the highly colored performance of Lon Chaney as *Singapore Joe*. . . . Chaney affects another of those bizarre make-ups. *Photoplay*

I went to view *The Road to Mandalay* with the preconviction that it would not please me, and I was delighted to find that my forebodings were not realized. For the kind of story it is, it is perfect, and Browning. . . . deserves only praise. . . . I was beginning to wonder if Lon Chaney could really act, but this picture cleared away the doubt. He can. *Film Spectator*

Unique regeneration theme worked out with some mighty powerful dramatic sequences. Exceptionally fine direction and great acting. . . . Chaney splendid, as usual. *Film Daily*

Outside of the technical arrangements, the marks of production, so to speak, which concern the settings, atmosphere, camera angles—and the straightforward progress of the story—this picture cannot be called any "great shakes". . . . Chaney saves it, however. He appears as a one-eyed derelict of Singapore, who rises from the depths only whenever he comes in contact with his pure and undefiled offspring—a girl reared in the sanctuary of sweetness and light. *Motion Picture Magazine*

They took a long running jump when they named the picture after Kipling's poem, because it has nothing to do with a "Burmah girl's awaitin'" or with "Come you back, you British soldier." It's a story of the underworld of Singapore. . . . Chaney has another of those characteristic roles. This time his deformity is a sightless, white eye. It is remarkable how this particular detail contributes a sort of mood and tempo to the whole production. . . . Chaney is splendid in a typical role. *Variety*

NOTES

The film's original working title was *Singapore*. Scenes that featured Chaney as a young and handsome Joe were deleted before the release of the picture. The worldwide box office gross was $724,000. Chaney's performance was voted one the best picks of the month by *Photoplay*.

Dr. Hugo Keifer, a Los Angeles optician, made the glass shield (similar to a contact lens) that Chaney wore to simulate a blind eye.[72] Two of these glass shields are in Chaney's make-up case at the Natural History Museum in Los Angeles.

A condensed version of *The Road to Mandalay* on 9.5mm with French title cards was later enlarged to 16mm. Prints of this version can be found at the Library of Congress, the Netherlands Filmmuseum, the Turner Film Library, and in some private film collections.

CHAPTER FIFTEEN

1927

Tell It to the Marines

Metro-Goldwyn-Mayer, 10 reels. 8,748 ft. *Released:* January 29, 1927. *Picture Code No.:* 266. *In Production:* June 7, 1926, to August 3, 1926, 57 days. *Retakes:* September 12, 1926, to September 16, 1926. *Producer:* Irving G. Thalberg. *Director:* George Hill. *Story and Scenario:* E. Richard Schayer. *Titles:* Joseph Farnham. *Photographer:* Ira Morgan. *Additional Photography:* Reggie Lanning. *Assistant Cameramen:* Cecil Cooney, Gordon Osbourne, Melio Caluori, Harold Lipstein, Bob Roberts. *Script Supervisor:* Harold Wilson. *Sets:* Cedric Gibbons and Arnold Gillespie. *Film Editor:* Blanche Sewell. *Wardrobe:* Kathleen Kay and Maude Marsh. *Assistant Director:* M. K. Wilson. *Second Assistant Directors:* Jack Tourneur, Arthur Rose. *Unit Manager:* Fred Leahy. *Still Photographers:* James Manatt, Homer Van Pelt. *Horse Wrangler:* Cy Clegg. *Set Musicians:* Sam and Jack Feinberg. *Cost of Production:* $433,000. *Profit:* $664,000.

CAST

Lon Chaney (*Sgt. O'Hara*), William Haines (*Pvt. "Skeet" Burns*), Eleanor Boardman (*Norma Dale*), Eddie Gribbon (*Cpl. Madden*), Carmel Myers (*Zaya*), Warner Oland (*Chinese Bandit Leader*), Mitchell Lewis (*Native*), Frank Currier (*General Wilcox*), Maurice Kains (*Harry*), Sgt. H. H. Hopple, USMC (*Marine*), Daniel G. Tomlinson (*Marine Major*), Willie Fung (*Chinese Man at Mission*), Dick Curtis (*Marine in Barracks*), M. K. Wilson (*Fight Referee*), Nola Luxford, Lori Bara (*Navy Nurses at Mission*), Buddy Rae (*Marine in O'Hara's Squad*). Sgt. Jiggs, USMC mascot, appeared as himself.

SYNOPSIS

En route to San Diego's Marine Corps Recruit Depot, "Skeet" Burns relates to a Marine general (traveling in civilian attire) that he plans to ditch the Marines and head to Tijuana to bet on the horse races. The general tips off Sgt. O'Hara at the train station, who attempts to take

Skeet to the Marine base but is given the slip. Several days later, Skeet shows up at the base without a dime and soon learns that being a Marine is tough work. He falls in love with naval nurse Norma Dale, who is also the object of Sgt. O'Hara's affection. After a rocky start, Skeet pledges his love to Norma before shipping out on sea duty. While stationed on Tondo Island, he is seduced by a local native girl, Zaya. Rebuffing her affections, he finds himself in a fight with the natives, but Sgt. O'Hara comes to his rescue. Later in Shanghai, Skeet meets Norma, who has called off their relationship after learning about the incident on Tondo Island. She seeks the advice of O'Hara, who, despite his personal feelings, urges her not to give up on Skeet. Norma is then ordered to go to Hangchow, the site of recent bandit trouble, to help with an epidemic. A few days later the Marines are ordered to evacuate the Americans from Hangchow, where Skeet and Norma are briefly reunited, before O'Hara's squad is assigned to protect the retreating escort at all costs. Here Skeet displays his courage and proves himself worthy of being a Marine. When his enlistment is over, Skeet and Norma marry and return to the Marine base to offer O'Hara a partnership in a ranch the couple own. The sergeant declines, proclaiming his heart belongs to the Marines.

CRITICS' CORNER
Excellent. It is, in fact, a better picture than any Mr. Chaney has ever been in. There are laughs and thrills, and in many situations deep emotional appeal. . . . Mr. Chaney's work is excellent. Eddie Gribbon, too, deserves mention for his comedy work. *Harrison's Reports*

A bear of a title, a bear of a story well done. . . . Chaney and William Haines so natural you forget it's a picture. *Film Daily*

It is of sure-fire hokum, but the M-G-M organization fell down woefully in handling it. It made a good picture, but could have been a rousing one if supervisor, scenarist and director measured up to the job they undertook. . . . Lon Chaney's performance in *Marines* is splendid. He is one of our very best actors and it is too bad that his leaning toward weird characterization is not curbed enough to allow us to see him in more such parts as he plays in this picture. . . . Lon has no superior on the screen as a pantomimist. *Film Spectator*

Lon Chaney's first appearance *au naturel* for many years and it makes one plead for more like it. He is a great actor and lifts himself out of the make-up artist class into real drama. . . . This picture will be a popular as any we have had in many a day, and will go down on record as one of Chaney's greatest. *Motion Picture Magazine*

Tell It to the Marines is a sure-fire boxoffice if there ever was one. It isn't $2 boxoffice stuff, but it is just what the doctor ordered when it comes to the picture houses. It's a special and that goes 100 percent. That it has Lon Chaney as the star isn't going to drive anyone away from the money window, for he certainly has a great boxoffice following, especially among the men. . . . The chances are that *Tell It to the Marines* will undoubtedly get from five to six months at the little Embassy and get money, too. When it reaches the picture houses it will be a clean up. *Variety*

NOTES

Portions of *Tell It to the Marines* were shot on location at the U.S. Marine Corps Recruit Depot in San Diego, California, aboard the battleship *USS California*, and at Iverson's Ranch in Chatsworth, California. The worldwide box office gross was $1,658,000.

The film was chosen as one of the top ten of the year by *Motion Picture Today* and the *New York Graphic*. The film, as well as Chaney's and Haines' performances, was voted one of the best picks of the month by *Photoplay*. While the *New York Times* did not chose the film as one of its top ten, it did single it out for honorable mention.

Because of his performance, Lon Chaney became the *first* actor to be made an honorary member of the United States Marine Corps. Sgt. H. H. Hopple, USMC, who appears in the film as a Marine, was Chaney's on-set technical advisor. The Marine mascot, Sgt. Jiggs, also appears in the film.[73]

Naval officers on the battleship *USS California* were shocked to see Admiral J. H. Hughes, commander of the Pacific Fleet, dining with a noncommissioned officer in the officer's mess, until they learned it was Chaney in costume.[74]

During the film company's stay at the Marine Corps Recruit Depot in San Diego, Chaney provided entertainment on several evenings by singing old songs from his musical comedy days, accompanied by his set musicians and long-time friends, Sam and Jack Feinberg.[75]

In 1937, M-G-M considered remaking *Tell It to the Marines* but never advanced beyond the discussion stage.

Prints of *Tell It to the Marines* can be found at the George Eastman House in Rochester, New York, the Turner Film Library, and in several private film collections.

Seventy-one years after making *Tell It to the Marines* at the Marine Corps Recruit Depot (MCRD) in San Diego, the film was given a special screening as the closing event celebrating the MCRD's seventy-fifth anniversary on June 19, 1997. Under the direction of CWO-3 Edward D. Harris, the Marine Band, San Diego, performed a special score to accompany the movie. Among the invited guests of Commanding General G. L. Parks was Chaney's great-grandson, Lon Chaney. A twenty-minute slide presentation about the making of the film preceded the screening.

Mr. Wu

Metro-Goldwyn-Mayer, 8 reels. 7,460 ft. *Released:* May 16, 1927. *Picture Code No.:* 301. *In Production:* November 30, 1926, to January 22, 1927, 41 days. *Producer:* Harry Rapf. *Director:* William Nigh. *Scenario:* Lorna Moon, from the play by Maurice Vernon and Harold Owen. *Titles:* Lotta Wood. *Photographer:* John Arnold. *Script Supervisor:* Willard Sheldon. *Sets:* Cedric Gibbons and Richard Day. *Film Editor:* Ben Lewis. *Wardrobe:* Lucia Coulter. *Assistant Director:* M. K. Wilson. *Set Musicians*: Sam and Jack Feinberg. *Cost of Production:* $267,000. *Profit:* $439,000.

CAST

Lon Chaney (*Mr. Wu/Wu's Grandfather*), Renee Adoree (*Nang Ping*), Louise Dresser (*Mrs. Gregory*), Holmes Herbert (*Mr. Gregory*), Ralph Forbes (*Basil Gregory*), Gertrude Olmsted (*Hilda Gregory*), Mrs. Wong Wing (*Ah Wong*), Anna May Wong (*Loo Song*), Sonny Lu (*Little Wu*), Claude King (*Mr. Muir*), Toshiye Ichioka (*Friend of Nang Ping*), Komaie (*Wu's Servant*).

SYNOPSIS

Wu's grandfather, a wealthy mandarin, agrees to let his grandson be taught the ways of the Western world. When Wu comes of age, he takes a bride; soon a daughter is born. Wu's wife dies in childbirth, and thereafter his daughter, Nang Ping, becomes the center of his life. When Nang Ping comes of age, it is arranged that she also will marry a mandarin, but she meets and falls in love with a young Englishman, Basil Gregory. He secretly visits her at her father's palace, and one day she reveals to him that she is carrying his child. A servant overhears the conversation and brings the news to Wu, who kills the servant. Wu confronts his daughter, who confesses everything to him. According to Chinese custom, he must take her life, which he does; then, because of his daughter's death, Wu seeks revenge upon the young man and his family by inviting Mrs. Gregory and her daughter, Hilda, to his palace. Wu is charming to the Gregorys until he reveals his plan that Basil will be killed and Hilda physically attacked. Mrs. Gregory offers her life in exchange for her children's, but Wu refuses. As he is about to strike a gong, signaling that his plans are to be carried out, Mrs. Gregory fatally stabs Wu and frees her children.

CRITICS' CORNER

Oriental melodrama improbable but it furnishes a lot of thrills. Attractive production creates proper Chinese atmosphere. . . . Lon Chaney an avenging Mr. Wu who suffers and makes others suffer in thoroughly convincing fashion. *Film Daily*

The appallingly slow tempo of this Chinese tragedy may have been calculated to reflect the calm and dignity of the Chinese spirit, the stoicism of the Chinese philosophy. But more likely it was designed to swell a very slight story to the proportions of a program picture. . . . Lon Chaney does not measure up to previous efforts. *Motion Picture Magazine*

From an artistic standpoint *Mr. Wu* cannot miss. But from a commercial standpoint it looks as though this Lon Chaney starring vehicle, even though the star is calculated to get them in, will not be a big box office attraction. . . . Chaney started by playing the grandfather of Mr. Wu in the initial scenes. Then Wu grew up and became a Mandarin with Chaney changing appearance and characterization in accord. It was a walk-away for him. *Variety*

In the pictorial conception of the play, *Mr. Wu*, the versatile Lon Chaney is in his element as a cultured but sinister Chinese mandarin, who, despite his Oxford indifference, when it comes to vengeance finds that he must abide by the letter of Chinese code. . . . Mr. Chaney is excellent in his performance, but his make-up might have been more effective, by less perfect eyebrows and more perfect Oriental eyes. His cunning is cleverly portrayed and this Mr. Wu is the personification of the man of culture who reverted to his kind. *New York Times*

Mr. Wu rises to sublime heights. But despite its failure to grasp its greatest opportunity, despite the mirth-provoking final shot showing Lon Chaney and Renee Adoree heading for heaven on a beam of celestial light—the silliest ending a picture ever had—*Mr. Wu* is a magnificent picture. . . . But the impression that stands out most boldly as I consider the picture in retrospect is the marvelous artistry of Lon Chaney's characterization. To me it is the greatest thing he has ever done on the screen. *Film Spectator*

NOTES

The ending in which Mr. Wu and his daughter ascend to heaven on a beam of light does not exist in any surviving prints. The worldwide box office gross for the film was $1,068,000.

Mr. Wu was originally a play in London and New York in 1914, with Matheson Lang playing the role of Mr. Wu. Matheson Lang played the title role in the 1921 Stoll Film Company version.

Script Supervisor Willard Sheldon was the guest of honor at the Silent Movie Theatre when the theatre presented the movie on May 25, 1996. It was the first time in 69 years that Mr. Sheldon had seen *Mr. Wu*.

Prints of *Mr. Wu* can be found in the Turner Film Library and in some private film collections.

The Unknown

Metro-Goldwyn-Mayer, 7 reels. 5,521 ft. *Released:* June 13, 1927. *Picture Code No.:* 305. *In Production:* February 7, 1927, to March 18, 1927, 35 days. *Producer:* Irving G. Thalberg. *Director:* Tod Browning. *Scenario:* Waldemar Young, from a story by Tod Browning. *Titles:* Joseph Farnham. *Photographer:* Merritt Gerstad. *Art Director:* Cedric Gibbons and Richard Day. *Film Editor:* Harry Reynolds and Errol Taggart. *Wardrobe:* Lucia Coulter. *Set Musicians:* Sam and Jack Feinberg. *Cost of Production:* $217,000. *Profit:* $362,000.

CAST

Lon Chaney (*Alonzo*), Joan Crawford (*Nanon*), Norman Kerry (*Malabar*), John George (*Cojo*), Nick de Ruiz (*Zanzi, Nanon's father*), Frank Lanning (*Costra*), John Sainpolis (*Doctor*), Mrs. Louise Emmons (*Gypsy Woman*). *Cut from the Release Print*: Polly Moran (*Landlady*), Bobbie Mack (*Gypsy*).

SYNOPSIS

Hiding from the police, Alonzo, disguised as an armless knife-thrower, performs in a Spanish circus. With his arms tightly bound to his sides, his freakish double thumb is concealed from everyone except his loyal friend and assistant, Cojo. Alonzo is in love with Nanon, the daughter of the circus owner. Nanon has a fear of men's hands and arms, but with Alonzo she is not afraid and so befriends him. Malabar, the strongman, is also in love with Nanon, but she rebuffs his advances because of her fears. Malabar, who thinks Alonzo is his friend, saves him from a brutal beating at the hands of Nanon's father. Believing Nanon will come to hate the strongman because of his advances, Alonzo proceeds to encourage Malabar to take Nanon in his arms. When Nanon's father discovers that Alonzo has arms as well as a double thumb on his left hand, Alonzo strangles the man. The murder is witnessed by Nanon, who can only identify the killer as a man with a double thumb. Cojo warns Alonzo that he could never have Nanon as a lover because she would not only discover that he has arms but also that he has a double thumb and is her father's killer. Alonzo therefore uses blackmail to force a doctor to perform a double amputation of his arms. Meanwhile, Nanon overcomes her fear of men's arms around her and falls in love with Malabar. When Alonzo returns, he has hopes and expectations that he and Nanon will marry. He is totally unaware of her change in outlook and is shocked and surprised when Nanon announces her plans to marry the strongman. Realizing he has maimed his body for nothing, Alonzo plots his revenge. In his new act, Malabar attempts to stop two horses on separate running platforms solely by the strength of his arms. Alonzo engages a brake on one of the platforms with the intention that the horse will tear the strongman's arm from his body. As Malabar's strength ebbs, Nanon attempts to quiet the rearing horse to save her lover. Fearing for her safety, Alonzo pushes her out of the way, and the horse stomps him to death.

CRITICS' CORNER

At the Capitol Theatre this week is presented a Lon Chaney picture which fascinates us, and then they make it so short that it left us bewildered and unsatisfied. . . . There is nothing that one can say of Mr. Chaney. His performances are always perfect. *New York Herald Tribune*

We think you will like it as an unadulterated shocker. . . . Like other Chaney pictures directed by Tod Browning, this has a macabre atmosphere. If you wince at a touch or two of horror, don't go to *The Unknown*. If you like strong celluloid food, try it. It has the merit of possessing a finely sinister plot, some moments with a real shock and Lon Chaney. *Photoplay*

Although it has strength and undoubtedly sustains the interest, *The Unknown*, the latest screen contribution from Tod Browning and Lon Chaney, is anything but a pleasant story. It is gruesome and at times shocking, and the principal character deteriorates from a more or less sympathetic individual to an arch-fiend. . . . Mr. Chaney really gives a marvelous idea of the Armless Wonder, for to act in this film he has learned to use his feet as hands when eating, drinking and smoking. *New York Times*

A gruesome and unpleasant picture. Like most films in which Lon Chaney and Tod Browning have been associated as star and director, it is artistically acted and skillfully directed. But those facts do not atone for the offence given by the feature to every normal-minded movie-goer. . . . Of Mr. Chaney's acting it is enough to say that it is excellent, of its kind. Similar praise might well be given the work of a skilled surgeon engaged in ripping open the abdomen of a patient. But who wants to see it? *Harrison's Reports*

A good Chaney film that might have been great. Chaney and his characterizations invite stories that have power behind them. . . . Another Chaney-Browning program release that will reinforce the value of this combination. *The Unknown* is a paradox, in that it is not as great a picture as it might have been, but will undoubtedly have its compensation in the gross rentals. *Variety*

NOTES

The film's original working title was *Alonzo the Armless*. The worldwide box office gross for the film was $847,000. *The Unknown* was chosen as one of the best picks of the month by *Photoplay*.

In some reviews, as well as on a studio credit sheet, Crawford's character is listed as Estrillita.[76]

Lon's feet were doubled by a man named Dismuki, who had been born without arms. Dismuki later toured with the Al G. Barnes Circus and Sideshow, billed as "The Man Who Doubled Lon Chaney's Feet in *The Unknown*," for a salary of $150 a week.[77]

The Unknown film was considered lost until a print was found in France in the early 1970s. Prints are housed at the George Eastman House in Rochester, New York (with English title cards), the Turner Film Library (with English title cards), Archives du Film du CNC in Bois d'Arcy, France, the Bulgarska Nacionalna Filmoteka in Sofia, Bulgaria, the Cinematheque Royale in Brussels, Belgium, Cineteca del Friuli in Gemona, Italy, Filmoteka Polska in Warsaw, Poland, and in several private film collections (with English title cards).

Mockery

Metro-Goldwyn-Mayer, 7 reels. 5,956 ft. *Released:* August 13, 1927. *Picture Code No.:* 320. *In Production:* May 19, 1927, to June 27, 1927, 33 days. *Producer:* Erich Pommer. *Director:* Benjamin Christensen. *Scenario:* Bradley King, from a story by Benjamin Christensen. *Titles:* Joseph Farnham. *Photographer:* Merritt Gerstad. *Sets:* Cedric Gibbons and Alexander Toluboff. *Film Editor:* John W. English. *Wardrobe:* Gilbert Clark. *Set Musicians:* Sam and Jack Feinberg. *Cost of Production:* $187,000. *Profit:* $318,000.

CAST

Lon Chaney (*Sergei*), Barbara Bedford (*Tatiana*), Ricardo Cortez (*Dimitri*), Mack Swain (*Mr. Gaidaroff*), Emily Fitzroy (*Mrs. Gaidaroff*), Charles

Puffy (*Ivan*), Kai Schmidt (*Butler*), Johnny Mack Brown (*Officer at Table*), Buddy Rae (*Russian Soldier*).

SYNOPSIS

Tatiana must deliver an important message to the Russian army during the 1917 Revolution. She meets Sergei, a dim-witted peasant, and promises him food and shelter if he will guide her safely to Novokursk, the Russian town where she is to deliver the plans. When she and Sergei are confronted by Bolshevik revolutionaries, Sergei claims the woman is his wife, although he receives a brutal whipping. After finding medical help for Sergei, Tatiana manages to secure him a menial position in the kitchen of the Gaidaroff family with whom she is staying. Then Sergei discovers that Tatiana has fallen in love with a Russian officer, Dimitri; and under the Bolshevik influences of Ivan, the cook, he comes to hate the countess and all rich people. When the army is called away, Novokursk is pillaged by the revolutionaries. The Gaidaroffs flee along with the other townspeople, leaving Tatiana alone with Sergei. He attempts to attack her but is stopped when the Russian army returns. All revolutionaries are ordered shot by Dimitri, but Tatiana pleads that Sergei be spared because he protected her. Sergei is overcome by Tatiana's compassion, and when the revolutionaries attack again, he proves his loyalty by defending her life with his.

CRITICS' CORNER

Star does good work but against a drab background and in a story that is generally not attractive. . . . Chaney first rate as the servant whose devotion knows no sacrifice. *Film Daily*

Chaney makes Sergei into an effective character. This star is the only film luminary who can play dumb gents minus sex appeal and ring the gong at the box office. Sergei is a big blunder and harelip man from the steppes with nothing to recommend him but Chaney's fine performance. . . . *Mockery* is hardly an authentic picture of the budding revolution but it is good melodrama held up to a keen edge of intensity by Lon Chaney's highly effective character playing. *Photoplay*

Like its central character, the narrative of *Mockery*, the latest production featuring Lon Chaney, is lumbering, dull-witted and, on the whole, unconvincing. . . . Mr. Chaney's individual efforts throughout this film are strikingly painstaking, and he undoubtedly looks the part of the greasy, long-haired rural derelict with a hare-lip. The fault lies, however, with Benjamin Christensen, the director, who has frequently called for action that is more surprising than logical. *New York Times*

Just like the last three or four Lon Chaney pictures—it is masterfully produced, but it is gruesome to the point of being repulsive. . . . Mr. Chaney again does wonderful work; but his part is extremely unsympathetic—he is presented as a peasant, filthy in body and dull in mind; and no one can feel sympathy for such a person . . . . Not for the family circle, and particularly not good for the children. *Harrison's Reports*

Lon Chaney is put through a routine of pug-ugly mugging, but even this flops, as somehow he hardly achieves the ferocious power of facial characterization he has often managed to convey in other productions. . . . The picture may be figured to draw on the strength of Chaney's box-office value the first half of the week. It lowers the star's batting average considerably. *Variety*

NOTES

The film's original working titles were *Terror* and *The Harelip*. The worldwide box office gross for the film was $751,000.

Chaney's performance was voted as one of the best picks of the month by *Photoplay*.

Johnny Mack Brown, who later became a popular Western actor, appears briefly as a Russian officer.

Prints of *Mockery* can be found at the George Eastman House in Rochester, New York, the Cineteca del Friuli in Gemona, Italy, the Turner Film Library, and in several private film collections.

London After Midnight

Metro-Goldwyn-Mayer, 7 reels. 5,692 ft. *Released:* December 17, 1927. *Picture Code No.:* 330. *In Production:* July 25, 1927, to August 20, 1927, 24 days. *Producer:* Irving G. Thalberg. *Director:* Tod Browning. *Scenario:* Waldemar Young, from a story by Tod Browning. *Titles:* Joseph Farnham. *Photographer:* Merritt B. Gerstad. *Set Design:* Cedric Gibbons and Arnold Gillespie. *Film Editor:* Harry Reynolds. *Wardrobe:* Lucia Coulter. *Assistant Director:* Harry Sharrock. *Set Musicians:* Sam and Jack Feinberg. *Cost of Production:* $152,000. *Profit:* $540,000.

CAST

Lon Chaney (*Burke*), Marceline Day (*Lucille Balfour*), Henry B. Walthall (*Sir James Hamlin*), Conrad Nagel (*Arthur Hibbs*), Polly Moran (*Miss Smithson*), Percy Williams (*Butler*), Edna Tichnor (*Bat Girl*), Claude King (*The Stranger*), Andy MacLennon (*Bat Girl's Assistant*), Jules Cowles (*Gallagher*).

SYNOPSIS

Unable to believe that Roger Balfour committed suicide five years earlier, Scotland Yard Inspector Burke has a plan to prove that Balfour was really murdered. Burke intends to prove his theory that a murderer under hypnosis will recreate his crime. Burke also uses the mysticism of vampires as a strategy to help ferret out the criminal. Since the death of Roger Balfour, his daughter, Lucille, has been looked after by Sir James Hamlin, Balfour's closest friend, who is secretly in love with the girl who is much too young for him. At first Burke suspects Arthur Hibbs is the murderer, but soon realizes that the young man is in love with Lucille and could not have murdered her father. Soon vampires are seen in the abandoned Balfour house, and Sir James suspects that Roger Balfour has returned as a vampire. Burke arranges the furniture at the Balfour estate exactly as it was when Roger was found dead, and with the menacing contribution of vampires in the abandoned Balfour home, Burke proceeds to hypnotize Sir James. Burke's theory is proven to be correct when Sir James acts out his killing Roger Balfour after his request to marry Lucille is flatly refused. Once Sir James is released from his hypnotic state, the vampire is then revealed to be Burke in disguise.

CRITICS' CORNER

Thrills and weird doings in profusion. Fine entertainment for the mystery lovers. Probably a trifle too spooky for the timid soul. . . . Lon Chaney is right at home in one of his unusual characterizations. Will please his following. *Film Daily*

Chaney is popular enough to drag them [the audience] out to see him here. . . . Tod Browning wrote it and Tod wasn't up to his usual good form . . . Several characters come under suspicion, which makes it ring with the necessary suspense. *Motion Picture News*

Lon Chaney is back, in a get-up which would make any sensitive girl quiver and quake on a dark night, but which doesn't require any contortions or self-torture. . . . This is a dark, foul mystery play, which has certain moment and certain elements as horrid as anyone could ask. But it's such a completely baffling mystery until almost the end, that you sit through it in a sort of creepy daze. *Motion Picture Magazine*

Lon Chaney has the stellar role in this mystery drama and the disguise he uses while ferreting out the murderer is as gruesome as any he has ever worn. The story attempts to prove that a murderer, when hypnotized, will enact again every detail of his crime. The suspense is marvelously sustained. Chaney plays a dual role, and when conventionally clad, is a little less convincing than usual. In the other role, perfect. *Photoplay*

Just like the last three or four pictures with this star—gruesome. Besides it has the disadvantage of having a nonsensical plot. . . . Mr. Chaney's make-up is at times hideous—enough to make one sick in the stomach. The picture succeeds in giving one a creepy feeling. . . . It should please the morbid. *Harrison's Reports*

NOTES

The film's original working title was *The Hypnotist*. The worldwide box office gross was $1,004,000.

London After Midnight marked the only time Chaney's make-up case ever appeared in a motion picture. At the end of the film, Burke is taking off his make-up for the Man in the Beaver Hat (the false vampire) as Lucy and Hibbs come to see him. Chaney's make-up case (according to production stills) can be seen sitting on a table.

Tod Browning remade *London After Midnight* in 1934 at M-G-M under the title *Mark of the Vampire*, with Lionel Barrymore and Bela Lugosi playing the two roles Chaney essayed.

This is one of most sought-after lost films from the silent era. It is also one of three films Chaney made for M-G-M—*The Tower of Lies* (1925), *London After Midnight* (1927), and *The Big City* (1928)—that is considered lost.

CHAPTER SIXTEEN

1928

The Big City

Metro-Goldwyn-Mayer, 8 reels. 7,277 ft. *Released:* March 24, 1928. *Picture Code No.:* 346. *In Production:* October 27, 1927, to November 19, 1927, 30 days. *Producer:* Irving G. Thalberg. *Director:* Tod Browning. *Scenario:* Waldemar Young, from a story by Tod Browning. *Titles:* Joseph Farnham. *Photographer:* Henry Sharp. *Art Director:* Cedric Gibbons. *Film Editor:* Harry Reynolds. *Wardrobe:* Lucia Coulter. *Set Musicians:* Sam and Jack Feinberg. *Cost of Production:* $172,000. *Profit:* $387,000.

CAST

Lon Chaney (*Chuck Collins*), Marceline Day (*Sunshine*), James Murray (*Curly*), Betty Compson (*Helen*), Matthew Betz (*Red*), John George (*The Arab*), Virginia Pearson (*Tennessee*), Walter Percival (*Grogan*), Lew Short (*O'Hara*), Eddie Sturgis (*Blinkie*), Clinton Lyle (*Mobster*), Alfred Allen (*Policeman*), F. Finch-Smiles (*Sunshine's Father*), George H. Reed (*Black Waiter*), Nora Cecil.

SYNOPSIS

Gangster Chuck Collins owns the Black Bottom nightclub in Harlem. When he learns that Red Watson, a rival gangster, plans to rob his guests, Collins outwits him by pulling off the robbery himself. Helen, Chuck's mistress, runs a dress shop as a front for his illegal activities and has just employed a naive girl named Sunshine, who knows nothing of Collins' criminal endeavors. After the robbery, she accidentally gives information to the detectives when they show up at the shop. Before acting on the information, the police wait in hopes of catching both gangs, and they follow Watson to Collins' nightclub. Collins' and Curly, his righthand man, escape before the police raid the club, taking refuge in Helen's apartment. It is there that Collins falls under the spell of Sunshine's goodness and decides to reform and return the stolen jewels and money to the police. Helen is jealous of the attention he is giving Sunshine and tips off Red Watson, who steals the jewels from Collins. Collins manages to recapture the goods and return them to police, and after he learns that Curly has proposed to Sunshine, he asks Helen to marry him. Greeted by Helen's eagerness, Collins retorts, "Listen! I ain't going to buy you nothin', I'm just gonna marry you."

CRITICS' CORNER

The Chaney-Browning team has made an altogether showmanly job of this melodramatic adventure in photoplay. . . . the Chaney fans and all fans will enjoy this one. *Motion Picture News*

Lon Chaney is a crook of no mean ability in this story. When one crook can step into a cabaret, undisguised, and capture the other crook's loot, conceal it in a dish of spaghetti and make his get-away, you have the acme of underworld intriguing. Lon wears his God-given face in this picture. The story is complicated but has good action. *Photoplay*

Lon Chaney's personality makes picture look better than it is. . . . Due to Tod Browning's capable direction and the finished performance of Lon Chaney, the picture manages to sustain fair interest. *Film Daily*

Minus horrid, blinded eyes, hunched back, and wooden legs, Lon Chaney remains true to his movie spiritual type. He never gets what he wants. Here he is a crook, smart, wise, set in a scenario complicated by the fact that everyone double crosses everyone. . . . It is all annoying. *Time*

Intelligent people will laugh at it; picture-goers of the rank and file may get some enjoyment out of it. One thing that is in favor of it at least is the fact that it is not of the gruesome sort, as the last three or four Chaney pictures have been. It is a crook melodrama, in which suspense is supposed to predominate. . . . Mr. Chaney is made ridiculous by being made to reform, and to make his confederates reform, too. *Harrison's Reports*

NOTES

The worldwide box office gross for this picture was $833,000. The exterior set of Chuck Collins' nightclub, the Black Bottom, was also used in as the nightclub in *While the City Sleeps*.

Clinton Lyle, who plays a mobster in *The Big City*, was one of Chaney's closest friends, dating back to their days in musical comedies. He also plays a gangster in *While the City Sleeps*. John George, who plays the Arab, appeared in several films with Chaney dating back to 1916, including *Outside the Law* (1921), *The Road to Mandalay* (1926), and *The*

Unknown (1927). He can be glimpsed as an extra in the bullpen sequence of Chaney's film biography, *Man of a Thousand Faces* (1957).

This is one of three films Chaney made for M-G-M—*The Tower of Lies* (1925), *London After Midnight* (1927), and *The Big City* (1928)—that is considered lost.

Laugh, Clown, Laugh

Metro-Goldwyn-Mayer, 8 reels. 7,064 ft. *Released:* April 14, 1928. *Picture Code No.:* 352. *In Production:* December 19, 1927, to February 2, 1928, 36 days. *Producer:* Irving G. Thalberg. *Director:* Herbert Brenon. *Scenario:* Elizabeth Meehan, from the play by David Belasco and Tom Cushing based on the Italian play *Ridi Pagliacci* by Gausto Martino. *Titles:* Joseph Farnham. *Photographer:* James Wong Howe. *Set Design:* Cedric Gibbons. *Film Editor:* Marie Halvey. *Wardrobe:* Gilbert Clark. *Assistant Directors:* Ray Lissner and Willard Sheldon. *Set Musicians:* Sam and Jack Feinberg. *Cost of Production:* $293,000. *Profit:* $450,000.

CAST

Lon Chaney (*Tito*), Bernard Seigel (*Simon*), Loretta Young (*Simonetta*), Nils Asther (*Luigi*), Cissy Fitzgerald (*Giancinta*), Gwen Lee (*Lucretia*), Emmett King (*Doctor*), Julie DeValera (*Nurse*), Helena Dime (*Lady at Luigi's party*).

SYNOPSIS

Tito and Simon are partners in a clown act that travels throughout the small towns of Italy. Tito finds a little girl who has been abandoned by her family and brings her up as his own child. When Simonetta grows up, he puts her into the act, against the wishes of Simon, who leaves Tito over this incident. It is then that Tito realizes that his fatherly affection for Simonetta has changed to passionate love. Certain that he cannot declare his feelings, he seeks a doctor to help him treat his overwhelming, forlorn emotions. At the doctor's office, he meets young Count Luigi, who is suffering from uncontrollable fits of laughter. The two men decide that they can help each other and become fast friends, and both are eventually cured of their afflictions. Tito finds Simon, and they reunite and become famous. Tito realizes that Simonetta and Luigi are in love, and he smothers his own feelings when he learns they are to be engaged. Seeing how despondent Tito has become, Simonetta insists on breaking off her engagement to Luigi to marry Tito. Knowing she does not speak from her heart, Tito purposely falls to his death while practicing his wire act, freeing Simonetta from her promise.

CRITICS' CORNER

It is not surprising, therefore, to note that the screen version of this *Laugh, Clown, Laugh*—which, it is only fair to tell you, was known as that several years before the inevitable song of the same name burst into accursed existence—provides a rather agreeable and frequently touching photoplay tragedy. . . . Mr. Chaney, discarding for the moment his usual propensity for distorted limbs, is a properly sentimental clown. *New York Herald Tribune*

This is the best work of Lon Chaney since *The Unholy Three*, and it is a great relief to have him minus his usual sinister make-up. His characterization of *Tito Flik* is perfect. *Photoplay*

The time has now definitely arrived when only a very small and insensitive urchin will be so mean as to laugh at one of Ringling's Pierrots. . . . Lon Chaney goes off on a tear in the part of the tragic Tito. While it puts some limit upon his metamorphic talent, he is able still to twist his face into many a contorted grin and to slobber frequently with sorrow. *Laugh, Clown, Laugh* is a trite picture and not a true one, but it succeeds surprisingly often in its lugubrious intentions. *Time*

Another romantic play with a semi-tragic finale, the fortunes of which are anybody's guess. In this case, Lon Chaney as the star should be almost an insurance of a draw. Star's name value is the film's best asset. Production is excellent in Herbert Brenon's best style. . . . Chaney does some splendid acting as the clown who makes the world laugh while his heart is breaking with a vain love. Sentiment sometimes gets a bit sloppy, but this actor always has the situation in hand and carries through some passages that call for dainty treatment and nice judgement. *Variety*

It is doubtful if Mr. Chaney has ever appeared in as good a picture. It is full of heart throbs. The story from the very beginning impresses one deeply; one feels that something worthwhile will happen in it. And one is not disappointed. . . . Mr. Chaney is superb as the clown. He makes one realize his mental state vividly. The closing scenes, where he is shown performing his death-defying act, and committing suicide, are the most pathetic of them all. . . . It should draw big crowds in any theatre and please them. *Harrison's Reports*

NOTES

Portions of this film were shot on location in Elysian Park, a suburb north of Los Angeles. The worldwide box office gross was $1,102,000. M-G-M also shot an alternative "happy ending" that does not exist in surviving prints. The existing incomplete print, in fact, has several scenes missing.

Laugh, Clown, Laugh was a popular stage play on Broadway, premiering at the Belasco Theatre in 1924, with Lionel Barrymore playing Tito. M-G-M was considering this film for Chaney as early as 1925 but held *Laugh, Clown, Laugh* back until sufficient time had elapsed after the release of *He Who Gets Slapped*.[78]

Julie DeValera, who played the nurse, was the premiere danseuse of the Imperial Ballet in Russia, and later at the Metropolitan Ballet in New York.[79]

Laugh, Clown, Laugh received an Academy Award nomination in 1929 for Best Title Writing, the first and last year for such a category.

While the movie did not make *Film Daily*'s top ten list, it was placed on its "Roll of Honor," a form of honorable mention. Chaney's and Ms. Young's performances were voted as one of the best picks of the month by *Photoplay*.

Prints of *Laugh, Clown, Laugh* can be found at the George Eastman House in Rochester, New York, the National Film and Television Archive in London, the Cinematheque Royale in Brussels, Belgium, the Turner Film Library, and in some private film collections.

While the City Sleeps

Metro-Goldwyn-Mayer, 9 reels. 7,227 ft. *Released:* October 20, 1928. *Picture Code No.:* 370. *In Production:* April 12, 1928, to May 18, 1928, 28 days. Released with sound effects and musical score (Movietone). *Producer:* Bernard Hyman. *Director:* Jack Conway. *Story and Scenario:* A. P. Younger. *Titles:* Joseph Farnham. *Photographer:* Henry Sharp. *Sets:* Cedric Gibbons. *Film Editor:* Sam S. Zimbalist. *Wardrobe:* Gilbert Clark. *Assistant Director:* M. K. Wilson. *Set Musicians:* Sam and Jack Feinberg. *Cost of Production:* $259,000. *Profit:* $399,000.

CAST

Lon Chaney (*Dan*), Anita Page (*Myrtle*), Carroll Nye (*Marty*), Wheeler Oakman (*Skeeter*), Mae Busch (*Bessie*), Polly Moran (*Mrs. McGinnis*), Lydia Yeamans Titus (*Mrs. Sullivan*), William Orlamond (*Dwiggins*), Richard Carle (*Wally*), Eddie Sturgis (*Skeeter's Driver*), Joseph W. Girard (*Captain of Detectives*), Fred Kelsey (*Detective in Shadow Box*), L. J. O'Connor (*Police Officer in Hallway*), Sidney Bracy (*Short Order Cook*), Sam and Jack Feinberg (*Men on Street*), Angelo Rossito, Eddie Kane, Buddy Rae, and Clinton Lyle (*Skeeter's Gang*), Scott Seaton (*District Attorney*).

SYNOPSIS

Dan, a New York City detective from the old school, is in love with Myrtle, a naive flapper and family friend. She has also caught the eye of

Skeeter, a well-known gangster. However, Myrtle is in love with Marty, a young man who has fallen in with Skeeter's gang. Skeeter is suspected of killing a jeweler, and Dan is more determined than ever to bring him to justice when he learns of the gangster's desires for Myrtle. Dan seeks the help of Bessie, Skeeter's former girlfriend, who has fallen on hard times, and convinces her to testify against her old lover. Dan arrests Skeeter and his gang, but Dan's case against Skeeter is dismissed when Bessie is found dead. Meanwhile, Skeeter sees Marty as a rival for Myrtle and arranges for him to be killed during a robbery, but Dan overhears his plot and is able to save him. Dan insists that Marty leave town, and Marty agrees after trying to have a note delivered to Myrtle. Skeeter intercepts the note and attempts to attack Myrtle in his nightclub but is interrupted when Dan shows up. Fleeing, Skeeter kills a police officer. When he tries to kill Myrtle, who can link him to the crime, Dan puts her up at his apartment for safety and soon professes his love to her. Out of gratitude, and because she does not know what has happened to Marty, she accepts his proposal of marriage. Dan and other officers corner Skeeter and his gang, and the leader dies in a rooftop gun battle with Dan. Marty returns to learn of Myrtle's agreement to marry Dan even though she doesn't love him. When Dan learns that Myrtle really loves Marty, he reunites the two lovers.

CRITICS' CORNER

While the City Sleeps is a better picture than its title, a picture which gives a reason for every thrill, which recognized the value of suspense and sudden change of pace. . . . Mr. Conway's direction, plus Mr. Chaney's splendid characterization, alone would insure success to this picture. . . . Mr. Chaney's characterization is carefully conceived and vividly portrayed, as only he could do it. In other words, we consider him one of the great figures of the screen. *Boston Herald*

Now and then Lon Chaney tosses his make-up kit over the fence and acts like a human being. He appears "as is" in this picture, which shows crook stuff at his highest tempo, dwarfing *The Big City* to the size of a newsreel, and proving that an occasional straight role is fine balance for big character actors. He gives a remarkable characterization of a tough dick. A well-knit story, exceptionally cast and directed. *Photoplay*

Though this is an underworld drama, the theme is exactly the same as that of *Laugh, Clown, Laugh*. And Lon Chaney is again the somewhat dilapidated looking would-be lover, who laughs while his heart is breaking. . . . Very exciting, but I think Lon Chaney should pick on girls nearer his own age. *Motion Picture Magazine*

Without even a limp or the suggestion of any make-up, Lon Chaney is to be seen this week at the Capitol Theatre in a thug's adventure called *While the City Sleeps*. Mr. Chaney is far better than the story. . . . It is Mr. Chaney who makes this picture at all interesting, for he gives a fine performance despite the weird incidents. *New York Times*

To begin with, Lon Chaney doesn't do at all in a semi-heroic role. You can't disassociate him from something monstrous and all the bizarre characters he has ever played come to confront the spectator. Good judgment ought to have barred Chaney from the role in the first place. Therefore, a misplaced star turns what might have been a stirring meller into second grade quality program output, wholly dependent on Chaney's name. *Variety*

NOTES

The film's original working titles were *Chinatown* and *Easy Money*. Portions were shot in downtown Los Angeles. The worldwide box office gross for *While the City Sleeps* was $1,035,000. It was released both silent and with synchronized musical score and sound effects. The existing print, which is the synchronized-sound version, is missing reel eight and exhibits signs of nitrate damage in several sections.

Richard Carle, Joseph W. Girard, Fred Kelsey, and Sidney Bracy, all veteran stage actors, also appeared in Chaney's only talking picture, *The Unholy Three* (1930).

Chaney's long-time set musicians not only worked behind the camera, but appeared in two sequences. The first one has them playing in the band at Skeeter's nightclub. The second sequence has them appearing as passer-bys on the street when Chaney discovers a very dead Mae Busch in front of the police station in a car.

Lt. Roy Harlacher of the Los Angeles Police Department served as Chaney's technical advisor.

The recently built City Hall building in Los Angeles made its movie debut in this picture. The building can be seen in the climatic rooftop gun battle. It would later be featured prominently in *War of the Worlds* (1953) and Jack Webb's *Dragnet* television series.

Prints of *While the City Sleeps* can be found at the George Eastman House in Rochester, New York, the Turner Film Library, and in some private film collections.

West of Zanzibar

Metro-Goldwyn-Mayer, 7 reels. 6,198 ft. *Released:* December 24, 1928. *Picture Code No.:* 378. *In Production:* June 25, 1928, to July 31, 1928,

31 days. Released with sound effects and musical score (Movietone). *Producer:* Irving G. Thalberg. *Director:* Tod Browning. *Scenario:* Elliott Clawson, from the play *Kongo* by Charles de Vonde and Kilbourn Gordon. *Titles:* Joseph Farnham. *Photographer:* Percy Hilburn. *Sets:* Cedric Gibbons. *Film Editor:* Harry Reynolds. *Wardrobe:* David Cox. *Set Musicians:* Sam and Jack Feinberg. *Cost of Production:* $249,000. *Profit:* $337,000.

CAST

Lon Chaney (*Phroso*), Lionel Barrymore (*Crane*), Warner Baxter (*Doc*), Mary Nolan (*Maizie*), Jacqueline Daly (*Anna*), Roscoe Ward (*Tiny*), Kalla Pasha (*Babe*), Curtis Nero (*Bumbu*), Chaz Chase (*Music Hall Performer*), Mrs. Louise Emmons (*Old Woman on the Street*), Rose Dione (*Owner of Zanzibar Dive*), Emmett King (*Stage Manager*), Art Winkler (*Stagehand*). *Cut from the release print:* Edna Tichenor (*Dancing Girl in Dive*), Dan Wolheim (*Man in Dive*).

SYNOPSIS

Phroso, a stage magician in an English Music Hall, loses the use of his legs after a fight with his wife's lover, Crane. His wife, Anna, returns months later but dies before Phroso reaches her. She has left behind a child that he suspects was fathered by Crane. He swears revenge on the man who maimed him and ruined his life and on his suspected child. An ivory trader, Crane, has returned to Africa, and Phroso follows his trail. Years later, he takes up residence in the Congo, using his magic tricks to mystify the local natives, who call him White Voodoo. He has the young girl, known as Maizie, raised in the worst dives of Zanzibar. Along with Doc, an alcoholic doctor, Tiny, and Babe, Phroso steals Crane's ivory. He then summons both Crane and Maizie to his compound. Maizie believes she is going to meet her father but is turned into an alcoholic wreck by Phroso. She witnesses a native funeral, where custom dictates that when the man of the family dies, either the wife or daughter must be sacrificed in a bonfire with the deceased. She falls in love with Doc, who is redeemed by her love. Phroso confronts Crane, telling him that Maizie is his daughter. Crane breaks into a fit of laughter and relates that Maizie is really Phroso's daughter. Overcome with grief, Phroso realizes that the natives intend to carry out his orders to kill Crane, and that the girl will be sacrificed according to their custom. While Maizie, Doc, Tiny, and Babe escape, Phroso uses one of his old magic tricks to stall for time. Holding the ceremony in his compound, he tells the natives that the white girl's funeral demands a coffin. Maizie is placed in the coffin, which has a revolving backboard that replaces

Maizie with a skeleton. The natives do not believe Phroso's magic, and the former magician cannot escape the fate from which he saved his daughter.

CRITICS' CORNER

Lon Chaney has gone cripple again for the sake of the public, but not for art's sake. Remembering his fine performance in a straight role in *Tell It to the Marines*, it seems a great pity that such a good actor should indulge in charlatan tricks. *Photoplay*

Not since that memorable screen melodrama *The Unholy Three*, have Messrs. Lon Chaney and Tod Browning, those eminent apostles of the macabre, been as successful in the demonstration of cinema terrors as in *West of Zanzibar*. . . . It is only fair to say that the film is a perfect vehicle for the unholy two. *New York Herald Tribune*

Lon Chaney is back at his old gruesome habits. This time he's a thing that crawls, dragging himself around on the palms of his hands with his useless legs behind him. And very convincing, too. . . . This is a mad, weird, grotesque, and completely nutty melodrama. You will get lots of laughs out of it, and I think it's far more entertaining than some of the Lon Chaney pictures that make sense. *Motion Picture Magazine*

This piece of filth is the stage play *Kongo*. And upon this play the Metro-Goldwyn-Mayer picture *West of Zanzibar* has been founded. How any normal person could have thought this horrible syphilitic play could have made an entertaining picture, even with Lon Chaney, who appears in gruesome and repulsive stories, is beyond comprehension. *Harrison's Reports*

In a grim, ingenious, but somewhat artificial tale, with a background of an African swamp festooned with cannibals, Lon Chaney once again returns to the impersonation of a cripple, a cheap music hall magician, whose legs are paralyzed by a fall. . . . It is a well concocted narrative and Mr. Chaney gives one of his most able and effective portrayals as he drags himself through scene after scene without using his legs. *New York Times*

NOTES

Upon its release, the editor of *Harrison's Reports* called for theatres to pull the film because of the lurid subject matter:

> If business is bad, don't attribute it to any business depression—people will, as a rule, deprive themselves of food rather than entertainment; what makes it bad is the quality of the pictures. What mother will allow her young daughter to set foot into your theatre again after learning that she saw a picture of the *West of Zanzibar* type?

The stupidity of producers seems to be unbounded. They know that ninety-five per cent of the people of the United States do not want such trash as they have been putting out. And yet they insist on putting it out. In no other industry do the manufacturers insist on producing an article that the consumers do not want. Only in the moving picture industry does this thing happen.

If you run *West of Zanzibar*, you will run it at the peril of alienating many of your regular customers. Demand that it be taken off your contract.[80]

The film's original working title was *Kongo*, the title of the play on which it was based. The worldwide box office gross was $921,000. During production, *West of Zanzibar* ran one day over schedule. It was released both silent and with synchronized musical score and sound effects.

Owen Moore was originally cast for the role of Doc, and Constantine Romanoff for the role of Tiny.[81] Warner Baxter and Roscoe Ward eventually played the parts.

Mrs. Louise Emmons, playing the old woman who watches Phroso go to the church to meet his wife, appeared in several small parts in many Chaney-Browning films, including, *The Blackbird* (1926) and *The Unknown* (1927). She had also appeared with Chaney in *Bobbie of the Ballet* (1916) at Universal.

West of Zanzibar was remade by M-G-M in 1932, under the original stage play title *Kongo*, with Walter Huston, who had essayed the role of Phroso on Broadway. In one sequence in the 1932 film, there is a brief clip from *West of Zanzibar*, showing Chaney (wearing a tribal mask) crawling out to a native burial ceremony.

Prints of *West of Zanzibar* are housed exist at the George Eastman House in Rochester, New York, the Turner Film Library, and in several private film collections.

M-G-M Home Video released *West of Zanzibar* (with the synchronized score), along with *The Unholy Three* (1930), on laser disc in 1993. The movie has been shown frequently on the Turner Classic Movies cable television channel. *West of Zanzibar*, along with *He Who Gets Slapped* (1924), *The Monster* (1925), and *The Unholy Three* (1925 version), were shown on several PBS television stations in the early 1970s.

Tell It To the Marines (1927). Lon and Eleanor Boardman.

Tell It To the Marines (1927). Lon, William Haines (holding rifle), and Eddie Gribbon (far right). This scene was filmed on the battleship USS *California*.

Tell It To the Marines
(1927). Lon and
William Haines.

Mr. Wu (1927). Claude King, Lon (in early age makeup of Grandfather Wu),
and Sonny Lu.

Mr. Wu (1927). Lon (as century-old Grandfather Wu) and Claude King.

Mr. Wu (1927). Lon and Ralph Forbes.

The Unknown (1927). Lon and John George. Note the "double thumb" on Lon's left hand.

The Unknown (1927). Lon and Joan Crawford.

The Unknown (1927). Lon and John Sainpolis.

Mockery (1927).

Mockery (1927). Lon and an unidentified player.

Mockery (1927). Lon and director Benjamin Christensen (standing under lights with white hat) prepare for a "dolly shot." The term refers to the large wheeled platform holding the cameras and lights. It allowed the camera to move with the actors and is still used today, although the device is more compact.

London After Midnight
(1927). Lon and Henry
B. Walthall.

London After Midnight
(1927). Lon and Edna
Tichenor.

London After Midnight (1927). Andy MacLennon, Claude King, Edna
Tichenor, Marceline Day, and Lon.

The Big City (1928). Lon and Betty Compson.

The Big City (1928). Lon, Marceline Day, and James Murray. The exterior set of the "Black Bottom" nightclub underwent a name change and served as the nightclub in Chaney's *While the City Sleeps*.

The Big City (1928). Lon and John George.

Laugh, Clown, Laugh
(1928). Bernard
Seigel and Lon.

Laugh, Clown, Laugh (1928). Lon and Bernard Seigel. In the early part
of the film, Lon wears a lighter base makeup to appear younger.

Laugh, Clown, Laugh (1928). Lon and Loretta Young. Notice the subtle graying of the hair to signify the character's transition of age.

While the City Sleeps (1928). Lon and Anita Page.

While the City Sleeps (1928). Lon and a very dead Mae Busch. The man looking over Chaney's left shoulder (holding glasses) is Sam Feinberg, one of Chaney's set musicians. The man on the far right without a hat is another friend of Chaney's and the film's assistant director, M. K. Wilson.

While the City Sleeps (1928). Lon and Wheeler Oakman (lying on ground).

West of Zanzibar (1928).

West of Zanzibar (1928). Lon and Jacqueline Daly.

West of Zanzibar (1928). Lionel Barrymore and Lon.

Where East Is East (1929). Lon and Lupe Velez.

Where East Is East (1929). Lloyd Hughes and Lon.

Where East Is East (1929).

Thunder (1929). Phyllis Haver and Lon.

Thunder (1929).

Thunder (1929). James Murray and Lon.

The Unholy Three (1930). Lila Lee, Harry Earles, and Lon.

The Unholy Three
(1930). Lon and
Charlie Gamora
(in ape suit).

The Unholy Three (1930). Ivan Linow, Harry Earles, Lon, and Lila Lee. Notice that not only Ivan Linow's shoes are built up for added height, but he is also standing on wooden boards that are covered by a carpet.

Lon Chaney's Home Movies (circa 1927; frame enlargement). Lon shows the title cards he uses in his home movies to a family friend. Hazel Chaney is in the background.

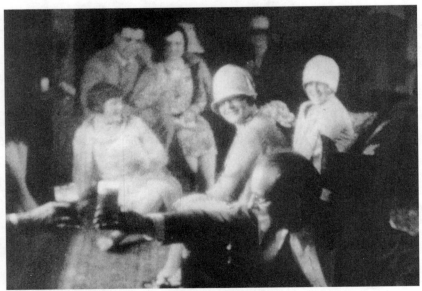

Lon Chaney's Home Movies (circa 1927; frame enlargement). Despite prohibition, Lon (front center) and family friends share a drink. In the background is Lon's son, Creighton, and next to him, Lon's wife, Hazel.

Man of a Thousand Faces (1957). Robert Evans, Elizabeth Flournoy, and James Cagney.

Man of a Thousand Faces (1957). Roger Smith and James Cagney.

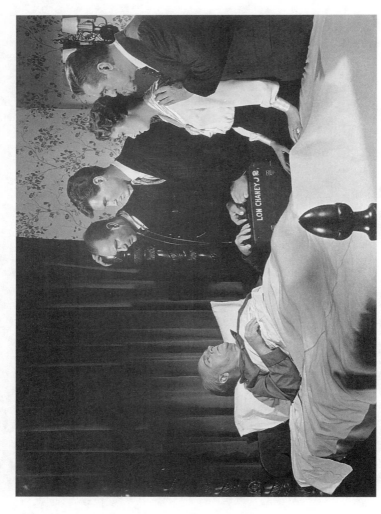

Man of a Thousand Faces (1957). The fictitious ending on Chaney's deathbed—it never happened. James Cagney, Jack Albertson, Roger Smith, Jane Greer, and Jim Backus.

This is one time that no motion picture camera ever captured of Lon Chaney: applying makeup to James Murray's face on the set of *Thunder* (1929).

Stars unwilling to pose for the paparazzi is nothing new. Upon his return from a vacation in New York, Chaney refuses to pose for photographers at Los Angeles Central Train Station (1928).

CHAPTER SEVENTEEN

1929

Where East Is East

Metro-Goldwyn-Mayer, 7 reels. 6,185 ft. *Released:* May 4, 1929. *Picture Code No.:* 415. *In Production:* January 5, 1929, to February 13, 1929, 33 days. Released with sound effects and musical score (Movietone). *Producer:* Irving G. Thalberg. *Director:* Tod Browning. *Scenario:* Richard Schayer, from a story by Tod Browning and Harry Sinclair Drago. *Adaptation:* Waldemar Young. *Photographer:* Henry Sharp. *Art Director:* Cedric Gibbons. *Film Editor:* Harry Reynolds. *Wardrobe:* David Cox. *Set Musicians:* Sam and Jack Feinberg. *Cost of Production:* $295,000. *Profit:* $283,000.

CAST

Lon Chaney (*Tiger Haynes*), Lupe Velez (*Toyo*), Estelle Taylor (*Mme. de Silva*), Lloyd Hughes (*Bobby*), Louis Stern (*Father Angelo*), Mrs. Wong Wing (*Ming*), Willie Fung (*Servant*), Duke Kahanamoku (*Wild Animal Trapper*).

SYNOPSIS

Tiger Haynes is a wild-animal trapper in Indochina and has the scars to prove it. His daughter, Toyo, is the light of his life and, like any father, he takes the news of her impending marriage to Bobby Bailey with mixed emotions. Bobby is the son of a circus owner who employs Tiger. With the return of Madame de Silva, Tiger's ex-wife and Toyo's mother, problems arise. While Toyo is delighted by her mother's return, Tiger is distrustful. Learning of her daughter's engagement to Bobby, Mme. de Silva attempts to lure the young man away from Toyo. Seeing his daughter's pain, Tiger releases a gorilla that Mme. de Silva had once treated badly. The ape attacks Mme. de Silva. Toyo urges her father to intercede to save her mother, but Tiger is too late; Mme. de Silva is killed. Although badly mauled, Tiger lives long enough to see his daughter happily married to Bobby and ready to start a new life in America.

CRITICS' CORNER

Good direction and acting may keep you from going home early in spite of the suspicion, later verified, that the best part of the picture was the opening sequence: Chaney catching a live tiger in a net which he and some Indo-Chinese helpers drop over it from a tree. *Time*

This picture simply couldn't happen any place but somewhere East of Suez, where the best is like the worst. And, believe it or not, for once Lon Chaney is a bad man with a good heart. *Screen Secrets*

Gather round, folks, for another Chaney bedtime story—something with a touch of Kipling and Poe. A very bad woman, the half-caste wife of a wild animal trapper, deserts her husband only to return later to steal the affections of the boy who loves her own daughter. Not nice at all, this woman, but Estelle Taylor plays her to perfection. Chaney is excellent and Lupe Velez lends fiery aid. *Photoplay*

Their [Chaney and Browning's] latest vehicle, however, though it may appeal to some of us through its silence, is a pretty feeble tale. . . . Mr. Chaney is always interesting to watch, but the story is too much in the mood of a cheap magazine sex tale of the Orient to be anything more than ordinary melodrama. . . . Whether or not Mr. Chaney doubles as the infuriated and rather comic looking animal [the gorilla] cannot be learned here. *New York Herald Tribune*

Not good entertainment! The endeavor of the producers to find suitable material for Mr. Chaney has led them to accept all kinds of gruesome stories. In *Where East Is East*, the main feature is the hero's letting loose of a gorilla on his ex-wife, mother of the heroine, tearing her to pieces. The actual killing is not, of course, shown; it is only implied. But the thought is there. And it is an unpleasant thought. *Harrison's Reports*

NOTES

The worldwide box office gross for *Where East Is East* was $920,000. During production, the film ran three days over schedule. It was released both silent and with synchronized musical score and sound effects.

Duke Kahanamoku, who played one of the animal trappers, later became an Olympic medal winner in swimming and a championship surfer.

Prints of *Where East Is East* can be found at the George Eastman House in Rochester, New York, the Turner Film Library (with the synchronized score), and in several private film collections. It has been shown frequently on the Turner Classic Movies cable television channel.

Thunder

Metro-Goldwyn-Mayer, 9 reels. 7,872 ft. *Released:* July 8, 1929. *Picture Code No.:* 425. *In Production:* March 3 to April 30, 1929. *Production halted:* April 30, 1929. *Resumed:* May 13 to May 23, 1929. *Retakes:* May 28, 1929, and June 1, 1929, 56 days. Released with sound effects and musical score (Movietone). *Producer:* Hunt Stromberg. *Director:* William Nigh. *Scenario:* Byron Morgan and Ann Price, from a story by Byron Morgan. *Titles:* Joseph Farnham. *Photographer:* Henry Sharp. *Film Editor:* Ben Lewis. *Script Supervisor:* Willard Sheldon. *Assistant Director:* Frank Messenger. *Unit Production Manager:* Jerry Mayer. *Still Photographer:* Bert Lynch. *Set Musicians:* Sam and Jack Feinberg. *Cost of Production:* $352,000. *Profit:* $272,000.

CAST

Lon Chaney (*Grumpy Anderson*), Phyllis Haver (*Zella*), James Murray (*Tommy*), George Duryea (*Jim*), Frances Norris (*Molly*), Wally Albright, Jr. (*Davey*), John MacIntosh (*Railroad Man*).

SYNOPSIS

Known for his determination to bring his trains in on schedule, "Grumpy" Anderson is the talk of the Chicago rail yards when his train is almost a half hour late. Along the way, he has refused to carry the private car of a wealthy businessman and has pushed his train to the limit. Zella, a nightclub singer and passenger on the private car, jumps into the cab of the train with the engineers and continues to ride with Grumpy and one of his sons, Tommy. Zella annoys Grumpy no end, but Tommy finds her attractive. Despite the delay, Grumpy manages to make up time and brings his train in on schedule, thus maintaining his reputation. Jim, Grumpy's other son, is killed in a train accident after working an overly long shift. Tommy blames his father for Jim's death and incites an argument while they drive the train carrying Jim's body. Their fight leads to an accident, and Grumpy as a result is relegated to the railroad's machine shop, where he oversees the repair of his own engine. Tommy, disgusted with railroad life, seeks out Zella, and a romance blooms. When the Mississippi River overflows its banks and causes widespread flooding, every engine and engineer is pushed into service to run supplies for the Red Cross. Grumpy and his engine are called in to help, and Tommy joins his father. Told that the tracks are under four feet of water, Grumpy ignores the warnings and drives his engine through the flood waters, saving not only Jim's widow and son but Zella as well. While Tommy and Zella are reunited, Grumpy, ever the professional, tends to his train.

CRITICS' CORNER

Weakest offering Chaney has yet made. Six reels built around a trick meller situation. Sound effects blah. . . . They had a trick situation where Chaney drives his engine through the flood district with tracks submerged and water rushing up over the old cab. The only kick in the whole film. But why try to build a feature film around that? *Film Daily*

Lon Chaney, who in his screen career has portrayed almost every calling, is now at the Capitol as a railroad engineer. Yesterday afternoon's audience seemed to find *Thunder* a good picture, even though it did appear now and then that coincidence was playing a bigger part in the railroad than the safety signal system. The picture is a silent one, save for sundry mutterings and moanings when trains are speeding across country. Sometimes the sound started before the train; sometimes the train got the jump and the sound came along like an echo. . . . When the picture gets away from railroad procedure, Mr. Chaney seems admirable. *New York Times*

Don't be skeptical. Lon Chaney actually drives that engine and, if you don't believe it, he'll show you his honorary membership in the brotherhood. His only disguise is grey hair and a moustache. As usual, he turns in a sturdy performance. . . . Snow storms, train wrecks and floods. Good entertainment. *Photoplay*

Mr. Chaney is antique and crotchety, rather than sinister, at the Capitol Theatre this week. He even goes in a bit for the quality described as "loveable," which certainly gives his latest film more than a touch of novelty. . . . A diffuse work, overwhelmed by detail, it can hardly be described as one of its star's best efforts. . . . Mr. Chaney gives a careful, sensible and entirely believable performance as the veteran engineer and the rest of the cast is helpful. *New York Herald Tribune*

There are many good incidents in *Thunder*, the story of which is entirely different from any story that has so far been given to Mr. Chaney—he is a railroad engineer this time—but the picture is so long that one becomes tired long before it is over. A careful pruning will, no doubt, speed it up considerably and make it hold the interest more tight. . . . It should give fairly good satisfaction everywhere. *Harrison's Reports*

Notes

Portions of *Thunder* were shot on location at the Chicago-Northwestern Railroad yards in Green Bay, Wisconsin; Chicago, Illinois; the Santa Fe Train Station and Roundhouse in Los Angeles; and San Bernardino and Inglewood, California. The worldwide box office gross was $1,018,000. The film ran 16 days over schedule during production, due to Chaney's illness. It was released both silent and with synchronized musical score and sound effects.

For years, *Thunder* was considered lost. While finishing this book, however, the author discovered that one to two minutes of footage from *Thunder* had been preserved by John Hampton, the former owner of the Silent Movie Theatre. The footage had remained buried in a can with other miscellaneous footage until the new owner of the Silent Movie Theatre, Lawrence Austin, discovered it.

This very brief film clip from *Thunder* was shown to the public, for the first time since the movie's original release, on May 25, 1996, as part of a Lon Chaney Super Evening at the theatre. The footage is that of Chaney in the repair shop of the railroad company. He regards the remains of his old engine, feels the pistons and drive shafts, and looks at some of the large wheels as the footage ends.

As this book went to print, additional footage (approximately 530 feet) was uncovered at the Library of Congress. The nitrate print, which should be restored shortly, includes scenes aboard Grumpy's engine featuring Chaney, James Murray, and Phyllis Haver. Other scenes include a brief clip at Grumpy Anderson's home, and James Murray visiting Phyllis Haver at a Chicago night club, as well as numerous shots of Grumpy's engine crossing the snow-covered country.

To make his character as believable as possible, Chaney obtained his engineer's certificate and became an honorary member of the Brotherhood of Locomotive Engineers.[82]

Thunder was Lon Chaney's last silent film.

CHAPTER EIGHTEEN

1930

The Unholy Three

Metro-Goldwyn-Mayer, 8 reels. 6,662 ft. *Released:* July 3, 1930. *Picture Code No.:* 494. *In Production:* March 26, 1930, to April 24, 1930, 27 days. *Retake:* April 30, 1930. *Producer:* Irving G. Thalberg. *Director:* Jack Conway. *Scenario:* J. C. Nugent and Elliott Nugent, from the novel by Clarence A. Robbins. *Photographer:* Percy Hilburn. *Art Director:* Cedric Gibbons. *Film Editor:* Frank Sullivan. *Recording Engineer:* Anstruther MacDonald and Douglas Shearer. *Wardrobe:* David Cox. *Cost of Production:* $279,000. *Profit:* $375,000.

CAST

Lon Chaney (*Echo*), Lila Lee (*Rosie*), Elliott Nugent (*Hector*), Harry Earles (*Tweedledee*), Ivan Linow (*Hercules*), John Miljan (*Prosecuting Attorney*), Clarence Burton (*Regan*), Crawford Kent (*Defense Attorney*), Richard Carle (*Barker at Sideshow*), Fred Kelsey (*Cop at Train*), Ray Cooke (*Sailor at Sideshow*), Joseph W. Girard (*Judge*), Sidney Bracy (*Butler*), Charlie Gamora (*Gorilla*). *Sideshow Performers*: Sylvester (*Sword Swallower*), De Garo (*Fire Eater*), Birdie Thompson (*Fat Lady*).

SYNOPSIS

Tweedledee (a midget), Hercules (a strongman), and Echo (a ventriloquist) perform in a local sideshow, while Rosie, Echo's sweetheart, picks the pockets of unsuspecting patrons. When the sideshow is shut down by the police, the three men form an alliance to commit robberies, calling themselves the Unholy Three. Using a bird store as their front, Echo poses as a kindly old woman who sells talking parrots. Using his skill as a ventriloquist to convince the customer that the birds really talk, he is also ensuring that there will be the expected complaints that the birds don't talk when they are taken home. Disguised as the old woman, Echo then goes to the customer's house pushing Tweedledee, masquerading as a baby in a baby carriage. Echo uses his ventriloquism to make the bird "speak" again, satisfying the customer. The criminals are then able to look over the premises with an eye to returning later to rob the home. They hire naive Hector MacDonald to work in the store, and he falls in love with Rosie. Echo's jealousy gets the better of him when he learns that Rosie loves Hector and has accepted his proposal of marriage. Meanwhile, the trio's crime spree continues successfully until one night the midget and strongman commit a robbery on their own and kill one of the victims. The trio realize that they could be caught, so they plant the jewels on the unsuspecting Hector. Rosie learns of their plan and tries to warn Hector, but she is abducted by the trio, who flee with her to a cabin in the mountains. Hector is brought to trial and faces the death penalty. Rosie pleads with Echo to help Hector, promising to remain faithful to him in return. After Echo leaves, Tweedledee overhears Hercules tell Rosie about the midget's plan to kill her and Echo. Tweedledee releases Echo's gorilla, but the strongman kills the midget before being killed by the great ape. Rosie escapes. In the courtroom, disguised as the old woman, Echo faces intense questioning by the prosecuting attorney. At one point, his voice slips into its normal deep tones, and the attorney rips off the wig to reveal his masquerade. Echo confesses everything and is sentenced to prison. Rosie and Hector see Echo off on the train that takes him to prison and it is there that Rosie promises to fulfill her part of the bargain. Echo realizes that she loves Hector and, as he boards the train, tells her to go to him.

CRITICS' CORNER

Lon Chaney back in talking version of film classic makes feature a great draw. Sound adds to picture's value. . . . Chaney and his varied speaking voices is the big draw in the billing. *Film Daily*

The finest thing about this picture is that it discloses Lon Chaney's natural voice just exactly as it should be—deep, vibrant, and perfectly poised. Chaney followers have eagerly awaited his first talking picture. Besides this, the silent version of *The Unholy Three* was one of Chaney's best, so this production was warmly anticipated. . . . You'll get thrills a-plenty! *Photoplay*

Chaney talks! And you'll talk, too, about Lon's first audible offering. . . . He's the same Lon Chaney with the added interest of a repertoire of voices to match his faces. *Screenland*

This was always one of the best picture plots ever seen and it still is, moving swiftly, logically, with the laugh and the shiver close together. . . . Lon Chaney proves once and for all that his popularity is based upon skillful acting and not grotesque make-up. *Motion Picture Magazine*

The bulletin matter regarding *The Unholy Three* is that in it Lon Chaney makes his formal bow to the more or less vocal screen. . . . Mr. Chaney has made a further contribution to the modern motion picture—although it may be a bit indelicate to mention it here. Like the two dozen students who swam the Hellespont and so ruined the beautiful legend forever, he has destroyed the effect of the phrase, "See your favorite actor; he speaks." For while others were loudly proclaiming the finding of a forgotten note, he quietly went fishing and came back with five. *New York Times*

NOTES

The worldwide box office gross for *The Unholy Three* was $988,000.

Chaney's performance and the film were voted one of the best picks of the month by *Photoplay*. While the movie did not make *Film Daily*'s top ten list, it was placed on its "Roll of Honor," a form of honorable mention.

George Hurrell, the noted still photographer, recalled that his first photographic sitting was with Lon Chaney. It was during the filming of Chaney's first and last talking picture that the two men met. Chaney arrived at the still gallery in his costume as Echo, with his ventriloquist dummy. Hurrell recalled that Chaney

> sat down, placed the dummy on his knee, and immediately assumed the character of Echo in the film. . . . Hurrell was impressed with this metamorphosis, an instantaneous change from the affable man who entered the gallery a moment before.
>
> During the shooting, Hurrell noticed that Chaney treated the dummy as an individual, not as a prop. When he wanted some shots of the star alone, he gently removed the dummy from Chaney's knee. "Now, how about some straight stuff?" Hurrell asked.
>
> Chaney's malevolent expression changed. He became affable again and laughed out loud. "Not today. I don't feel comfortable being photographed as myself." He got up, shook Hurrell's hand with a sort of finality, and tenderly picked up the dummy. At the door he paused and turned. "Good-bye," he said, plaintively, and disappeared down the stairs.[83]

Prints of *The Unholy Three* can be found at the George Eastman House in Rochester, New York, the Turner Film Library, and in several private film collections. M-G-M Home Video released this film, along with *West of Zanzibar* (1928), on laser disc in 1993. It has been shown frequently on the Turner Classic Movies cable television channel.

Unrealized Projects

The following consists of documented projects planned for Lon Chaney. The reasons why these productions were not produced vary. Many that Lon proposed for his film company were not made because of lack of funding. Those at M-G-M are more problematic; many projects were bought but for various reasons (script problems, scheduling, Lon's illness and subsequent death, etc.), the films eventually were put on hold.

The Sacrifice

Originally planned in 1921 as a film project for Lon's proposed film company deal with Abe Stern, Julius Stern and Louis Jacobs. It was described as an Italian love story written by Chaney and Perley Poore Sheehan (who later wrote Chaney's *The Hunchback of Notre Dame*). After negotiations collapsed, Chaney and his business manager, Alfred Grasso, offered the project to another independent financier, H. A. Berg. That deal also fell through.

God's Lightning

This project originally was to be produced by George Loane Tucker, director of *The Miracle Man*. It would feature Chaney as a deformed cripple with "a tremendous regeneration theme." With Tucker's death in 1921, the project was offered as part of Chaney's own film company deal, first to H. A. Berg in 1921, then to Associated First National in 1923.

Untitled Gouverneur Morris Story

The untitled story would feature Lon Chaney as a man who impersonates four or five different characters in the story. The project was associated with the 1921 H. A. Berg deal, and later with Associated First National in 1923.

The Man Who Lived Twice

Story written by Darryl F. Zanuck exclusively for Chaney. Universal Studios and Irving Thalberg had expressed interest in making the project. The reason why it was never produced remains unknown.

The Lancashier Witches

Around 1921, Chaney and English producer George Dewhurst were in negotiations to produce a film based on *The Lancashier Witches*. Chaney was to be guaranteed a salary of $20,000 for four weeks of work, and would be paid an additional $2,750 a week if the film ran over schedule. There was an option for one more additional picture before the expiration of the agreement at the same terms. The film would be filmed entirely in England with "a 1st class American Producer" [euphemism for director], and "will support L[on] C[haney] with 1st class leading cast of English actors and a leading American ingenue."[84] For reasons that remain unknown, the deal was never consummated.

Welford Beaton Original Story

This project, described as having a regeneration theme based on *Return Good for Evil*, was offered as part of the proposed deal with Associated First National in 1923.

Little Church Around the Corner

Based on the 1902 play by Marion Russell. Produced by Warner Bros. Pictures in 1923. Chaney was offered the role of Jude, but was forced to turn it down because of scheduling conflicts with *The Hunchback of Notre Dame*.

Where's Haggerty?

Based on the novel by Frank L. Packard, author of *The Miracle Man*. Part of the proposed four-picture deal with Chelsea Pictures Corp. in 1922. *The Hunchback of Notre Dame* was to be produced by the company, but the entire deal collapsed, probably because of financial problems.

The Thug

Based on the novel by Fred R. Beechdolt. Part of the proposed four-picture deal with Chelsea Pictures Corp. in 1922.

The Scar

Based on the novel by M. F. Gordon. Part of the proposed four-picture deal with Chelsea Pictures Corp. in 1922.

The Shooting of Dan McGrew

Based on the 1907 poem by Robert William Service. Produced by Sawyer-Lubin Productions in 1923. Chaney was offered the role of Jim but was forced to turn it down because of scheduling conflicts with *The Hunchback of Notre Dame*.

The Span of Life

Based on the stage play by Sutton Vane, Chaney was originally signed to play the role of Derringer, an ex-convict clown. Chaney signed a contract in May 1923 with Louis B. Mayer Productions, but the movie was not made. In 1926, two years after the merger of Metro and Goldwyn companies with Mayer's company, it was announced that Chaney would star in the film, along with Pauline Starke and William Haines. When M-G-M failed to produce the film as planned, they announced that *The Road to Mandalay* would be released in its place.

Hate

Based on the novel *The Four Stragglers* by Frank Packard, author of *The Miracle Man*. Originally announced by M-G-M for release in 1926, and later in 1927. In this film, Chaney plays "the feared and brutal leader of a band of Apaches that dominate the underworld of Paris, and woe to the foe who sees the flash of his quickly drawn knife. The fortunes of war throw Chaney and his enemies into an intimate entente, and finding themselves comrades in the same regiment, there is a war within a war that leads to drama of the most intense order." Tod Browning signed as director, but the project was shelved. *The Big City* was announced as the Chaney film to take *Hate*'s place on the release schedule.

Seven Seas

Based on the character Cheri-Bibi in the novel of the same name by
Gaston Leroux, author of *Phantom of the Opera*, the story plunges him
into swirling action that seethes aboard a convict ship on its way to
Devil's Island. A revolt among the prisoners throws into Cheri-Bibi's
hands the man responsible for his plight, and the man's sardonic revenge is tempered only by the softening influence of the girl who is the
one redeeming breath of beauty in his life. Originally announced as a
1927 release, it was later rewritten as a sound film and was to be Chaney's second talking picture. It was eventually made in 1932 under the
title *Phantom of Paris*, with John Gilbert.

Ordeal

Based on the high-seas novel by Dale Collins. Announced for 1928 release. The picture was scheduled to commence production after completion of *London After Midnight* (October 1927).

The Wandering Jew

Based on the popular novel by Eugene Sue about a man who is forced
to roam eternally without rest because he struck Christ on the day of
the Crucifixion. The May 5, 1921, issue of *Motion Picture News* announced that Louis B. Mayer Productions would produce a film based
on the novel. It later became one of many stories absorbed by the three
film companies during the formation of M-G-M. In 1921, there was no
announcement of who would play the title role. It was announced as a
1927 release for Chaney.

The Bugle Sounds

Based on the novel by Major Linovi Pechkoff of the French Foreign
Legion. Chaney and Wallace Beery were announced to star in the production as rival officers in the Foreign Legion; the Chaney character
dies valiantly destroying the captured cannon and killing the native
leader. Originally announced as a silent picture, set to go into production on August 2, 1929. George Hill was signed as director. Because of
Chaney's illness, several other actors were announced, but the project
was shelved. It was rewritten as a sound film and announced as Chaney's third talking picture. The title was eventually used for the 1941
World War I picture starring Wallace Beery.

The Sea Bat

Originally announced in May 1929 as a "weird story about tropical life and jungle voodoo." Tod Browning was signed as director. The project was made in January 1930 with Charles Bickford and Rachel Torres, directed by Wesley Ruggles. The movie had little to do with jungle voodoo.

Brother Officers

Based on a story by Lt. Commander Frank "Spig" Wead. Chaney would play a tough English army sergeant in India. He befriends young Lt. Gerald and they form a close friendship. The sergeant becomes a commissioned officer and he and the lieutenant vie for Lady Diana's hand. Hoping to dash his rival's romantic interest in Diana, Gerald convinces the Colonel that Chaney is the best man for the remote outpost along India's northern border. Chaney pulls strings and has Gerald assigned to his remote post. During a fierce battle, Chaney forgets his rivalry with Gerald and distinguishes himself in the line of combat. Gerald and Diana are reunited, and Chaney learns that his actions will be rewarded with a promotion. Originally announced as a silent film in June 1929. Fred Niblo was assigned to direct.

Sgt. Bull

Based on a story by Hans Kraly and Dale Van Every, was to feature Chaney as Sgt. Bull, an officer in Her Majesty's army in India in 1912, meeting a young lieutenant who becomes his rival for a girl's love. The climax of the picture takes place during the World War, when Bull has chosen the young officer for a suicide detachment. Bull later realizes the woman that the young officer is married to is his own former intended. When the officer refuses to leave the detachment, Bull shoots him in the shoulder and takes his place. Originally planned for production as a silent film in January 1930. Jack Conway was assigned to direct.

Cheri-Bibi

See *Seven Seas* for description.

Lon Chaney's Other Film Appearances

Aside from his film roles, Lon Chaney appeared in several newsreels and home movies. The following list is compiled from documented material known to have survived.

Life In Hollywood #3

This series was produced circa 1923–1924 and featured a tour of Universal Studios. It opens with an aerial shot of Hollywood, the camera flying over Universal Studios. The area leading to the studio commissary is shown, populated with numerous character types and familiar faces. The exterior of *The Hunchback of Notre Dame* set is shown before we see Lon Chaney (in a three-piece suit and cap) escorting a man on the set. He describes how he made his entrance in the epic film and proceeds to demonstrate the feat. His companion is amazed at Lon's ability, and Lon offers the man a cigar. They then walk to his car as Lon waves goodbye to someone off camera. The rest of the short shows other stars, such as Reginald Denny, Mary Philbin, and Baby Peggy, at work. Prints of this film are housed at the Library of Congress and in many private film collections.

1925 Studio Tour

The M-G-M studio tour features many aspects of the major studio at work. We are shown the developing lab, prop department, wardrobe, and the studio back lot. Many of the studio's stars are featured in close-ups as well as gathering on the studio lawn in one long line. As the camera slowly pans by, we see a bespectacled Lon Chaney in a lively conversation with another actor. Chaney's back is to the camera, and he briefly turns around to give the audience a quick glimpse of himself. Prints of this film are housed at the Library of Congress and in many private film collections.

Lon Chaney and His Wife at the Grauman's Chinese Theatre Ceremonies

This short shows Norma Talmadge breaking ground for Grauman's new theatre. In attendance are Charlie Chaplin, Sid Grauman, and Anna May Wong. Lon and his wife are briefly shown approaching the camera and smiling. This clip was sold for many years to film collectors by Blackhawk Films.

Movie Memories

Released in the early 1930s by Paramount, this short film presents clips from the studio's silent films, including a brief clip from *The Miracle Man* in which Thomas Meighan tells Betty Compson, Lon Chaney, and J. M. Dumont his plan to use the blind faith healer. The healing sequence from the film is also included, albeit condensed. This is the only known footage of *The Miracle Man* to exist.

Lon Chaney Showing His Camera to the Prince of Sweden and the Prince of Denmark

Lon Chaney is shown wearing his khaki uniform from *Tell It to the Marines* and walking toward a group of people while filming them with his 16mm camera. Another close-up shows him displaying his camera to the Prince of Sweden and Prince of Denmark as studio executive Louis B. Mayer watches. Where this brief clip originated remains a mystery. Most likely it was from a newsreel, possibly produced by M-G-M. It is included in an episode of the 1960s television series *Hollywood and the Stars*.

Lon Chaney's Home Movies

These films, not distributed to the public, show another side of the actor. The films were in the possession of William N. Dunphy, whose grandfather was a close friend of Chaney's. Taken around 1927, they show the actor, his wife, and the Dunphys at Saboba Springs, in the backyard of Chaney's Beverly Hills home, hosting a small party at their house (featuring a young Creighton Chaney), and at Saratoga Springs. Portions of the home movies can be seen in the Kino Video *Lon Chaney: Behind the Mask* (1995).

The Hollywood Revue of 1929

Lon Chaney does not appear in this film although entertainer Gus Edwards, accompanied by several women, sings "Lon Chaney's Gonna Get You, If You Don't Watch Out." The dance number features several male dancers sporting masks that somewhat resemble Chaney's famous visages.

Man of a Thousand Faces

1957

Man of a Thousand Faces

Universal-International Picture. *Released:* August 14, 1957. *Picture Code No.:* 1844. *In Production:* November 7, 1956, to December 27, 1956, 35 days. *Additional Days In Production:* January 9 and 10, 1957. *Producer:* Robert Arthur. *Director:* Joseph Pevney. *Scenario:* R. Wright Campbell, Ivan Goff and Ben Roberts, from a story by Ralph Wheelwright. *Photographer:* Russell Metty. *Art Directors:* Alexander Golitzen and Eric Orbom. *Sound:* Leslie I. Carey and Robert Pritchard. *Sound Mixer:* Bob Pritchard. *Recorder:* Don Cunliffe. *Mikeman:* Ed Hall. *Film Editor:* Ted J. Kent. *Musical Score:* Frank Skinner. *Orchestrator:* Joseph Gershenson. *Costume Supervision:* Bill Thomas. *Mr. Cagney's Wardrobe:* Marilyn Sotto. *Women's Wardrobe:* Rose Brandi. *Men's Wardrobe:* Truman Eli. *Make-Up Artists:* Bud Westmore, Jack Kevan and Vince Romaine. *Hair Stylists:* Merle Reeves and Virginia Jones. *Special Effects:* Clifford Stine. *Script Supervisor:* Adele Cannon. *Camera Operator:* Phil Lathrop. *Camera Assistant:* Ledge Haddow. *Key Grip:* Dean Paup. *Second Grip:* Ken Smith. *Gaffer:* Max Nippell. *Best Boy:* Virgil Proctor. *Property Master:* Bob Lazlo. *Still Photographer:* Roland Lane. *Set Dresser:* Julia Heron. *Publicist:* Lon Jones. *Assistant Directors:* Phil Bowles and Ray De Camp. *Unit Manager:* Edward Dodds. *Sign Language Technical Advisor:* Marjorie Ramsey.

Dance Director: Kenny Williams. *Dialogue Director:* Bill Chatham. *Running Time:* 122 minutes. Filmed in Cinemascope.

CAST

James Cagney (*Lon Chaney*), Dorothy Malone (*Cleva Creighton Chaney*), Jane Greer (*Hazel Bennett Chaney*), Marjorie Rambeau (*Gert*), Jim Backus (*Clarence Locan*), Robert J. Evans (*Irving Thalberg*), Celia Lovsky (*Mrs. Chaney*), Jeanne Cagney (*Carrie Chaney*), Jack Albertson (*Dr. J. Wilson Shields*), Nolan Leary (*Pa Chaney*), Roger Smith (*Creighton Chaney at 21*), Robert Lyden (*Creighton Chaney at 13*), Rickie Sorensen (*Creighton Chaney at 8*), Dennis Rush (*Creighton Chaney at 4*), Simon Scott (*Carl Hastings*), Clarence Kolb (*Himself*), Danny Beck (*Max Dill*), Phil Van Zandt (*George Loane Tucker*), Hank Mann (*Comedy Waiter*), Snub Pollard (*Comedy Cook*), Larry J. Blake (*David T. Stone*), Hank Patterson (*Scotty, Stage Door Man*), Marjorie Bennett (*Vera*), Leo Needham (*John Chaney*), Hugh Lawrence (*George Chaney*), Elizabeth Flournoy (*Thalberg's Secretary*), Billy Curtis (*"Unholy Three" Midget*), Robert Brubaker (*"Unholy Three" Director*), Harry Antrim (*Cleva's Birth Doctor*), William Hudson (*Dave Anderson, Reporter on "Miracle Man" set*), Russ Bender (*Divorce Judge*), Tom Kennedy (*Man in Audience at Eulogy*), Charles Cane (*Studio Guard*), Forrest Taylor (*Miracle Man*), James Gardinet (*Assistant Director on "Miracle Man" set*), John Bryant (*William R. Darrow, Jr.*), June Blair, Anne Carroll, Evelyn Ford, Della Malzahn, Carol Morris [Miss Universe of 1957], Jeane Strangis, Joyce de Brott, Louise Lane, Betty Jeffrys (*Chorus Girls*), Harold Bostwick (*Piano Player*), Michael Dale, Alan Pinson, Ken Terrell (*Reporters at Chaney's House*), David Sharpe (*Photographer at Chaney's House*), Helen Brown (*Mrs. Heinley*), Hal Taggart (*Chaney's Divorce Lawyer*), Donald Kerr (*Stage Hand*), Edwin Parker (*Studio Guard Greeting Thalberg*), Paul Powers (*Studio Executive*), George Pembroke (*Mr. Tait*), Frances E. Williams (*Louisa, Cleva's Maid*), Nicky Blair (*Cameraman on "Unholy Three" set*), Mike Lally (*Soundman on "Unholy Three" set*), Bob Forrest (*Policeman on "Unholy Three" set*), Charles Horvath (*Strongman on "Unholy Three" set*), Mike Portanova (*Assistant Director on "Unholy Three" set*), Walter Lawrence (*Stage Hand*), Jess Kirkpatrick (*Police Lieutenant in Hospital*), Herbert C. Lytton (*Emergency Room Doctor*), Jack Tessler (*Orchestra Leader*), Karl Linares (*Stage Performer*), George Ramsey (*Assistant Director Speaking to Locan*), George Peters (*"Hunchback of Notre Dame" Director*), Dave Kashner (*Flogger on "Hunchback of Notre Dame" set*), William Flaherty (*Assistant Director on "Hunchback of Notre Dame" set*), Forrest Phinney (*"Phantom of the Opera" Director*), Nancy Kilgas (*Leading Lady on "Phantom of the Opera" set*), Jerry Hartleben (*Lon at 8*), Lei Lani Sorensen (*Carrie at 6*), Clem Fuller, Walter Lawrence (*Cowboy Extras in Bullpen*), Virginia Eubanks (*Dowager Extra*), Fred Somers, Jack Chefe, Harry Wilson (*Extras in Bullpen*), John George (*Extra in Bullpen*), Sammee Tong (*Chinese Extra in Bullpen*), Anna Yip (*Chinese Woman Extra in Bullpen*), Spencer Chan (*Chinese Extra in Bullpen*), George Mather (*Bullpen Assistant Director*), Troy Donahue, Richard Emory, Robert Hoy, Joe Merrit (*Assistant Directors in Bullpen*), Ralph Montgomery (*Director in Bullpen*), James Seay (*Extra Casting Director*), Tom Gibson (*Studio Gate Guard*), Steve Drexel (*Messenger Boy*), Helene Drake ("*Laugh, Clown, Laugh*" *Script Supervisor*), Heinie Conklin (*Man in Audience*), Penny Parker (*Contortionist Double for Cagney in* "*Miracle Man*" *scene*), Bill Chatham (*Shadow Dancer*), Dorene Taylor (*Singing Double for Dorothy Malone*). *Cut from Release Print:* Natalie Masters (*Nurse*), John Halloran (*Proprietor of Small Saloon*).

SYNOPSIS

Eulogizing the great Lon Chaney after his untimely death, studio executive Irving Thalberg recalls Chaney's humble beginnings and his birth to deaf parents. Years later, Lon is a struggling performer in vaudeville with his singer-wife, Cleva. One night he learns of her pregnancy and takes her home at her urging to meet his family. Frightened by meeting his deaf parents and fearing their affliction may be hereditary, Cleva withdraws from her husband. They go to San Francisco, where Lon has accepted a job with the Kolb and Dill company. After the birth of their son, Creighton, the rift between Lon and Cleva widens. Despite the fact the child was born normal, Cleva leaves the boy in the care of his father as she pursues a singing career in the local cabarets. Lon is adamant that she stay home and take care of the young boy. Jealousy erupts when Cleva sees Hazel Hastings, a chorus girl in Lon's show, helping take care of the boy. After learning that Lon had her fired from her job, Cleva seeks revenge by swallowing poison on the stage while Lon is performing. When Cleva disappears from the hospital, Lon files for divorce and is forced to place Creighton in an orphanage. Down on his luck, Lon enters the growing movie industry as an extra, eventually obtaining character roles because of his unique ability with make-up. With the role of the fake cripple in *The Miracle Man*, Chaney becomes a successful character actor in Hollywood. Lon is reunited with Hazel and they soon marry, bringing young Creighton home from the orphanage. Lon Chaney becomes a major star after appearing in *The Hunchback of Notre Dame* and other hits, including *Phantom of the Opera*. Cleva suddenly reappears, begging to see her son, who believes his mother has died. Lon has never forgiven her and refuses. He is devastated when Creighton leaves home to live with her. Talking pictures arrive and Chaney is destined to become as big a star in the new medium as he was in silent movies. A recurring throat problem proves to be cancer, and Lon is given a few months to live. He is reunited with his son shortly before his death, and his dying gesture is to give his make-up kit to Creighton, launching him on his own career as an actor.

CRITICS' CORNER

The boys at Universal have come along with a biography of Lon Chaney, called *Man of a Thousand Faces*, and someone on the lot had the wit to put James Cagney in the leading role. This, in three words, saves the picture. . . . Cagney pulls off a minor miracle, projecting himself into the turmoiled life of Chaney and making it believable. *The New Yorker*

Man of a Thousand Faces, as presented in the Robert Arthur production, emerges as an unashamed soap opera tearjerker. This is not meant in a disparaging sense, for it is this very quality which will probably find favor with general audiences. . . . As Chaney, Cagney gives one of his most notable performances. He has immersed himself so completely in the role that it is difficult to spot any Cagney mannerisms. *Variety*

Cagney is overwhelming in his portrayal. . . . There is strong, almost melodramatic stuff in *Man of a Thousand Faces* and in the last analysis it is Pevney's exceptional direction that has prevented it from ever seeming anything but fine drama, highlighted and relieved by comedy and tenderness. *The Hollywood Reporter*

Thanks to a dandy performance by James Cagney in the role of the great silent-film star, Lon Chaney, there is drama and personality in *Man of a Thousand Faces*. . . . Joseph Pevney's direction has a curious affection for cliches, but Mr. Cagney rises above it. He etches a personality. *New York Times*

Man of a Thousand Faces is as delightful a surprise as finding a $20 bill at the back of a discarded wallet. . . . [The film] is honest, romantic, sometimes brutal, often ideal. I was held by every moment. . . . Cagney, always a player who gets far below the surface of a character, has never been more dynamic or appealing than he is as this star. *Los Angeles Examiner*

NOTES

The movie biography of Lon Chaney was filmed on the Universal-International Studios lot and on location in Toluca Lake, California. The movie was reissued in 1964.

All the theatre sequences were filmed on the original *Phantom of the Opera* stage at Universal, commonly known as Stage 28. According to the daily production report, the recreation of the famous unmasking scene for *Phantom of the Opera* was also filmed on Stage 28.[85]

Man of a Thousand Faces was nominated for an Academy Award for Best Original Screenplay but lost to *Designing Women*. The Department of Health, Education and Welfare chose the film to be closed-captioned for the deaf. James Cagney composed the music for the two dance numbers in the film.[86]

This was the last time that James and Jeanne Cagney appeared together in a picture.

Man of a Thousand Faces was released by MCA Home Video on videotape and in a letterbox laser disc in 1994.

Epilogue

Almost thirty years ago, I saw Lon Chaney's film biography, *Man of a Thousand Faces*, and two days later I was scouring the local libraries for information about this fascinating person. I was disappointed, to say the least, that no books had been written about Chaney. Material in encyclopedias was vague and often repeated the same myths about his life and how he created his famous faces.

But I didn't give up hope. In 1971, Robert G. Anderson published the first book dealing with Chaney's life and art, *Faces, Forms, Films: The Artistry of Lon Chaney*. Even though he left many questions unanswered about the actor's life, I (along with other Chaney fans) was elated by the more than 150 photographs that illustrated his book. Over the years, Mr. Anderson and I have shared a friendship based on our mutual admiration of Chaney, and he once confided to me that he hoped his text "would get the ball rolling" for another book on the actor. In the 1980s, two self-published volumes appeared. One offered numerous photos many of us had never seen before, but its text and captions left a lot to be desired; the other volume repeated many of the same old myths and offered little hard research.

In a 1930 interview, Lon Chaney stated that he would never write his own life story and proudly proclaimed that he "would fix it so nobody else will write my biography after I'm gone, too." I, of course, sensed a challenge. At first, the assembly of information began as just another facet of my fascination with this actor's life and career. After sharing some stories with Burt Lancaster on the set of *Tough Guys*, he suggested that I write a biography of Chaney. I shrugged it off, saying that I didn't feel comfortable authoring a book, but he remained firm in his suggestion. It was a suggestion that stayed with me for years.

It is no secret that I have championed Lon Chaney and his memory. I remember that ten-year-old boy who wanted to know more about the man of a thousand faces as well as a line from Woody Allen's *Radio Days*. A radio performer is looking over the New York skyline and wistfully asks a fellow actor, "I wonder if they'll [the public] remember us?" As the years roll by, many old film stars are forgotten by the general public, leaving only their admirers to keep their memories alive.

Although I never intentionally planned on becoming a lobbyist for Chaney, I found myself in that unfamiliar capacity when I urged my make-up union to honor Chaney's make-up achievements, and I was given the honor of presenting a plaque to his grandson, Lon Ralph Chaney. The desire to keep Chaney's memory alive propelled me to beseech Lon's hometown of Colorado Springs to finally honor the memory of their famous native. A theatre was named in his honor and a marquee adorns the side of the building, reminding Colorado Springs residents that Chaney was an integral part of their city. Inside the lobby, several cases of pictures and memorabilia demonstrate Chaney's unique talent. (Although it was not the bronze statue I had hoped for, it was the best offer one could get from an unresponsive city government.)

On a recent morning news show, I was asked by the entertainment reporter why I chose to write—at that time—two books on Lon Chaney. I answered then as I do now: I don't know. Part of it has been for that ten-year-old boy who couldn't find anything at the library. Part of it has been to document, as factually as possible, the life and career of a man who had a definite impact not only on motion pictures but also on his many admirers—including me. I was also reminded of the words of Gwen Thomas:

> I often wish I could speak into the ears of the dead the gratitude which was due to them in life and so ill-returned.

Lon Chaney may have hoped to "fix it" so that no one could write his biography after he was gone, but I feel my trilogy has been able to document factually what the man was like away from the camera, how he created his famous make-ups, and what a truly unique talent he was.

It is for the next ten-year-old who will not be faced with disappointment when he wants to know more about Lon Chaney—as well as with a nod of gratitude to the actor and man behind the thousand faces— that I wrote these books.

Notes

1. Universal Picture Code Book, Margaret Herrick Library of the Academy of Motion Picture Arts and Sciences, Beverly Hills, California.

2. *Universal Weekly*, December 6, 1913.

3. Ibid.

4. Ibid.

5. Universal Picture Code Book, Margaret Herrick Library of the Academy of Motion Picture Arts and Sciences, Beverly Hills, California.

6. *Lon Chaney: The Man Behind the Thousand Faces* (New York: The Vestal Press, 1993).

7. Universal Picture Code Book, Margaret Herrick Library of the Academy of Motion Picture Arts and Sciences, Beverly Hills, California.

8. Ibid.

9. Ibid.

10. Ibid.

11. Ibid.

12. Ibid.

13. Ibid.

14. Ibid.

15. Ibid.

16. Ibid.

17. Ibid.

18. Ibid.

19. Ibid.

20. Ibid.

21. Ibid.

22. *A Blind Bargain* (New Jersey: MagicImage Filmbooks, 1988).

23. Ibid.

24. Universal Picture Code Book, Margaret Herrick Library of the Academy of Motion Picture Arts and Sciences, Beverly Hills, California.

25. American Film Institute Catalog. *Feature Films 1911–1920* (University of California Press, 1988).

26. Universal Picture Code Book, Margaret Herrick Library of the Academy of Motion Picture Arts and Sciences, Beverly Hills, California.

27. Ibid.

28. Ibid.

29. *Motion Picture News*, April 20, 1918.

30. Universal Picture Code Book, Margaret Herrick Library of the Academy of Motion Picture Arts and Sciences, Beverly Hills, California.

31. *Motion Picture News*, July 13, 1918.

32. *Lon Chaney: The Man Behind the Thousand Faces* (New York: The Vestal Press, 1993).

33. Universal Picture Code Book, Margaret Herrick Library of the Academy of Motion Picture Arts and Sciences, Beverly Hills, California.

34. *Lon Chaney: The Man Behind the Thousand Faces* (New York: The Vestal Press, 1993).

35. Bob Birchard to the author, February 1989.

36. *Motion Picture News*, August 3, 1918.

37. Universal Picture Code Book, Margaret Herrick Library of the Academy of Motion Picture Arts and Sciences, Beverly Hills, California.

38. Priscilla Dean to the author, September 1987.

39. Mitch Trimboli to the author, June 1995.

40. *The Hollywood Reporter*, September 16, 1996.

41. *Treasure Island* pressbook. Author's collection.

42. American Film Institute Catalog. *Feature Films 1911–1920* (University of California Press, 1988).

43. *A Thousand Faces: Lon Chaney's Unique Artistry in Motion Pictures* (New York: The Vestal Press, 1995).

44. Leo McCarey, interview by Peter Bogdanovich, Louis B. Mayer Foundation Oral History Program, American Film Institute.

45. *Motion Picture News*, February 5, 1921.

46. Ibid.

47. *Motion Picture News*, April 23, 1921.

48. Ibid.

49. Universal Picture Code Book, Margaret Herrick Library of the Academy of Motion Picture Arts and Sciences, Beverly Hills, California.

50. *The Night Rose* pressbook. Author's collection.

51. *Lon Chaney: The Man Behind the Thousand Faces* (New York: The Vestal Press, 1993).

52. American Film Institute Catalog. *Feature Films 1911–1920* (University of California Press, 1988).

53. *Lon Chaney: The Man Behind the Thousand Faces* (New York: The Vestal Press, 1993).

54. *Motion Picture News*, October 1, 1921.

55. *A Thousand Faces: Lon Chaney's Unique Artistry in Motion Pictures* (New York: The Vestal Press, 1995).

56. *American Cinematographer*, November 1922.

57. Letter from the Alfred Grasso family collection.

58. Universal Picture Code Book, Margaret Herrick Library of the Academy of Motion Picture Arts and Sciences, Beverly Hills, California.

59. Taking that into account, as well as the rate of inflation for ticket prices, the film's gross is probably much higher.

60. *Classic Movie Monsters* (New Jersey: The Scarecrow Press, 1978).

61. *A Thousand Faces: Lon Chaney's Unique Artistry in Motion Pictures* (New York: The Vestal Press, 1995).

62. Virgil Miller, interview by Robert S. Birchard, Louis B. Mayer Foundation Oral History Program, American Film Institute.

63. Sidney Singerman to Don Krim, July 1995.

64. *He Who Gets Slapped* pressbook. Author's collection.

65. *The Motion Picture Guide: Silent Films 1910–1936* (Illinois: Cinebooks, Inc., 1986).

66. Brian Anthony to the author, August 1996.

67. Letter from the Alfred Grasso family collection.

68. Tom Weaver to the author, August 1996.

69. *A Thousand Faces: Lon Chaney's Unique Artistry in Motion Pictures* (New York: The Vestal Press, 1995).

70. *The Hollywood Reporter*, October 29, 1993.

71. *Tower of Lies* pressbook. Author's collection.

72. *Lon Chaney: The Man Behind the Thousand Faces*, (New York: The Vestal Press, 1993).

73. *Tell It To the Marines* pressbook. Author's collection.

74. Ibid.

75. Thomas Butler to the author, April 1993.

76. Credit sheet from author's collection.

77. *Lon Chaney: The Man Behind the Thousand Faces*, (New York: The Vestal Press, 1993).

78. From a reader's report dated April 10, 1925. M-G-M Collection. USC Cinema and Television Library.

79. *Laugh, Clown, Laugh* pressbook. Margaret Herrick Library of the Academy of Motion Picture Arts and Sciences, Beverly Hills, California.

80. *Harrison's Reports*, January 5, 1929.

81. Notes from the May 17, 1928, and June 7, 1928, scripts. Author's collection.

82. *A Thousand Faces: Lon Chaney's Unique Artistry in Motion Pictures* (New York: The Vestal Press, 1995).

83. *50 Years of Photographing Hollywood: The Hurrell Style* (New York: Greenwich House, 1983).

84. Business proposition from Alfred Grasso family collection.

85. *Man of a Thousand Faces* daily production report. Universal Collection. USC Cinema and Television Library.

86. *Lon Chaney: The Man Behind the Thousand Faces* (New York: The Vestal Press, 1993).

Bibliography

American Film Institute Catalogue, Feature Films 1911–1920, University of California Press, 1988.

American Film Institute Catalogue, Feature Films 1921–1930, R. R. Bowker Co., 1971, New York.

Anderson, Robert G., *Faces, Forms, Films: The Artistry of Lon Chaney*, A. S. Barnes & Co., 1971, New York.

Blake, Michael F., *Lon Chaney: The Man Behind the Thousand Faces*, The Vestal Press, 1993, New York.

Blake, Michael F., *A Thousand Faces: Lon Chaney's Unique Artistry in Motion Pictures*, The Vestal Press, 1995, New York.

Bodeen, DeWitt, *"Lon Chaney: Man of a Thousand Faces," Focus On Film*, May-August 1970, 21–39.

Braff, Richard E., *"A Lon Chaney Index," Films In Review*, April 1970, 217–228.

Chaney, Lon (possibly ghostwritten), *"My Own Story," Movie Magazine*,
Part I—September 1925, 42–44, 108–110
Part II—October 1925, 55–57, 86–89
Part III—November 1925, 55–56, 74–75

Connelly, Robert, *The Motion Picture Guide: Silent Films 1910–1936*, Cinebooks, Inc., 1986, Illinois.

Eames, John Douglas, *The MGM Story*, Crown Publishers, Inc. 1975, New York.

Edmonds, I. G., *The Big U*, A. S. Barnes & Co., 1977, New York.

Glut, Donald F., *Classic Movie Monsters*, Scarecrow Press, 1978, New Jersey.

Hirschhorn, Clive, *The Universal Story*, Crown Publishers, Inc., 1983, New York.

Marx, Samuel, *Mayer and Thalberg: Make-Believe Saints*, Random House, 1975, New York.

Miller, Patsy Ruth. *My Hollywood: When Both of Us Were Young*, O'Raghailligh Ltd. Publishers, 1988, New Jersey.

Riley, Philip J., *A Blind Bargain*, Magic Image Filmbooks, 1988, New Jersey.

Riley, Philip J., *London After Midnight*, Cornwall Books, 1985, New York.

Rosenthal, Stuart, *The Hollywood Professionals: Tod Browning*, A. S. Barnes & Co., 1975, New York.

Slide, Anthony, *Nitrate Won't Wait*, McFarland & Co., Inc., 1992, North Carolina.

St. Johns, Adela Rogers, *"Lon Chaney, A Portrait of the Man Behind a Thousand Faces," Liberty*,

Part I—May 2, 1931, 16–20,22, 24–25.

Part II—May 9, 1931, 28–36.

Part III—May 16, 1931, 28–34.

Part IV—May 23, 1931, 36–37, 40–44.

Part V—May 30, 1931, 39–44.

Stine, Whitney, *50 Years of Photographing Hollywood: The Hurrell Style*, Greenwich House, 1983, New York.

Turner, George, *"A Silent Giant: The Hunchback of Notre Dame," American Cinematographer*, June 1985.

Waterbury, Ruth, *"The True Life Story of Lon Chaney," Photoplay*,

Part I—December 1927, 32–33, 110–114.

Part II—January 1928, 36–37, 119–121.

Part III—February 1928, 56–57, 94, 112–113.

About the Author

Michael F. Blake has been called "the walking encyclopedia" on the life and career of Lon Chaney. His two previous books on Chaney, *Lon Chaney: The Man Behind the Thousand Faces* and *A Thousand Faces: Lon Chaney's Unique Artistry in Motion Pictures*, are considered to be the definitive works on the famous actor.

Michael's knowledge of Chaney's life and career has made him a sought-after guest speaker and production consultant on many projects. He served as a consultant for the Kino International Video Lon Chaney film series and supplied material for the recent documentary on Universal Studios, *The Universal Story*. In the summer of 1994, he appeared as a guest speaker during a film tribute to Lon Chaney at the International Mystery Film Festival in Italy. He is currently helping the Library of Congress to restore fragments of a nitrate print of Chaney's last silent film, *Thunder*.

Michael was responsible for the 1986 renaming of a theatre in Chaney's honor in the silent-film star's hometown of Colorado Springs, Colorado. The author was also instrumental in the Hollywood Make-Up Union's posthumously honoring Chaney's achievements in motion picture make-up by presenting the award to the actor's grandson, Lon Ralph Chaney, during a film retrospective at UCLA in 1983. Michael is also the first make-up artist to be allowed to examine Chaney's make-up case, at the Natural History Museum in Los Angeles, as part of a story for the French Television show, *Hollywood*.

He has lectured extensively and written many articles pertaining to Chaney for *Filmfax, Performing Arts, Monsterscene, Cult Movies,* and *Leatherneck: Magazine of the Marines*. Michael has been featured discussing Lon Chaney on several television shows, including *Entertainment Tonight, AMC in Hollywood, Sci-Fi Buzz, Movie Magic, CNN Showbiz Today, A&E's Biography,* and the Japanese NHK special, *100 Years of Cinema Magic*. His collection of Lon Chaney memorabilia is considered to be the most extensive in the world and includes 120 lobby cards, 10 posters, more than 1,900 photographs, and 4 autographed photographs.

For the past 19 years, Michael has worked as a professional make-up artist on such productions as *Star Trek VI, Strange Days, Tough Guys, Sister Act I & II, Soapdish, Magnum, P.I., Happy Days,* and the recent *Independence Day.* Before that, he worked as a child actor appearing in *The Munsters, Adam-12, Bonanza, The Lucy Show, Bewitched, Kung-Fu,* and *Marcus Welby, M.D.* He has also performed several times as a guest clown with the Blue Unit of Ringling Bros.-Barnum and Bailey Circus.

Between make-up assignments, Michael is at work writing *Greasepaint to Prosthetics: Conversations with Hollywood Make-up Artists, The Adam-12 Log Book, The Hunchbacks of Hollywood,* and *A Movie Buff's Guide to Hollywood.* He lives with his wife, Linda, and dog, Tara, in Los Angeles, California.